# Exotic Appetites

ch 4 + intro : p 60 - 88
ch 11    p 193 - 217
epilogue    p 279 - 222

# Exotic Appetites

## Ruminations of a Food Adventurer

Lisa M. Heldke

Routledge
New York and London

Published in 2003 by
Routledge
29 West 35th Street
New York NY 10001
www.routledge-ny.com

Published in Great Britain by
Routledge
11 New Fetter Lane
London EC4P 4EE
www.routledge.co.uk

Routledge is an imprint of the Taylor & Francis Group.

Printed in the United States of America on acid-free paper.
10  9  8  7  6  5  4  3  2  1

Portions of this book appeared in the form of two earlier articles by the author;
they are reprinted here by permission of the publishers. "Let's Eat Chinese" ©
2001 by the Regents of the University of California; reprinted from *Gastronomica*
vol. 1, no. 2, by permission of the University of California Press. "Let's Cook Thai,"
reprinted from *Pilaf, Pozole and Pad Thai: American Women, and Ethnic Food,* ed.
Sherrie A. Inness (2001), by permission of the University of Massachusetts Press.

Library of Congress Cataloging-in-Publication Data

Heldke, Lisa M. (Lisa Maree), 1960–
Exotic appetites : ruminations of a food adventurer / Lisa M. Heldke.
        p. cm.
Includes bibliographical references and index.
ISBN 0-415-94384-1 (hb : alk. paper)— ISBN 0-415-94385-X (pb : alk. paper)
1.  Heldke, Lisa M. (Lisa Maree), 1960—Biography. 2. Gastronomy.  I. Title.

TX649.H45 A3 2003
641'.01'3—dc21

2002156317

# Contents

There is in some few men of every land a special hunger, one which will make them forego the safe pleasures of their own beds and tables, one which initiates them into that most mysterious and ruthless sect: the adventurers.

—M. F. K. Fisher

I always mix my cultures. After all, we built an entire country mixing enchiladas and gefilte fish.

—Overheard in the IBM cafeteria

# Acknowledgments

This book began more than a decade ago. During the time I have been writing it, the discipline of food studies has arrived on the academic scene, in a (small) flurry of books, journal issues, and conferences. Whereas ten years ago only home economists, anthropologists, folklorists, and rural sociologists addressed food as a serious topic of academic study, now the joint meetings of the Association for the Study of Food and Society (ASFS) and the Agriculture, Food and Human Values Society feature papers from a host of disciplinary perspectives, including literature, cultural studies, history, and yes, even philosophy. This emerging field of study has given me a context in which to think and write, and its practitioners have given me much to think and write *about*. Thank you to the regular contributors on the ASFS e-mail list, on which I am a faithful lurker. And a deep and most heartfelt thank you to the members of Convivium: the Philosophy and Food Roundtable—particularly Ray Boisvert, Carolyn Korsmeyer, Glenn Kuehn, and Jeremy Iggers—who prove with their own work that the philosophy of food is *not* an aberration or a gimmick.

I appreciate the audiences—at conferences, at colleges and universities, and at dinner tables—who heard and commented on portions of this work over the years; their responses very profoundly shaped the evolution of my thinking. Thanks specifically to audience members at the World Conference of Philosophy in Nairobi; Hamline University; LeMoyne College; the Society for Women in Philosophy (SWIP); the Popular Culture Association; Moorhead State University; the International Association of Women Philosophers; the Society for the Advancement of American Philosophy; the Oral Fixations Conference at George Washington University; Pacific Lutheran University; the Association for the Study of Food and Society; the Agriculture, Food and Human Values Society; and the Shop Talk Program at Gustavus Adolphus College.

I was able to work on this project full-time during two leaves from my job at Gustavus Adolphus and during several summers as well, thanks to generous faculty development grants and the college sabbatical program. Thanks to Dean Richard Fuller, Dean Elizabeth Baer, and the Gustavus Adolphus Faculty Development Committee for affording me these opportunities.

I spent the eight months of a sabbatical at the Center for Advanced Feminist Studies (CAFS) at the University of Minnesota. Thanks to Claire Gravon, Mary Lay, and Karen Moon of the administrative staff of CAFS for their generous hospitality. While in residence at CAFS, I participated in Sophia, the reading group of the feminist philosophy graduate students and faculty at the university. Thanks to members of that group, including Lisa Bergin, Jan Binder, Melissa Burchard, Heidi Grasswick, Katy Gray Brown, and Naomi Scheman, for reading and discussing one of my chapters with me. My office mate at CAFS, sociologist Chris Atmore, is the best, most stimulating office mate I've ever had; the project made several significant conceptual leaps thanks to her insightful questions, apt suggestions, and useful textual suggestions—all delivered over many plates of mock duck.

The Lily Library at Indiana University and the Schlessinger Library at Radcliffe College both possess superb collections of cookbooks; I am grateful for the opportunity to have used these excellent resources. I particularly appreciate the careful bibliographic work done by William Koeggel, director of the Lily collection.

Particular thanks to editor Damon Zucca, editorial assistant Robert Byrne, and production editor Julie Ho of Routledge, for their matter-of-fact enthusiasm for, and support of, this book—and for their lucid and unambiguous advice during the revision process.

I have spent the last several summers in Maine, on the Blue Hill Peninsula, where I have been able to interrupt my work on the manuscript in order to look out the window at Herrick Bay. Thanks to those who have made life there especially congenial—Ellen Anthony, Bob Hines, James Schwartz, Tim Boggs, Roxanne Sly, and Patty and V. B. Chamberlain.

More than anything else, my work on this book has been improved as a result of conversations with friends, family, colleagues, casual acquaintances, and total strangers. I will no doubt leave out many of the friends (and all of the strangers) in attempting to name them, but I'll do it anyway. Thanks to these people for reading and commenting extensively on entire drafts of the manuscript at various stages of completion along the way: Jay Benjamin, Mariangela Maguire, Carolyn O'Grady, Alison Bailey, Julie Johnson, and Joanna Kadi. Thanks, in particular, to four reviewers—Paul Thompson, Bonnie McKay, Sherrie A. Inness, and an anonymous individual—for their insightful recommendations for revision. Thanks to Darra Goldstein and Sheila Levine for their work on behalf of the manuscript.

Members of a short-lived, never-named feminist philosophy writing group read and provided extensive comments on large sections of this work. Its members include Corrinne Bedecarré, Amy Hilden, and Anne Phibbs. Thanks especially to Corrinne for her valiant efforts to get me to stop writing as the world's most plodding philosopher.

Claudia Card suggested that I think about writing a book after hearing me read a paper on food colonialism at a SWIP conference. Carol Mickett gave an early, extremely thoughtful response to the paper from which this book grew. Uma Narayan was perhaps the first philosopher to take up my work and to respond to it in her own writing. Kathleen Fluegel brought me up short over a dinner table conversation one night. Margot Backus put me on the trail of *The Original Thai Cookbook,* and got me started thinking about including cookbooks in this work. Greg Kaster put me on the trail of several books that turned out to be incredibly important in my thinking (and I had many wonderful food conversations with him and Kate Wittenstein over the dinner table at their house). Barb Heldke and Colette Hyman were terrific sources of anecdotes, remarks overheard in restaurants, articles, websites, and all manner of other food-related ephemera. Joanne Waugh made me start thinking about why people are upset by some kinds of culinary exchanges and not by others. Marti Crouch presented me with the living example of someone for whom food really *is* the center of her life—and has fed me, intellectually and physically, in innumerable ways. Brian Johnson read and responded to pieces of this work with creativity and insight at a time when I felt extremely discouraged. Stephen Kellert helped me to flesh out the earliest ideas for this book, and continued to challenge and encourage me along the way. Many friends offered encouragement at Bleak Moments during my search for a publisher: Kathy Matz, Dawn Ulrich, Erin Dana, Lauren Fleer, and Betsey Larson. And of course there's the Jenkins family.

Two friends stand as profound influences upon my life and my philosophical work. Bruce Norelius has been my intellectual companion since I was fourteen years old. He has talked with me about my work as only someone who has known me long and well could do; I appreciate the insights of his architect's mind. And Abby Wilkerson has been my most deeply engaging philosophical companion, as well as my most constant source of recipes, since I met her at a SWIP conference fifteen years ago. I quite genuinely don't know what sort of thinking I'd be doing these days in the absence of Abby's influence; I'm glad I won't have to find out.

Food is a deep interest of most everyone in my family, which includes a food scientist (my sister Sybil), a licensed buttermaker and creamery manager (my dad Richard), a stupendous pie maker (my mother Carol), a stupendous pie eater (my "outlaw" Jay), and one of the only people I know who still cooks actual meals every day (my sister Barb). They are present in this book in the form of stories and anecdotes, but also in the passion I bring to my study of food. Thanks goes to them for inspiring and supporting my love of food from the beginning.

Finally, thanks to Peg O'Connor, who has read, commented, suggested, critiqued—and told me to press the *print* key. For seven years, she has provided me with unflagging encouragement, cheerfulness, and a home full of love, all while enduring my endless sighs over her rather *selective* food habits with more equanimity than I could ever muster.

This book is finite. It is with a sense of utter astonishment that I have finally come to realize that its finitude means that, no matter how long I work on it, I will not be able to say everything I ought to say about this topic, answer every question or objection, reflect on every comment I've heard. I apologize in advance for those things I obviously should have said and didn't. And I promise writers reading this that I will approach their books with much more sympathy, humility, and generosity than I would have in the past. Your books will be finite, too. You won't have said everything you should have said either. I forgive you in advance.

# Leaving Home: One Girl's Story

When I was in graduate school studying philosophy, and later, when I first began teaching philosophy, I hosted large Thanksgiving dinners for my friends. Each year, I insistently—and obsessively—cooked all the food myself, because I wanted the dinner to be just the way *I* liked it, the way Thanksgiving is *supposed* to be. I spent a lot of time thinking about the attitude with which I approached the meal. Why, exactly, was I making such a big deal out of this meal—a meal commemorating a holiday with which I was becoming decidedly uncomfortable, showcasing a large dead animal, something with which I was also increasingly uncomfortable?

I finally reached the conclusion that I liked Thanksgiving dinner so much—hosting it at my house, cooking all the food myself, and eating it—because I never wondered what to fix. I prepared virtually the same meal every year: roast turkey (cheesecloth covering the breast to keep it from drying out while still making the skin crispy), bread stuffing (white bread, not corn bread, no oysters, and *no giblets*), mashed potatoes (mashed with cream, please, but no garlic at Thanksgiving), gravy (thickened with flour, not corn starch), and pumpkin and mince pie (homemade crust, of course). I allowed myself a certain amount of latitude with the vegetables (squash this year?), the cranberries (raw relish, or cooked sauce?), and the bread (popovers? muffins?), but for the most part, the meal looked just like the meal I'd eaten every Thanksgiving since childhood. My mom still cooks this meal, too; in fact, most of the years I cooked those large dinners, we would talk to each other on the phone several times during the morning, to remind each other to baste under the cheesecloth, or to ask whether a Pyrex pie pan can go right into the oven from the freezer.

And there, I finally decided, was the heart of my attachment to Thanksgiving dinner. I had been eating this meal one day a year for my entire life, but over the years, it had come to be one of the only meals that my mother and I "cook in common." It remained as one of the strongest threads tying me to my cooking and eating heritage—along with Christmas cookies, potato pancakes, and the practice of using butter in everything.

What happened that severed me from my food roots? A couple of big things. First, there was the fact that I wanted to stop eating meat as much as possible. My mom has always been a meat cook; I'd grown up eating beef roasts and pork tenderloin, hamburgers and fried chicken. But I'd never enjoyed meat, to put it mildly; even as a child, I'd invented all sorts of elaborate strategies to avoid taking my share of meat at the dinner table. So when I went away to college and ate in the cafeteria, I mostly stopped eating it. When I attended graduate school and started cooking for myself, I never cooked meat, though I would eat it when I went to someone's home, or in a restaurant. In recent years, my consumption dropped to nearly zero. My decision to minimize meat was and is simultaneously ecological, ethical, political, and aesthetic. I am always in the process of evaluating and reframing it.

I realized early on that living out this decision would mean relinquishing some parts of my food heritage and complicating my relationship to my family's eating habits. Indeed, one of the reasons I hadn't made the move to eliminating meat from my diet earlier was that I found it too difficult, too much of an imposition, and too much of a source of tension to refuse to eat meat when my mother was cooking for me. But when I set up house for myself, I decided I was willing to relinquish some parts of my food heritage in order to live out this choice.

The second thing that contributed to my departure from my eating heritage was that when I went away to graduate school, I entered a world of experimental-cooking-and-eating, a world heavily populated by academics, and by people with some disposable income who like to travel. It's a world where entire cuisines can go in and out of vogue in a calendar year, where lists of "in" ingredients, cuisines, techniques, and restaurants are published in glamorous magazines that feature pictures of gorgeous food on their covers and articles inside about how saffron is harvested. It's a world in which people whisper conspiratorially about the great little place serving Ethiopian—well, actually Eritrean—food that just opened up. (But pray that it doesn't get a good review in the newspaper, because we all know what happens then!) The world of food adventuring was a wonderful world, full of tastes, textures, and smells I had never, ever encountered growing up in Rice Lake, Wisconsin.

In my hometown, meat-potatoes-and-vegetable meals predominated in most homes, and an "ethnic" meal most likely meant spaghetti with red sauce at the Bona Casa in Cumberland, fifteen miles away. As a 4-Her, my favorite project had been cooking, and my favorite year was the year I was enrolled in a cooking project called "International Foods." In it, I learned how to make chili with V-8 juice and Swedish Christmas cookies. Moving to Evanston—right next to Chicago!—for graduate school was like moving to a culinary Disneyland for me. Within the first few months I jettisoned the box of instant mashed potatoes and cans of Campbell's soup I'd brought with me, and started stocking my cupboard with bulgur and tree ear fungus. And I was scouring the *Chicago Reader* for two-for-one restaurant coupons at interesting ethnic restaurants that I could get to on the el.[1]

Thai restaurants were opening in large numbers in Chicago about this time, and I can still remember my first visit to one. My roommate's parents were in town, and they took us to dinner at the Thai Star Cafe on State Street. I remember tasting kai thom kha—a chicken soup made with coconut milk, lemon grass, and kha or galangal, a spice related to ginger—and realizing "I have never tasted anything like this in my life before." And I hadn't; the food I experienced that evening probably contained at least six spices with which I'd never come in contact. Even familiar foods were used in ways I'd never have imagined (the things they'd done with peanut butter and ketchup!). After the meal, the four of us sat around marveling at how wonderful the food had been—and how very *inexpensive*, too. (Now, I marvel at the fact that I can buy a powdered kai thom kha mix in my local food co-op.)

So, between arriving in Chicago at the dawn of the Thai Food Era and my decision to nix the hamburgers, I found myself eating less and less like I'd grown up eating. I was having a wonderful time, but I never knew what to cook when I invited people over for dinner. Sometimes my indecision would render me nearly incapable of acting. (It's the night before my dissertation advisor is coming over for dinner, and the floor of my apartment is covered with cookbooks, all of which are bristling with bookmarks marking menu possibilities. I've sketched out five potential menus, each of them featuring foods of a different nationality, most of them consisting of several dishes I've never cooked before—maybe never even heard of prior to leafing through this cookbook.) My mom would never have found herself in this predicament. She has a standard repertoire of foods, many of which she grew up cooking, and that she still cooks. When she has dinner guests, she selects a menu from among her standards, preparing foods she's prepared and enjoyed countless times before, knowing that once again they will turn out well and everyone will enjoy the meal. At the height of my experimental phase, I found myself missing that, even envying it—especially when I spent three hours trying to decide on a menu, or when I tried out a new dish for company and it turned out to be awful.

Dinner envy aside, I was becoming a food adventurer, and I (mostly) didn't look back. After eating my way through the inexpensive ethnic restaurants of Chicago and Evanston during graduate school (the weekend I defended my dissertation I celebrated with meals at both an Indian and a Peruvian restaurant), I moved to a small town in Minnesota, and then to another small town in Minnesota. In these towns I found my food adventuring activity curtailed; the few restaurants in them tended toward pizza, burgers, and the occasional steak, and in the grocery stores, food from major American conglomerates dominated the shelves. Of course some of my colleagues, who were not products of the Upper Midwest, did find the foods of the area weird—and often unappetizing; they *did* feel like food adventurers when they found Jell-O with peas in it on the restaurant salad bar, or when they went to a lutefisk dinner sponsored by the local Lutheran church. But for me, Jell-O salad and lutefisk were very old, as well as very unappetizing, news.

Despite the dearth of opportunities for food adventuring in my own town, I managed to scrape by. On weekend visits to Minneapolis/St. Paul, trips to professional conventions, sabbaticals in other towns, and summer vacations, I collected eating adventures in restaurants serving all sorts of ethnic cuisines, ranging from the relatively routine (Vietnamese food in Minneapolis/St. Paul) to the more unusual (Tibetan food at "America's Second Only Tibetan Restaurant" in Bloomington, Indiana). By scouring the "restaurants by ethnicity" section of the Manhattan Yellow Pages, I found a place serving Burmese food in walking distance from the hotel at which I was staying for the American Philosophical Association convention. Following a friend—a newspaper food critic and self-described food adventurer who was on an "eat your way around the world" tour for his paper—through the streets of Cochin, India, late one night, I landed at a neighborhood family restaurant featuring Mogul food. And when I had dinner in

Minneapolis with another friend, we would eat at her favorite comfort food restaurant—an Ethiopian restaurant right near her office at the university.

"Experiment" was my middle name; I'd try (nearly) anything once, and I actively sought any and all opportunities to increase the number and range of eating adventures I had. Experimentation had its risks and dangers—the dangers of ordering a dish that was too spicy, too full of "weird" foods—but that risk was just part of the experiment, part of the adventure. I was not alone on my quests; wherever I adventured, I could always be sure of company. No matter what crowd I was in, there was always someone else like me, eager to eat things they'd never heard of before.

Over time, though, I started to have some suspicions about my food adventuring. For one thing, various experiences made me feel uncomfortable about the easy acquisitiveness with which I approached a new kind of food, the tenacity with which I collected adventures—as one might collect ritual artifacts from another culture without thinking about the appropriateness of removing them from their cultural setting. Other experiences made me reflect on the circumstances that conspired to bring these cuisines into my world in the first place. On my first visit to an Eritrean restaurant, for example, I found myself thinking about how disturbing and how complicated it was to be eating the food of people who were in the middle of yet another politically and militarily induced famine. An offhand remark in a murder mystery I was reading started me thinking about the *reasons* there were so many Vietnamese restaurants in Minneapolis/St. Paul, reasons directly connected to the Vietnam War and the resultant dislocation of Vietnamese and Hmong people.[2]

## Cultural Colonialism: What Is It?

Eventually, I put a name to my activity, to my penchant for cooking and eating ethnic foods—most frequently and most notably the foods of economically dominated or "third world" cultures.[3] The name I chose was "cultural food colonialism" because, as I had come to see, my adventure eating was (and continues to be) strongly motivated by an attitude with deep connections to Western colonialism. When I began to examine my tendency to go culture hopping in the kitchen and in restaurants, I found that the attitude with which I approached such activities often bore an uncomfortable resemblance to the attitude of, say, nineteenth- and early twentieth-century European painters, anthropologists, and explorers who set out in search of ever "newer," ever more "remote" cultures that they could co-opt, borrow from freely and out of context, and use as the raw materials for their own efforts at creation and discovery. Richard Burton and Henry Schoolcraft, for example, "discovered" the headwaters of the Nile and Mississippi River, respectively—with the help of local folks who already knew what Burton and Schoolcraft had come to discover.[4] Paul Gauguin went to Tahiti in order to "immerse [himself] in virgin nature, see no one but savages, live their life . . ." in order that he might make "simple, very simple art"—using their lives and art as his raw material.[5]

Of course, my eating was not simply colonizing; it was also an effort to play, and to learn about other cultures in ways I intended to be respectful. But underneath, or alongside, or over and above all these other reasons, I could not deny that I was motivated by a deep desire to have contact with, and to somehow own an experience of, an Exotic Other, as a way of making myself more interesting. Food adventuring, I was coming to decide, made me a participant in cultural colonialism, just as surely as eating Mexican strawberries in January made me a participant in economic colonialism.

Furthermore, I came to think that cultural colonialism helped to support and normalize economic colonialism—and that my unthinking participation in the former thus had an effect on the latter as well. So I started paying attention to cultural colonialism—in particular, cultural food colonialism. What was it, really? (*Was* it, really?) What were its symptoms? Its activities? Its cures? Would I have to stop eating out? Who did it? Where? Why?

This book attempts to answer some of these questions. It is my effort to make the notion of cultural food colonialism at once subtler and nuanced, and more clear and compelling as an explanation of the practices in which many of us sometimes engage. It is also my attempt to make understanding these activities seem like an important thing to do—to reveal this set of practices-and-attitudes in ways that make them seem obviously in need of thoughtful, reflective attention from everyone who eats and cooks.

## *Cultural* Food Colonialism?

Food colonialism is a familiar notion—but in ordinary usage, it refers to things such as the disruption of local, self-sufficient food systems and their replacement with export economies, or the practice of multinational food firms moving their growing and production facilities "offshore" in order to exploit cheap labor and land.[6] Such material or economic food colonialism produces real poverty, malnutrition, and starvation in dominated economies, even as it produces artificially cheap foodstuffs for inhabitants of dominant economies. As such, it merits—and has received—considerable attention from both academic and nonacademic writers.

In contrast to such a familiar form of colonialism, identifying a form of colonialism as *cultural* might seem odd, even positively wrong to some readers; isn't colonialism *by definition* an economic or political relationship? A woman once responded to my discussion of various cultural forms of food colonialism quite angrily by saying, "Exploitation happens in our culture because our economy rewards multinational corporations such as Dole, not because I sometimes eat in a Chinese restaurant." She went on to say "'Cultural food colonialism' as distinct from economic food colonialism is a speculative construct which depends on someone else's reading of my motives. . . ."[7] In other words, cultural colonialism has no objective, external manifestations; it goes on—if at all—only in my head. As such, its existence can never be strictly verified, and its effects surely cannot be very damaging (to colonizer or colonized) if or when it does occur.

I disagree. As one way to make the notion of cultural colonialism comprehensible, if not compelling, consider a concept that is its close relative— the familiar notion of cultural imperialism. Cultural imperialism refers to the practice through which an economic or political power imposes its social or cultural practices and belief systems on another culture. Cultural imperialism both supports and is supported by economic and political forms of imperialism; it helps to make those other forms effective and powerful.[8]

In the most extreme forms of cultural imperialism, the imperial power may, as a matter of explicit policy, root out indigenous practices and replace them with its own in order to subdue and control a people. A notorious example of this in the United States was the system of boarding schools (often missionary schools run by the Catholic Church) for Native American children. Euroamerican governmental and religious officials forcibly removed Native children from their homes, and sent them to faraway schools from which they often were not allowed to return for years at a time. At school the boys' long hair was cut (a direct assault on the sacred traditions of many Native nations), and boys and girls were forbidden to speak their languages, eat their own foods, or engage in their own spiritual practices. They were forbidden to observe all the most central, daily, routine, and significant ways in which their cultural selves were defined and encouraged; in short, they were not allowed to be Lakotah, Ojibwe, Navajo, Hopi.

In other cases the imposition of the imperial culture may appear (even to inhabitants of the indigenous culture) less a systematic attempt to destroy the indigenous culture and more of a supposedly "benign," or even "welcome" side effect achieved in the process of pursuing other goals. Consider the "creation of a demand"—notice the absence of an agent in that phrase!—for U.S. fast foods, U.S. movies, and U.S. clothing in many contemporary third world nations. While first world businesses like McDonald's and Coca-Cola do not explicitly state as their goal the obliteration of indigenous foodways in places where they set up outlets, the erosion of those foodways and their replacement by desires for french fries and hamburgers constitutes an effect that is by no means simply accidental.

Cultural imperialism refers to the *imposition* of cultural practices by an economic or political power; cultural colonialism, as I shall be using the term, refers to the *appropriation* of such practices by such a power. In both cases, the cultural forms exist alongside, and work in the support of, economic and political forms.

This book focuses on cultural forms of food colonialism; by choosing this focus, I do not suggest that they are more important than more familiar economic forms. I *do* mean to show that the cultural forms in which many of us participate have serious consequences, and are worthy of our serious examination.

## What Might Anticolonialism Look Like?

To describe a culture's cuisine as colonized suggests that there exists such a thing as an uncolonized or anticolonized cuisine—an ideal, perhaps, toward which the would-be anticolonizer aims. What would it mean for a culture not to be colonized? My answer to that question must remain provisional for the time being; a more robust answer must await the analysis of colonialism to which it will respond. An uncolonized cuisine is not one that has been subject to no outside influences, one that has not been changed by the introduction of new dishes, new foodstuffs, new spices, or new cooking techniques from another culture. There are no such cuisines. Cuisines are not static entities that remain unchanged over time, nor is each one rigidly separated from other cuisines such that we can tell where that one stops and this one starts. Practitioners of some cuisines may aspire to such hermetic isolation, or may even insist that their cuisine *is* unchanging, but in practice, even the most strictly rule-bound cuisines—French haute cuisine, Chinese imperial cuisine, Middle Eastern home cuisines,[9] for example—experience numerous small and large changes throughout their histories, as a result of the creativity of insider cooks and (more important for the present point) as a consequence of contact with other cuisines. If the notion of an uninfluenced cuisine ever made sense historically, it does not now. Countless numbers of food crops have crossed and recrossed the world, ending up far from the places they were originally cultivated: the potato, first grown in the Andean highlands, is now grown and eaten in the Himalayas; peanuts, originally grown in North America, are now grown and used extensively in Southeast Asia and West Africa.[10] Dishes and preparation methods travel in similar fashion: many researchers believe that pasta, ubiquitous to Italian cooking, was actually a borrowing from the Chinese. I first encountered the dish called satay—thin strips of chicken or beef that are barbecued and served with a spicy peanut sauce—in a Thai restaurant, so I assumed it was native to Thailand. I subsequently learned it is more often considered to be Malaysian, although it is likely of Arabic origin, and the word "satay" may be a variation on the word "steak." So perhaps this "authentically Thai" dish I loved so much actually had its origins in a dish that imitated the American tradition of steak on the grill.

These examples do not change the fact that, in some cuisines, dishes have persisted for centuries in nearly the same form. Claudia Roden, in *A Book of Middle-Eastern Food*, discusses a thirteenth-century manuscript of recipes, the *Kitab al Wusla il al Habib*, which is probably of Syrian origin. She notes, "I was thrilled to trace the origin of several of my own family's recipes" to this seven-hundred-year-old recipe book![11] But despite such examples, it must be admitted that purity, understood as absence of outside influences, is not possible in a cuisine.

Purity is no virtue in a cuisine, either—even a cuisine that would describe itself as uncolonized. Lack of influence is not, in and of itself, desirable. One can unearth countless examples of the ways in which food exchanges have enriched, expanded, perhaps even improved cultures' cuisines. Not all of these exchanges have been free and open ones, but some of them have. And let it be noted that colonized cultures have taken advantage of even their forced exposure to the foods of the colonizer, to enrich their own cuisine. Vietnamese cuisine, for example, adopted, with great success, many elements of French cuisine during the French occupation of Vietnam. Is Vietnamese cuisine then "better off" because of the French occupation? This is hardly the lesson I would draw from the example. Rather, I would suggest that it points to the possibilities for creative and flexible resistance to oppression that are present even in a culture's cuisine.

So the notion of an uncolonized cuisine must acknowledge the fact that cuisines can and do grow in healthy ways as a result of outside influences. The question, then, for the would-be food anticolonizer is not "Must such culinary cultural exchanges happen?" but "Under what sorts of conditions ought they happen?" The ideal is not a cuisine under a bell jar, but a cuisine that influences and is influenced by other cuisines in ways over which its practitioners (those who can most properly be said to have the right to de-termine its future form) have some control. I will have much more to say about anticolonialism in part 4 of this volume.

## Who Are the Food Adventurers?

Before I answer that question, let me explain why I use the term "adven-turer" here, rather than "colonizer," the word I've used up to this point. Cul-tural food colonialism—like any other kind of colonialism—assumes many forms, depending upon the interests, assumptions, and aims of those partic-ipating in it. For example, some of us are moved by an impulse to homoge-nize an ethnic cuisine in order to make it appeal to "the American consumer"—an impulse that may prompt the entrepreneurs among us to package that cuisine into mass-marketable restaurant franchises (Chi Chi's, Lee Ann Chin) or seasoning packets (A Taste of Thai). In contrast, others may see ourselves as protecting a cuisine from such profit motives, and pre-serving it in its original state (like a nature preserve), by frequenting authen-tic restaurants, but keeping their locations to ourselves. These two impulses tend to work at odds with each other to produce different consequences. Colonizing is not a unified set of activities with a single goal, but a many-

tentacled activity with diffuse—sometimes competing, sometimes supporting—goals.[12] Indeed, its diffuseness and variety account for its tenacity and
resilience; there is no single front on which to attack it.

In this book I pay particular attention to those people for whom eating is
an expedition into the unknown, a pursuit of the strange. They—we—are
the food adventurers. But while the group of food adventurers stands at the
center of my account, it is connected in myriad ways to other groups whose
members' activities also support and reinforce colonizing kinds of relations.
I invite you as readers to find yourselves in these pages—even if you don't fit
the precise profile of a food adventurer I sketch here.

We food adventurers are often people who believe that we have no culture of our own, people who sometimes blithely refer to ourselves as "nothing," "neutral," or "ordinary" (as did my graduate school roommate, a
middle-class woman of English heritage).[13] We see our culture or cultures
reflected around us so frequently and so widely that we come to think of
them as no culture at all, as a kind of default or background against which
other cultures can be displayed.[14] We are often persons who, as children,
would not have had the experience of being described by our peers as weird
or different because of the foods we ate at home. (In contrast, my friend
Clare, whose family was Italian, reports that she hated her breakfasts of hot,
milky coffee and hard rolls, not because she didn't like the way those foods
tasted, but because they were not what her friends ate for breakfast; she
begged for corn flakes.) We are often Euroamerican, Christian-raised persons for whom immigration is a (relatively) distant event—something undertaken by great grandparents, perhaps. We often find the foods that we
ate growing up or that we eat on a daily basis to be boring; we long to spice
up our diets (literally) with the flavors of exotic cuisines.[15] (Jane and
Michael Stern use even stronger language; they describe white Americans as
possessed of "a strong streak of . . . self-loathing"; in the 1960s, they suggest, this boredom with our own foods spawned the gourmet food craze.)[16]

After reading my description of food adventurers, several people have
asked whether, say, Vietnamese or African-American or Indian people can
ever be food adventurers—or is this just a "white thing?" Certainly cultural
food colonizing is not a whites only activity. I take seriously the issue, raised
by Joanna Kadi, that "many people of color are just as inattentive to these issues [of cultural appropriation] and thus act inappropriately toward each

other," and that focusing only on relations between whites and some other group(s) of color "support[s] the lie that we [people of color] can only be discussed in relation to white people, that our only important relationships exist with white people."[17] Nevertheless, I have chosen in this work to focus primarily on white cultural food colonizing, on whites' relations to various peoples of color through their food. I do so partly because I rely heavily on my own experience as a white eater in order to do this analysis; I want to think about my relations to the people I colonize through food.

I also do so because I think there are important differences between, say, the acquisitiveness of a white adventure eater in a Burmese restaurant and that of a Korean adventurer in an Indian restaurant, differences that do not preclude the possibility that the Korean eater is engaging in cultural appropriation, but that do not allow the two instances to be conflated into a single phenomenon either. In the United States, white privilege is a ubiquitous feature of the society, influencing every interaction taking place in it, even as class and gender further shape the character of that privilege. The actions of a white eater are situated against a historical backdrop of European colonialism, and take place in the context of contemporary Euroamerican neocolonialism. Whites do not have a monopoly on ignorance or acquisitiveness, but the impact of our ignorance and acquisitiveness is different from (and generally greater than) that of persons of color, who, whatever else characterizes their actions, are always also on the receiving end of racism.

Eating in restaurants and engaging in experimental cooking as a hobby generally require a certain amount of economic privilege in the United States; thus, food adventurers tend to be persons with middle-class status— or persons who pass as, or aspire to, the middle class. The food adventurers with whom I am most familiar also tend to be persons with a significant amount of education; we are often academics and other professionals. A study produced by the National Restaurant Association, entitled *Ethnic Cuisines: A Profile*, supports my observation. The report identifies one of three segments of ethnic food consumers as "culture-oriented" consumers, a category that overlaps considerably with my food adventurers. According to the report, this segment of consumers is "the most highly educated, has the highest mean income, and the greatest percentage of managerial/professional workers."[18] The food adventurers I know don't actually have high incomes. (Most of them are teachers and students.) But food adventuring,

unlike travel or art collecting, is a cultural activity you can do for relatively
little money. Many ethnic restaurants are inexpensive—especially those
serving cuisines that seem most distant from mainstream white American
food culture. Food adventuring probably particularly appeals to academics
and other middle-income professionals because, much as we may not like to
admit it, many of us snobbishly see ourselves as above the hoi polloi. But we
must mark that status with cultural indicators that don't require overlarge
incomes. Sports cars, gigantic houses, and expensive jewelry are not within
our budgets; dinner is.[19]

    Food adventurers score culture points for our erudition; we gain sta-
tus—albeit a somewhat countercultural status—for knowing what galangal
is. And the status we acquire is increasingly less countercultural, because
ethnic foods are "hot"; eating ethnic foods, the culinary and travel magazines tell us, is a very popular thing to do.

    Although both men and women engage in food adventuring, being a
food adventurer often has a decidedly manly caste to it; we tend to describe
a willingness to try new foods as bravery. Bravery is especially required if
one is to eat unusual animals, the targets of much food adventuring (and a
topic I will pursue in part 2). Furthermore, food adventuring is frequently
described as a quest, and the food adventurer as an explorer; indeed, the
rhetoric of the activity is often the rhetoric of conquest. To be a food adventurer is to be masculine in certain ways, even when one is a woman.

    An anecdote may serve to illuminate my suggestion. My roommate in
graduate school was a chemistry student, nearly the only woman in her lab.
This lab, like many, established an unwritten code of behavior that empha-
sized hard-core dedication to doing chemistry, as evidenced chiefly by the
amount of time one spent in the lab. My roommate strove to prove that she
belonged in it by making sure she was the first one there in the morning the
last one there at night, and the only one there most weekends.

    The lab relaxed on Friday nights by going out to eat as a group. But even
their recreating exhibited both hard core and experimental qualities; they
always went to restaurants that featured spicy foods.[20] Members of the
group vied with each other to find the restaurants featuring the most unusual and/or the fieriest cuisine with which to impress the other members of
the group. To me as an outsider, this Friday night activity appeared to be an
extension of the laboratory. In both, a masculinist ethos of intensity, single-

mindedness and drive prevailed; and in both settings, I saw my roommate working overtime to prove that she was entitled to participate.

As should be clear by now, I consider myself—a white academic from a hybridized working class-middle class family who spends a lot of time at conferences and who loves to travel—to be a card-carrying, if deeply uneasy, member of the food adventurers' club. Despite my deep misgivings about food adventuring, and despite my efforts to remake my own activity into something less exploitive, it is clear to me that I am still a food adventurer, still a cultural food colonizer in important and significant ways. Thus, I speak of *we* and *us* rather than *they* and *them* when I refer to food adventurers throughout this work.

Unlike me, many readers of this book may not find their particular eating or cooking habits depicted in the chapters ahead; for such readers, unfamiliar ethnic cuisines may hold little allure. But although adventure eating may be unfamiliar, the colonizing attitude in which it is undertaken may nevertheless be quite familiar to such readers. Colonizing impulses pervade contemporary American culture. The adventure eater may be an unusual breed of cultural colonizer—unusual in her choice of object. But she finds many fellow travelers who are also infatuated with Things Other—with the art, craft, music, religion, story, and locale of other ethnic and racial groups. Food adventuring, then, can serve as a very illuminating window through which to examine the more general phenomenon of cultural colonizing.

## Philosophy, Feminist Theory, and Food

Some readers may be surprised to find a philosopher taking a professional interest in food, for while the study of food has long been at the center of disciplines such as anthropology and home economics, and has recently experienced tremendous growth in others such as literature, religion, and cultural studies, and while gastronomy has even come to be a separate department in some academic institutions, the philosophical study of food is still something of a novelty act—regarded as such particularly by philosophers themselves. This remains true despite the appearance, in recent years, of a number of books in the philosophy of food, and the establishment of a philosophical society devoted to the study of food.[21]

I hope that my philosopher's interest in food will also be met with at least some relief—both by some practitioners of food studies and some philosophers. Why relief? Philosophy is a discipline that, among its tasks, concerns itself with questions about fundamental features of human existence—and surely our multifaceted relationship to food is one of the most important of such features. As such, I believe philosophy has much to contribute to the growing field of food studies. It is not because philosophy has the capacity to "solve" problems in food studies where other disciplines have been unable; philosophy, as I understand it, is centrally a discipline devoted to asking questions—asking them in a way that enables one to reframe one's perspectives on the world. Therefore, I think the principle kind of contribution that philosophy can make to the study of food is to raise questions that reveal different layers of the issues, different aspects of the terrain of food studies. Obviously philosophers' work will be informed by those disciplines with long-standing interests in the study of food—but just as obviously, it will not necessarily ask the questions or frame the issues in ways that those other disciplines believe are the most appropriate. Philosophers' methods are not those of ethnographers, for example, who may at times find themselves scandalized by philosophers' tendency toward abstract generalization, our tendency to see the development of a point as necessitating more theory rather than more examination of concrete circumstance. Abstraction and theorizing can make important contributions to the study of food, by enabling patterns to emerge, connections to be drawn.

To reverse the terms of the equation, I also believe that the study of food has much to contribute to the study of philosophy,[22] for while it is true that philosophy has been concerned with fundamental matters of human existence, it is also true that at least Western philosophy has often ignored that concern when the matter at hand has been literally material—when it has concerned the body. I hope that philosophical attention to food can, among other things, contribute to the philosophical project of exploring the *bodily* being of human being, with all its temporality, routine, fallibility, and ordinariness.

While my interest in food does seem to require some explanation when I describe myself as a philosopher, when I describe myself as a feminist philosopher—or, better yet, a feminist theorist—my interest may seem obvious to the point of being virtually necessary, given the degree to which food-making is seen as women's work. For at least several decades now, feminist theorists have been exploring those domains of human experience traditionally identified as "belonging" to women.[23] Reproductive issues, childbirth, the work of mothering, housework, sex work, sexuality itself, pornography, women's health, and any number of other features of human life have come to be taken seriously as academic subjects in large part because of the efforts of feminists, who have understood these "women's issues" as relevant theoretical concerns.

In the spirit of those endeavors, some feminist theorists have begun to turn serious attention to food, cooking, and eating. In the first expressions of interest, many feminist theorists sought to explore and explain the increasingly troubled relationships between women and food that came to be manifested in anorexia, bulimia, compulsive eating, and other eating disorders.[24] More recently, feminists have also turned attention to such varied topics as the emergence of cookery as a "domestic science," the roles of food in popular cultural representations of womanhood, food and religion in medieval European women's lives, and the historical relationships between fasting and eating disorders.[25]

So far, however, my discussion of the relations among philosophy, feminist theory, and food has proceeded only at the level of generality. What about this book in particular? This is a philosophical account of a set of concrete, ordinary daily activities in which some people engage. The kinds of questions I ask are ethical and sociopolitical questions that are familiar to philosophers, even though the subject matter to which I attach them—food—is not. As such, I see it as both an invitation to philosophers to consider food a philosophically relevant topic and also a kind of offering from a philosopher to the interdisciplinary study of food—an example of one sort of food question a philosopher might ask and explore.

This is, at core, a work rooted in feminist thought. Ironically, however, it is the very centrality of feminist theory that may make it appear, initially, as if my work "isn't feminist, isn't about women at all." My work is *not* about women, when that phrase is understood to mean "about women by not being about men, about women by talking about women, women's work, and women's experiences exclusively." Instead, the questions of this book emerge most directly, not from existing feminist work on food, but from feminist work on race and racism. My work takes up challenges posed particularly by strands of feminist theory developed by feminists of color, and third-world feminists including bell hooks, Trinh T. Minh-Ha, Uma Narayan, and Joanna Kadi. One of the most important lessons white feminists began to learn from the work of feminists of color in the 1980s was that women's oppression always exists along multiple axes simultaneously. To put the matter most simply, there is no way to sort out the part of a Black woman's experience of oppression that arises from her being a woman, and the part of that oppression that arises from her being Black; oppression simply doesn't work like a component stereo system. This means that white, middle-class feminists must take racism and classism seriously as central features of *women's* oppression—not as add-ons that can be considered after the "real" challenges of women's (read: white, middle-class women's) oppression have been met.

In the 1990s that feminist lesson further evolved to emphasize the importance of investigating one's own privilege within systems of oppression. Peggy McIntosh's now nearly canonical article, "White Privilege and Male Privilege: Unpacking the Invisible Knapsack," began to explore the similarities between the unearned benefits of whiteness and the unearned benefits of masculinity as a way of making visible to herself the reality of her own white privilege. Ruth Frankenberg's later book *White Women, Race Matters* explores her hypothesis that "race shapes white women's lives" in such deep and multifaceted ways that it is possible to say, without hyperbole, that racism is "a system that shapes [white women's] daily experiences and sense of self."[26] White women in feminism came to learn that we, too, have a race (that we are "raced"), just as, earlier, men in feminism came to understand themselves as gendered.

My work in this book takes up the feminist project of interrogating my own location in systems of privilege and oppression—specifically, systems of racist colonialism. These systems variously privilege and marginalize me, a white woman with considerable educational and economic privilege who grew up in a "mixed marriage" of working-class and middle-class parents. I explore cultural food colonialism as one way into understanding my own privilege—and also because food represents one concrete, daily site at which I can engage in the project of resisting, undermining, transforming, and otherwise fiddling with that privilege.

Even as I understand this as a work written firmly from the perspective of a feminist philosopher, at the same time it is deeply indebted to work in many other disciplines. One anecdote may illustrate this disciplinary debt. When I began to work on the project, I was using the resources of the

Northwestern University library, which is housed in a building comprised of three separate towers, each one five stories tall. During the course of that initial research, I found myself, at one time or another, looking for a book on every floor of every tower—an architectural illustration of the multidisciplinarity of my inquiry. To some this observation might amount to an admission that I am always trespassing—or that I am always a dilettante, never speaking with any authority or expertise. However, I understand my approach to illustrate the fact that I operate from a position that recognizes that there are always other ways of asking the same question, always other kinds of questions to be asked.

In addition to philosophy and feminist theory, the fields that most deeply inform this book include colonial and postcolonial theory—particularly that done by political theorists—and development theory. Other influences obviously exist as well, drawn from cultural studies, literary theory, anthropology, and even musicology and art criticism. I have found insights and illustrations for my analysis of cultural food colonialism in the theoretical analyses of imperialist and colonialist exploitation in travel, music, literature, art and the collecting of cultural property. These cross-pollinations serve as further evidence that the phenomenon of food adventuring is not simply the bizarre pastime of some utterly isolated subgroup, but in fact is part of a system of cultural colonizing activity in which vast numbers of us participate.

Food is something that many people in the United States think about constantly, while never really giving it much thought whatsoever. We talk about food, we watch it on television, we see it in magazines, we hear about it on the radio, we can buy it everywhere—in more forms than have been available to any other society in history. Americans are infamous snackers—Europeans think of us as the people who eat constantly, who eat in our cars, who eat between meals, who eat on our way to dinner. Some segments of the population buy stacks of cookbooks, dining guides, calorie and nutrition primers. But despite all this attention to food, we pay astonishingly little *reflective* attention to it—where reflection might mean something as simple as thinking about who grows one's oranges, or wondering whether Thai people would find the menus in American Thai restaurants to be odd.

We as a society have become considerably more reflective about food in recent years. Environmental concerns have at least temporarily captured our

elusive attention, and we have come to worry about some of the environmental consequences of the typical American diet—in the last ten years, we
have worried publicly (if briefly) about rain forest beef, alar in our apples,
mad cow disease, and bovine growth hormone. I draw on and depend upon
this increased public interest in and attention to food-in-general. But I also
want to invite readers to consider different kinds of concerns—cultural and
social concerns, in addition to these environmental ones.

"But what difference could a book like this possibly make?" I've been
asked this question frequently, in tones of varying politeness. The subtext of
the question is often, "Why would you devote yourself to something this
trivial, when there are genuinely important food and/or colonialism issues
to which you could turn your attention? How is my thinking about the way
we eat going to change the world?"

For those who find the most power in a philosophical answer to that
question, I draw upon John Dewey, who observed that "every act has potential moral significance, because it is, through its consequences, part of a
larger whole of behavior. A person starts to open a window because he feels
the need of air—no act could be more 'natural,' more morally indifferent in
appearance. But he remembers that his associate is an invalid and sensitive
to drafts. He now sees his act in two different lights, possessed of two different values, and he has to make a choice. The potential moral import of a
seemingly insignificant act has come home to him. . . . There is no hard and
fast line between the morally indifferent and the morally significant."[27]
Everything—even the most trivial acts—potentially carries moral weight.

But such a philosopher's answer can only tell us that the matter of one's
dining habits *can,* under the right circumstances, be morally relevant; it
does not tell us that we are, here and now, under the right circumstances,
nor that the moral relevance is of such a magnitude as to warrant devoting
an entire book to it. For this kind of answer, I turn to the audiences to
whom I've presented my work. In reply to the "so what?" question, the people who have heard me talk about cultural food colonialism—including
people both inside and outside academia, people who count themselves as
food adventurers and people who don't—have responded by vigorously engaging with the issues. They have puzzled aloud about how their own eating
practices fit my claims—or offered arguments for why they didn't. They've
provided limit case examples and extenuating circumstances that enabled
my argument to become more complex and nuanced—or showed its limita-

tions. They've offered models of resistant eating for my consideration. They have vocally, sometimes angrily, refused my invitation to become reflective about yet one more thing in their lives. But whatever shape their response has taken, they have responded—vigorously and with deep involvement. I choose to take their responses as evidence that the questions I am asking are questions that matter, questions that are worth thinking about for anyone who lives and eats in contemporary American culture.

My hope is that this book continues that discussion by inviting you as readers to reflect on the eating practices that surround you and in which you participate, in a way that enables you to see the many stranded connections between your attitudes and practices and the ideologies and practices of social and political institutions both large and small. It does so through the specific attitudes and practices we call food adventuring, an activity that supports and is supported by social and cultural ideologies.

PART ONE

# Let's Eat Chinese

WHILE VACATIONING IN IRELAND ONE SUMMER, MY PARTNER AND I FOUND OURSELVES ravenously hungry very early one evening in Dublin. Five-thirty is an inconvenient time to be hungry in Ireland; most restaurants don't open for dinner until a much more fashionable hour, so unless you can satisfy yourself with pub food, your only option is to tough it out—or wander the streets in hopes of finding someplace open. Luck, however, was with us that evening; we stumbled upon an open Thai restaurant.

Finding a Thai restaurant in Ireland felt oddly like landing on home turf. When we are at home in Minnesota, we eat Thai food whenever we get the chance—which means whenever we can manage to be in Minneapolis or St. Paul around dinner time. Walking into this restaurant, we were strangely confident after days of moving tentatively through an unfamiliar world of pub lunches and full Irish breakfasts. I remember walking into the restaurant thinking, "Well, at least I'll know how to behave here; I know how to behave in Thai restaurants." Armed with this sense of belonging, of being in the know, I immediately began deciding which features of the restaurant's decor were genuinely Thai, and which were of obvious Irish origin— this, despite my never having been in Thailand in my life, and having spent a grand total of six days in Ireland so far. I found myself chuckling just a bit smugly at the sight of the redhaired, freckled Irish teenager dressed in traditional Thai shirt and trousers who filled our water glasses. What in the world did those wacky Irish think they were trying to prove by dressing up in traditional Thai costumes? Surely they didn't think they were passing for Thai with that hair!

In the midst of my complacency, however, I also found myself confused and a bit ill at ease. Here I was, staring in the face of a cross-cultural entrepreneurial enterprise that did not in any (apparent or necessary) way involve the United States, or a U.S. influence. Some Thai people apparently just moved to Ireland and opened a restaurant—and it looked like they didn't even pass Go (a.k.a. the United States) to do it. How could this be?

While I assessed the restaurant and its staff, another part of me (the part that was supposed to be writing this book) observed myself at work, and wryly noted my eagerness to neatly separate the restaurant's authentically Thai elements from its "Irish Thai" ones, despite the fact that only a couple weeks earlier I'd been furiously writing away on the spuriousness of authenticity. I was surprised—and embarrassed—to realize how willingly and easily I slipped into my food adventurer ways, with all the presumptions and ideological underpinnings that go along with them.

I realized that I regarded myself as knowledgeable about the difference between authentic Thai and Irish-influenced Thai restaurants quite literally because my Thai food experience had been restricted almost entirely to the United States. Unintentionally—indeed, despite my best and most highly reflective efforts—I had slipped into conceiving of the United States as culinarily neutral, as a beige backdrop against which other cuisines could display their features. According to this line of thinking, when a Thai restaurant appeared on the U.S. scene, it would not in any way bear the imprint of its locale; it would be just like a Thai restaurant in Thailand. By this line of reasoning, I, as an inhabitant of the United States, was in a perfect position from which to judge authenticity, since I'd seen Thai food cooked in a culturally neutral atmosphere—surely the next best thing to seeing it cooked on its native turf. My culture is a plain white plate—perfect for setting off features of a cuisine without imparting any flavors of its own.

I had also slipped back into conceiving the United States as Culinary Central— as the place through which any "foreign" cuisine would have to pass, before relocating in another "foreign" locale; this presumption produced my discomfort over seeing Thai and Irish culture linked together without any mediation by the United States. This particular food adventurer belief of mine even comes with its own mental image: a wheel with spokes radiating out from its axis to points on the periphery. The United States is the axis, and all other countries (and all subcultures within the

United States) are points on the periphery. Peripheral cultures can only connect with each other by traveling on a spoke, through the center, down another spoke to the other culture. They cannot simply travel around the outer ring to engage with each other without involving the center.

Sitting in this Irish Thai restaurant, I recalled having had the same "How can They do it without Us?" feeling several years earlier, when I'd eaten in a Thai restaurant in Nairobi. How could Thai food have made it to Kenya without any (apparent) help from Us?[1] How could two cultures interact with each other without the United States being somehow involved?   — same problem w/ fusion .

The United States, on the cultural food colonialist view from which I was operating, was both centrally important and transparent, both a necessary party to any cross-cultural dialogue and an entirely neutral party.

And I was having a classic food adventurer moment.

## Colonizing as an Attitude Problem

Food adventuring, as I conceive of it, is in part an attitude, a particular spirit or disposition I embody as I go into a restaurant or a grocery store, as I read a cookbook or talk with a friend about a meal. What do I mean when I describe food adventuring as an attitude? Before I turn to examine the specific features of the food adventurer's attitude, it's worth briefly examining my use of this term.

### Attitudes Involve Practices

The term "attitude" may seem an odd choice here, because we often tend to think of attitudes as purely mental entities—private, internal possessions that have no tangible outward manifestations. On this view, we can "keep our attitudes to ourselves"—hiding our evil ones behind a façade of polite and friendly behavior, for instance. If attitudes were purely mental, purely internal, it would not be useful to describe food adventuring as an attitude. Such an identification would isolate attitudes from actions, leaving them with virtually no explanatory power.

But attitudes are not purely mental. I do not simply carry them in my mind; I carry them on my face, in my posture, and (crucially) in my interactions with others. I constantly display my attitudes in the ways I approach the world. (That doesn't mean we can *never* keep our attitudes to ourselves—I can at least temporarily conceal an attitude from you, for example, by pretending to have a different one.) Attitudes are in principle always at least partly public—open to observation, scrutiny, praise and criticism. Behavior is *part of* the attitude itself, not just the outward manifestation of it. More than a promissory note for action, an attitude is best understood as a kind of action. Any activity into which I carry a particular attitude will, therefore, come to be shaped by that attitude. Any activity into which one carries a colonizing attitude becomes structured by colonizing. The reverse is also true; that is, attitudes manifest themselves in actions; and actions are shaped and formed by attitudes.

Pragmatist philosopher John Dewey provides further insight into this relationship. In describing it, Dewey variously uses the notions of "attitude and act," "motive and consequence," and (most often) "character and conduct." In an early work, we find this definition of character and conduct (a definition in which Dewey even uses the word "attitude"): "If we take the moral feelings, not one by one, but as a whole, as an attitude of the agent toward conduct, as expressing the kind of motives which upon the whole moves him to action, we have character. And just so, if we take the consequences willed, not one by one, but as a whole, as the kind of end which the agent endeavors to realize, we have conduct."[2] Character, then, is the entire package of motives and aims, out of which spring our various actions. These various actions, taken together and understood in turn as the consequences of our motives and aims, comprise conduct.

In a dichotomy-smashing move that is familiar to readers of Dewey, he defines character and conduct as "morally one and the same, first taken as effect and then as causal and productive factor."[3] Character, to oversimplify, is "yesterday's conduct," while conduct is "tomorrow's character." The two cannot be understood in isolation from each other, and indeed, they are formed (and continually reformed) in intimate relation to one another. "In a word, character is the unity, the spirit, the idea of conduct, while conduct is the reality, the realized or objective expression of character."[4] What Dewey holds for character and conduct I likewise maintain for attitude and action.

Understanding attitudes in this way means that when two people engage in what is ostensibly the same activity but with different attitudes the activities are *not* the same in the two cases. A group of people eating in an ethnic restaurant are not all doing the same thing, but are engaging in a host of different activities that are infused with the attitudes of those who participate in them. On Dewey's terms, conduct differs because character differs.

What follows from this analysis of the relation between attitude and action? Simply this: sometimes eating in an ethnic restaurant actively supports and advances colonialism, and sometimes it does not; sometimes it even resists colonialism. If attitudes can be colonizing, then surely they can be anticolonizing as well; and if anticolonizing attitudes were to shape eating practices, then activities that are vehicles of colonization could be transformed into vehicles of anticolonialism. Once we recognize attitude and action (character and conduct) as mutually constitutive, we must also recognize that activities do not carry their moral meaning and worth independent of the attitudes of those who carry them out; it is not the case that some actions are "anticolonialist in principle." Challenging food colonialism will not be accomplished by my simply forswearing some set of activities (no more eating in ethnic restaurants, no more shopping in ethnic grocery stores)—or even swearing *on* to some other set. The relation between attitude and action makes any such simple moral commandments impossible.

I'll return to this topic in much more detail in part 4.

### Attitudes and Ideologies

I understand attitudes to be individual embodiments of culture-wide ideologies. Paolo Freire, the Brazilian radical philosopher of education, describes the relationship, noting that "the dominant ideology 'lives' inside us and also controls society outside."[5] The ideology of colonization that pervades and controls a particular society also lives inside us as a colonizing attitude.

Thinking of attitudes in this way connects the macroscopic level to the microscopic; it links large scale political and economic systems to individuals' actions and beliefs. Such links are vital because, without them, we are left to understand systems like colonialism either as large scale systems of oppression only (an understanding that obscures the ways in which individuals perpetuate those systems) or as individual acts entirely (an account that hides the powerful institutions linking individuals' actions, and that makes it look as though individual action alone can transform the world).[6]

In exploring and confronting a phenomenon such as food colonialism, it is important to stress the relationships between large and small, between ideology and attitude. To see why, consider this example from my work as a teacher. I teach courses on racism and sexism, in which I focus on large-scale systems of oppression. I do this as a way to counter my students' tendency to see oppression only in the individual attitudes of bad people. However, I have also learned that if I focus exclusively on systems, I tend to immobilize students, who become confounded by the sheer size of the problems they confront, and end up feeling that their own actions are of no consequence whatsoever. I have come to appreciate the importance of interweaving discussions of systems of oppression with discussions about how the attitudes and actions of individuals can work to support or resist oppressive systems. Otherwise, students disengage from the problems they confront, figuring that they as individuals are no (meaningful) part of the problem, and thus cannot be any (useful) part of a solution.

That same principle carries over to my thinking about food adventuring. Without question, we must understand the ways that colonialism shapes the world food system on the macro level (think, for example, of the ways in which entire local economies are given over to the production of luxury crops for export, leaving local farmers in the position of paid workers who cannot afford to purchase the foods they once grew). But if we locate colonialism only in such large-scale relationships, ordinary individuals within colonizing societies may well feel that we are innocent of any participation in colonialism, or are at least powerless to do anything about the colonizing relationships that do exist. (I, personally, don't control any multinational food companies, and the trifling amount of stock I hold in such companies surely can't make any difference, can it?) In an effort to resist such disengagement, I think food adventurers are warranted in devoting attention to the ways that individual attitudes and actions manifest and reinforce colonizing relationships.

## Food Colonizing Attitudes

There is no single set of beliefs, dispositions, and behaviors that can be called "the colonizing attitude," just as there is no one thing called "the ideology of colonialism." The ideologies and attitudes we call colonialism have as many faces, as many aspects, as there have been colonizing relationships in history. It would be not only impossible, but also foolhardy, to try to characterize all colonialism in terms of a single ideology.[7] Instead, I choose to focus on two elements that play an important role in the attitudes of many contemporary Euroamerican food adventurers and other cultural colonizers: their often obsessive interest in and appetite for the new, the obscure and the exotic; and their treatment of dominated cultures not as genuine cultures, but as resources for raw materials that serve their own interests. These two elements are linked together by a third element that plays a supporting role: the adventurer's intense desire for authentic experiences of authentic cultures.

In this section of the book, I explore each of the three aspects of the food colonizer's attitude in some detail, beginning with the quest for novelty and exoticism in chapter 1, and ending with the Other as resource in chapter 3. In this initial description of the three, I will draw my examples primarily from diners' experiences in restaurants—my own experiences and those of people with whom I've talked. In parts 2 and 3 I will reexamine these three aspects of colonialism through the lenses of restaurant writing and cookbook writing, to see what more we can learn about each of them if we consider other food adventuring activities.

*Chapter 1*

# The Quest for Novelty

> Within commodity culture, ethnicity becomes spice,
> seasoning that can liven up the dull dish that is main-
> stream white culture
> —bell hooks, *Black Looks: Race and Representation*

FOOD ADVENTURERS ARE ALWAYS LOOKING FOR SOMETHING NEW TO EAT. WE'D rather try a new dish than eat the same one we had last time—even if we loved the one we had last time. We'd rather try a new restaurant than eat at an old standby. And, more than anything else, we love to try cuisines we've never had before. I used to think that everyone sought out variety in their diet—everyone, that is, except for children and picky eaters, whose eating habits were anomalous and in need of special explanation. The rest of us, I assumed, just tried new foods as a matter of routine.

But humans do not universally desire novelty. Many eaters—including many ethnic food fans—place a high premium on constancy in their diet.

## I'll Have the Usual: The Virtues of Tradition

In many cultures of the world, people eat the same *kinds* of foods for gener-ations, coming to define themselves in terms of their relations to those tradi-tional foods. A South Indian waiter explained to me once that "South Indians are rice people; North Indians are wheat people." To him, South In-dian cuisine, in all its variety and complexity, could still be understood in terms of one single, staple, *defining* food. In many cultures, a single starchy food plays such a central role in the culture's foodways that its absence means there is no meal. To ask, in Chinese, if one has eaten, you literally say

"Have you had rice?" When I was growing up among Lutherans, the joke
was that you only had to say a prayer before eating if there were potatoes—
no potatoes, no meal. Within this kind of eating context, variety—at least
variety in staple foods—is accorded little value.

Some cultures place such value on the traditional preparation of their
cuisine that their members tend to systematically reject new ways of preparing foods. Cookbook author Claudia Roden writes that "Cooking in the
Middle East is deeply traditional. . . . Its virtues are loyalty and respect for
custom and tradition, reflected in the unwavering attachment to the dishes
of the past. Many have been cooked for centuries, from the time they were
evolved, basically unchanged."[1] She notes that when an outsider suggests a
variation in a recipe, the outsider is likely to be met with incredulity, scorn,
or laughter.

Such aversion to new food preparation techniques or new foods sometimes has considerable political and social significance, as it does when a
colonizing culture rejects the foods of the people it has colonized—or vice
versa. Nineteenth-century European colonials living in Asia and Africa often
pointed to the food of the colonized as yet more evidence of their heathen-
ish and subhuman ways. Only inferior beings could possibly eat such weird
and revolting foods; they would stick to the foods of home, no matter how
difficult they were to procure.[2] (Of course, while some colonizers were busy
snubbing the food of the locals and waiting for their shipments of foodstuffs
from home, others were lapping up every new dish their native cook could
put before them—and asking for recipes to take back home. This was particularly the case for many British people in India, a topic I'll explore later.)

Conversely, colonized cultures often have adhered to their own food
practices as one important symbolic way to resist colonial incursion. Land,
labor, and resources may be in the possession of the colonized, but if they
are able to prepare familiar foods, dress in familiar ways, and practice traditional art forms, then people still control their own cultural life on at least
some levels. Food represents one important way to sustain that life, both literally and figuratively. Indeed, given the importance of cultural practices to
cultural identity, it is easy to see why cultures emerging from colonialism
may work vigorously to reinstate all such cultural practices that have been
forbidden or demeaned by the colonizer. Leaders, recognizing the power of
such practices have even at times mandated their return—as did Mobutu

*but also a way for colonizes to mark them difference*

Sese Seko in Zaire when he required its citizens to wear their traditional dress. While such a mandate proved highly unsuccessful for understandable reasons, it is also not surprising that Mobutu attempted it.

Even in a variety-obsessed culture such as my own in the United States, some people eat the same foods every day—often out of economic necessity, but frequently for other reasons as well. Health constraints sometimes dictate a strictly uniform diet. At a conference banquet, I met a man whose doctor had prescribed that he eat exactly the same foods every day as a way to manage a health problem. Ironically, he was seated next to a man who had been told to vary his diet every day—also for health reasons. And sometimes necessity has virtually nothing to do with a decision not to vary one's diet. When Gerald Ford was president, the nation learned that he ate the same lunch every day, which he made for himself. (As I recall, it involved cottage cheese and ketchup.) My partner Peg O'Connor had a grilled cheese sandwich and a glass of ginger ale for lunch every day every summer of her childhood; by graduate school, she had expanded her lunch repertoire only slightly, to include four or five items. She, in her own defense, is quick to invoke the case of Ludwig Wittgenstein, the brilliant but eccentric twentieth-century philosopher who reportedly didn't care what he ate—provided it never varied from day to day. And even among experimental eaters, many have the same thing every day for breakfast.

Variety is not universally desirable. Sometimes, familiarity breeds not contempt but comfort and security, ease and facility. The term "comfort foods" in fact refers to just those familiar foods that we turn to, in order to soothe ourselves after a hard day, or to treat ourselves on a Sunday morning.

While it might be tempting to assume that only the foods one has eaten since childhood could achieve such familiarity, in fact once-unfamiliar ethnic foods sometimes achieve this status as well. I know several Euroamericans for whom various Ethiopian dishes have become comfort food. Many diners in ethnic restaurants featuring ethnicities other than their own turn out to be there in search of their own version of a comfort food—*not* something they've never eaten before. The National Restaurant Association report confirms this observation. *Ethnic Foods: A Profile* places ethnic restaurant eaters into one of three "attitude segments." Only among the "culture-oriented" segment—the segment most similar to food adventurers—does there exist a strong interest in new, novel foods. Members of the other two

segments—the "restaurant-oriented" and "preparation-oriented" consumers—
in fact express little desire to try new things; restaurant-oriented consumers,
for example, *are seeking food they know and like*," while preparation-oriented
consumers exhibit "a reluctance to venture into unknown territory."[3]

## I'll Have the Unusual: The Fascination with Novelty

Unlike those who favor familiarity, food adventurers like nothing better than
unknown territory. We search through restaurant lists in phone books and
magazines, looking for unfamiliar restaurants with promising names. We
devise ingenious methods to learn where They go to eat, and what they eat
when they get there. We read ethnic newspapers, to find restaurants that ad-
vertise in them. We swap tips on Internet newsgroups (carefully keeping
our *real* favorites to ourselves, for fear that popularity will ruin them). Indeed, the Internet has proven to be an incredible resource for food adventurers, something the essayist and self-described "big hungry boy" Calvin
Trillin recognized as early as 1974, when he wrote about an investment banker
who "could summon data on four hundred [restaurants in New York] simply by strolling over to a computer terminal he had installed in a small office
one flight above his bedroom and punching a few keys—having first dialed
a special number in California on the telephone and placed the receiver next
to what passes for the machine's ear."[4] Nowadays, even the casual food adventurer might avail herself of the vast resources of the Internet, where any
number of e-mail lists and websites are devoted to helping their readers
"discover" the best Cantonese/Tex-Mex/Central American restaurant in New
York/North York/New York Mills, advising travelers on where to eat in Singapore and Buenos Aires, and directing cooks to the best sources for nam
pla, chipotles, and harissa. Accessibility has made certain aspects of food adventuring much easier.

Of course, accessibility is a double-edged sword for the food adventurer,
whose motive for all this information gathering is to discover foods that
aren't yet known—where "known" is understood to mean "known to most
members of white, middle-class America." We go on quests for dining experiences our friends have never had, for there is a social profit to be made by
being the first among one's friends to have eaten Tibetan food. Like the explorers Richard Burton and Henry Schoolcraft, contemporary white Ameri-

can food colonizers set off on brave adventures down unfamiliar streets filled with people-who-aren't-white in search of the newest, most exotic dining experience possible. We are bold, willing to eat anything—once—and to go anywhere—so long as we're the only ones of Us there once we arrive.

So why do some of us require such a constant infusion of new flavors? Why does the novel hold such fascination for food adventurers?

## Because I've Never Had It Before!

Food adventurers crave the new in part simply *because* it is unusual, unexpected, or different, and differentness is something we have come to value and even demand. We tend to consider "novel" and "ethnic" as somehow synonymous. The National Restaurant Association study on ethnic cuisines, for example, identifies the quest for novelty as one of the *primary* characteristics of the group it labels "culture-oriented," a group whose members "see the enjoyment of ethnic cuisines as part of learning and participating in a culture other than one's own" (4). Sixty-three percent of culture-oriented consumers strongly agree with the statement "I am constantly looking for new tastes and cuisines to try," and 41 percent strongly agree that they would be "really distressed if there were no more new cuisines or dishes to try" (51). According to the authors of this study, desire for a constant influx of new experiences counts as evidence of a culture orientation. Why? Is my fascination with novelty *really* equivalent to an interest in cultures (whatever that might mean)? I'm frankly suspicious. When food adventurers flatfootedly equate interest in cultures with a desire for new dining experiences, the results are problematic, both for diners and for those whose foods they consume.

*well duh .*

One problem with novelty is simply that it cannot remain novel. That which is novel quickly becomes ordinary, prosaic, even—gasp—common. In a capitalist, consumerist economy like that of the United States, yesterday's new exotic cuisine becomes tomorrow's supermarket special. I have watched this happen with Thai food during the time I have been working on this book. It has gone from being a cuisine featured in only a few out-of-the-way restaurants in big cities to being something I can make at home, thanks to handy foil pouches of "Thai seasonings." In the process, Thai food has ceased to be glamorously, mysteriously novel for the hard-core food adventurer; it may well be on its way to becoming everyday—as ordinary as spaghetti and tacos. And that, for the food adventurer, spells disaster—even as it spells "commercial success" for the Thai ingredient import business, and "safe to eat" for other consumers who prefer their dining adventures a little bit more scripted.

The novel, when it loses its novelty, becomes uninteresting, undesirable. By the time he can buy a manufactured version of it in the frozen food section of his supermarket, the food adventurer's interest in the food dissipates, and he abandons it to the profit makers. When this happens, the adventurer must set out again to find something else new to replace it. If I desire the novel only for its novelty, I tend to become bored with each new thing rather quickly—a tendency that the food-writing industry happily reinforces. Glamorous food magazines often feature articles that inform their readers (in all seriousness) as to which cuisines and ingredients are now "out" and which have come "in." In a single article, the daily diet of millions of Thais can be declared passé, no longer cutting edge. Living on the front of the wave is highly situational, for the wave doesn't crest simultaneously at all places in mainstream culture. It's far easier for me to be the most adventuresome person in the room when I'm among friends in my small Minnesota town than when I visit friends in cosmopolitan Washington, D.C.

But wherever they live, adventurers who place a high premium on novelty must continually be on the lookout for something to take the place of the cuisine on its way to becoming old and familiar. This means never eating the same cuisine for long—and thus never acquiring much familiarity with it.

The fact that food adventurers lose interest in a cuisine at the point at which the American consumerist machinery starts to kick in has given us a false sense of moral purity about our activities. Since we tend to avoid ethnic food once it has been franchised, we also tend to think we are not part of the colonialist project to exploit other cultures' cuisines; exploitation is what Taco Bell has done to Mexican food, not what I do when I eat Peruvian food at the little place down the street. (In this, we adventurers are rather like those who refer to themselves as "travelers," rather than "tourists.") But the new food junkie is as much a participant in colonialism as is the taco franchiser. Valuing a colonized culture's cuisine primarily because I find it novel fosters a harmful relation to that culture—harmful to me and to members of that other culture.

The harm to the colonized is primarily cultural, not economic.[5] To value
a culture simply because it brings me into contact with something different
from my own is to value it because of an incidental fact about *myself*; such a
form of appreciation makes my experience the most relevant aspect of the
exchange, and makes me the only relevant measure of the interest of a cuisine. But when my unfamiliarity is the measure, other cultures become interchangeable insofar as they are all equally unfamiliar to me. This makes
my interest in them a function of my ignorance rather than of anything about
the cultures individually.

It is relatively easy to understand that such an exchange is at least disre-
spectful, if not downright injurious, to the culture being consumed for its
novelty. What may be less evident is that food adventurers also harm ourselves through such exchanges. The food adventurer who valorizes novelty
and difference purely for their own sakes tends to devalue the importance of
tradition and continuity in her own life. Certainly tradition and continuity
are not valuable at all times and in all places, any more than novelty is always harmful; food traditions can become straitjackets that stifle creativity
and destroy the life of a cuisine. But the adventuring food colonizer tends to
radically undervalue the importance of her own food traditions, to see in
them only boring sameness, and to disregard the ways in which those traditions have contributed to her identity.

I once talked with a woman who had grown up in a Scandinavian household in Minnesota, and who had welcomed the appearance of any new cuisine to the region as a way to alleviate what she saw as the unremitting
boredom of the predominant food. She saw variety as an unproblematically
positive thing to seek. I could sympathize; having grown up in a nearby region, I know that "white food" doesn't refer to a racial classification. But at
the same time, I felt disappointed that she regarded her own heritage only as
a limit, as something to be outgrown or cast aside. While I spent a number
of years assiduously ignoring all the foods I grew up eating, in recent years
I've found myself returning to some of these foods—a move that coincides
with my philosophical turn toward theorizing about my own white identity.
I see this exploration of my food heritage as in part an attempt to understand and connect myself to my particular ethnic location within the white
racial system. As such, it is not an unthinking, romantic return to my roots,
but rather a critical, reflective attempt to come to terms with those roots, to

*but it provides livelihood*

understand how they continue to shape my current ways of being in the world.

It would be grossly simplistic to say that rejecting one's culinary heritage is akin to refusing to acknowledge one's racial or ethnic identity. However, I do think there is something suspicious and troubling about a white person who valorizes all "ethnic" cuisines while simultaneously denigrating her own. Like the Euroamerican who idolizes the noble savage of North America and bemoans the loss of innocence in one's own culture, the food colonizer who has no time for her own food heritage creates a false image of both her own culture and the other's.

## Cultural Capital

Because the quest for newness qua newness can never, by its very nature, be permanently fulfilled, questers motivated by novelty for its own sake may end up using the cuisines of other cultures like disposable towels—terrifically handy for the moment, but of little or no value once they've been used once or twice. But food adventurers—most of us, anyway—don't value novelty only for its own sake. The novel also provides us with a kind of capital we can use to enhance our cultural status—"cultural capital," to use social theorist Pierre Bourdieu's term. By sampling a cuisine none of your friends has tasted, you accumulate a bit of sophistication that you can bank, and invest later in a social situation in which it is important to raise your stature.

The importance of a cultural capital reserve is perhaps best observed in its absence, as this passage from *The Restaurant Lover's Companion* illustrates: "Not long ago, Steve was invited to dine at a fancy Indian restaurant by an important business contact. He ordered a dish new to him, a vegetable *thali*. When [it arrived] he realized he didn't know whether he should dump the little dishes onto the silver platter, spoon them onto his plate, or just eat straight out of them. . . . He would have given anything to have known the right answer because being unsure made him nervous throughout the entire meal."[6] The fact that *The Restaurant Lover's Companion* is one of a growing number of ethnic dining guides on the market that speaks to the perceived importance of amassing enough information specifically about ethnic cuisines to be able to function with ease in social and business settings. That such books provide information that would usually be available for the asking in an ethnic restaurant is a fact worth noting. Why didn't Steve believe he could ask someone what to do? Why are people buying this book, and studying it at home before going out to eat with their business colleagues— or sneaking into the restaurant bathroom to read it between courses?

When novelty is valued for its ability to net me cultural capital, it turns out that I achieve status because I display familiarity with a cuisine that others haven't discovered, or are just now discovering. It is, paradoxically, my familiarity with that which others find novel, my ability to treat it as old hat, that gives me this status. "Peruvian food? I had it for the first time about fifteen years ago, in a place in Chicago that had just opened up. I've had it several times since then, but nothing has ever been as good as that first meal, back before *anyone* had even *heard* of Peru." (And so much the better if most of us still haven't eaten Peruvian food; to treat as passé something that is still in the realm of the unknown to most of your coworkers doubles your cultural capital.) In the world of travel, it is similarly my familiarity with a place that makes me a "traveler" as opposed to a "tourist"—a distinction that, as Michael Gorra notes, "depends on having some tourists around to avoid."[7]

Here again we must continually replenish our supply of new, novel eating experiences, because others will always catch up with us. Ethnic dining guides represent perhaps the ultimate catch-up tool; once someone else can read up on Nigerian food before he's even arrived at the restaurant, it's hard for me to score many points for having actually eaten the food and knowing something about it as a result of that experience. And if the game we're playing is Displaying Your Familiarity, then book knowledge may be practically interchangeable with experiential, gustatory knowledge—an observation that should indeed give us pause. Again, we confront the fact that the quest for novelty must remain unfulfilled—or, more accurately, always only temporarily fulfilled. When you're in the business of amassing cultural capital, once everyone knows what ghee is, *your* knowing what it is ceases to have any value. It's a tough game, this staying one jump ahead of everyone else in the restaurant.

## Novel = Exotic

Novelty has other attractions as well, however. It appeals to adventuring food colonizers because we see in it the presence of the exotic; I reckon that this is one of its most important meanings for food adventurers. The earliest meaning of the word "exotic" is simply "not native to the place where found."[8] Plant species are exotic, for example, if they have been introduced to a region (palm trees in Ireland; sumac in Minnesota). We can understand cuisines as exotic in this sense as well—although it might be problematic to ascertain what a "native cuisine" is.[9] Vietnamese food, for example, is not native to the North American continent, but it certainly is "native" to many of the people on this continent who have grown up cooking and eating it on a daily basis. This notion of exoticism obviously provides a strong connection to novelty; exotic food might be described simply as food that is novel—because not native—to members of a particular culture.

A more recent definition of the exotic takes us beyond the notion of foreignness alone: "strikingly or excitingly unusual or different" (436). Connecting the two definitions, we find that which is not native to a place becoming "excitingly unusual"—fascinating and desirable because of its "foreignness." It is worth noting that there is nothing necessary about the move from "not native" to "excitingly unusual." Exotic plant and animal species, for example, are regarded as pests that are neither exciting nor desirable. Similarly, immigrants to this country often meet with open hostility from those already located here; some of that hostility takes the form of revulsion in the face of the new immigrants' foods. *Excitingly* unusual exotic things are in a class all their own.

Catherine Lutz and Jane Collins, in their book *Reading National Geographic*, address this notion of the exotic when they note, "The eye of *NG*, like the eye of anthropology, looks for cultural difference. It is continually drawn to people in brightly colored, 'different' dress, engaged in initially strange-seeming rituals or inexplicable behavior. This exoticism involves the creation of an other who is strange but—at least as important—beautiful"— or, in the case of food, strange but delicious. Lutz and Collins conclude that "The exotic other is by definition attractive. . . ."[10] (And tasty.) Skim the pages of *Saveur,* the glossy magazine with the motto "Savor a world of authentic cuisine," and you might think you are looking at *NG.* Pictures of delicious foods from a particular region vie for your attention with shots of the "interesting" natives of that region—just the thing to spice up the "dull dish" of mainstream white culture.

Note that the definition of "exotic" as excitingly unusual includes no explicit reference point; it does not specify that something must always be unusual or different *to someone in particular*. I suggest that the reference here is excluded because, in the context of contemporary white adventure eating, things come to be treated as if they were exotic in principle—unusual and different per se, regardless of perspective. But perspective is not at all irrelevant, and the "nonperspectival" perspective from which cuisines get defined as exotic is the perspective of the Euroamerican eater. Hamburgers are never defined as exotic in the United States, even though they are indeed a strikingly different food to many people living in the country. Pad thai, however, is exotic (by definition!), even though it is a common, ordinary snack food for Thai people—many of whom now live in the United States. Perspective disappears for Euroamerican adventure eaters, not because it is irrelevant, but because we come to assume the universality of our own point of view.

While perspective *is* obviously relevant to the issue of differentness, the ways in which we use the term "exotic" mask or elide the question, "From whose perspective is it different?" The perspective is, in fact, still there—it is the perspective of a middle-class Euroamerican—but it is left unstated. Rather than a perspective, we who occupy it treat it as the wallpaper, as the default, as ground zero. (Recall my musings in the Thai restaurant in Dublin for an example of this attitude.) The result is that I come to define Thai food as exotic food—exotic, somehow, even to Thais who have consumed it every day of their lives. Thai food is different-in-principle because different-to-Us.

In fact, the term "difference" is instructive here. In present usage, we find this term referring to people of color, with no mention of those *from whom* they differ. In higher education, for example, there is much talk of "respect for difference," which I am to understand as meaning "respect for people who are not like me-a-white-person." White people are virtually never the "different" ones who are to be extended respect; whites are the universal standard(s) against which difference is revealed.[11]


### Domesticating the Exotic

Food adventurers may be enthralled with the exotic, but there *is* a limit to our adventurousness. We need to whittle the exotic down to size, so it isn't too odd for us; we like our exoticism somewhat familiar, recognizable, *controllable*. It needs to fit into some known category for us before we can even be fascinated by it. While we may pride ourselves on our openness to novelty, we who inhabit the cultural norm always want that novelty explicable in terms of the norm as well. We're like those visitors to a new city who

ask the locals "So, where's your Soho here? Where's the Village?"—attempting to understand this new place by superimposing their map of New York
City upon it. The fact that even adventurers seek familiarity in the midst of
our adventuring reminds us that we aren't really so different from other, less
intrepid eaters; the difference is more than anything a matter of the degree
of familiarity we require in our dining experiences. Here again, context is
relevant; one may be more or less of an adventurer depending upon the spirit
of those around you. The borders between adventuring consumers of ethnic
cuisines and other kinds of cultural colonizers are permeable and situational.

The exotic itself has to fit into some fairly well-delineated categories in
order for it even to be detectable as exotic by Euroamerican food adventurers.
Understanding exoticism in this way, we must conclude that some cuisines
might simply be beyond exotic—so far outside of our ken that we have no
place for them, no way to assimilate them. At the extreme end, we (or at least
various less-intrepid subsets of us) may not see them as cuisine, or even as edible. "Birds' nests? Duck webs? *Insect eggs?*" If a food is too far removed from
the territory of exoticism that we have identified, then it remains invisible, uninteresting, or distasteful to us. The lines of demarcation are highly individual;
one man's bird's nest is another woman's ethnic comfort food.

But the exotic cannot be too tame, or too familiar, either, or it will cease
to be exotic. It is thus unsurprising to realize that foods continually move
into and out of the realm of the exotic for us, as they become more and less
familiar to us. One example that brings this home to me is pizza. My mother
reports that our family first ate this food a few years before I was born. At
that time, it was a deeply foreign food in northern Wisconsin—and it was
*not* a big hit with the family. But by the time I was a small child, pizza had
assumed a regular place in the family diet—although Aunt Loretta would
still remark "Ach, that old pie-za," whenever it appeared in her presence.
We still thought of it as Italian, however. Now, you can buy pizza in every
shopping mall, and my young niece and nephew probably would describe it
as American food—which it has become.

There is a class hierarchy—a kind of snobbery, if you will—manifested
in the degrees of exoticism that one is willing to experience or enjoy. And it
is a hierarchy rooted not particularly in money, but in cultural capital—the
stuff with which we academics end up being rather well endowed, no matter how recent and tenuous (or even artificial) our membership in the middle class may be. A wide cultural gulf separates the people who eat Chun

King frozen entrees and visit Mexican franchise restaurants from the people who are willing to go to "real" restaurants, frequented by "natives," but who still tend to stick to the safe dishes. Still another gulf separates them from the people who pride themselves on eating the weirdest (to mainstream, white eyes) food on the menu—or who want to eat what They really eat. There is prestige to be gained from being the one willing to eat the most exotic thing. The less familiar, the less domesticated, the greater the adventure value of a meal, a restaurant. What experience is at the top of this hierarchy? It is the experience of the undomesticated exotic, which we also know as the authentic—the true cuisine, unmediated by any outside influences. (Never mind for the moment that no such thing exists.)

What role do members of the society of the colonized Other play in establishing the boundaries of the exotic? Do they have a role in deciding which aspects of their culture are selected as being exotic enough—or, for that matter, which entire cultures are paid attention to and which are ignored? It might be tempting to claim that the colonized have no power over this whatsoever, but such an answer wouldn't be accurate or illuminating. Market-savvy ethnic restaurateurs, for example, may have tremendous power to direct consumers' tastes in a particular direction, for whatever reason. Perhaps they want to deflect consumer interest away from certain dishes because they are too labor intensive or require ingredients that are too difficult to obtain or too expensive; perhaps they want to encourage tastes for dishes that rely on abundant foods, are easy to prepare or that showcase something in a cuisine about which the restaurateur is particularly proud. Just as it is hopelessly naive to describe the transfer of foodstuffs and recipes as a completely free and equal exchange, so too is it wrongheaded (and disempowering) to suggest that members of colonized societies are all and only helpless pawns in the exotification process.[12] The fact that they are not—that they employ all manner of techniques to influence the ways in which their cuisine is taken up by the Euroamerican consumerist machinery—is an important potential source for resistance to food colonialism, a possibility to which I will return in part 4.

*Only Ignorance Is Bliss*

Examining the connection between novelty and exoticism affords one more opportunity to discuss the way in which an obsession with difference springs from, and encourages the preservation of, ignorance about that other culture. I can preserve the exotic allure of a cuisine best by remaining ignorant of its particularities; shrouded in mystery, it has the power to tantalize me. If I investigate the sources of that enticing aroma, its power to entice me diminishes. Graham Huggan makes a similar point in a discussion of postcolonial literature. He writes, "Exoticism relieves its practitioners . . . from the burdensome task of actually learning about the 'other' cultures. As Tzveetan Todorov says, 'The best candidates for the exotic label are the peoples and cultures that are most remote from us and least known to us. . . . Knowledge is incompatible with exoticism, but lack of knowledge is in turn irreconcilable with praise of others; yet praise without knowledge is precisely what exoticism aspires to be. This is its constitutive paradox.'"[13]

*Praise without knowledge*: the phrase aptly describes the enchantment with which food adventurers greet a new dish, a new style of cooking, a new cuisine—and then lose interest in it when it becomes too well known to us.

## Rehabilitating Novelty?

My discussion of the quest for novelty-cum-exoticism has characterized it as primarily problematic, a desire the would-be food anticolonizer should seek to overcome.

Problematic though it is, I recognize that to reject novelty is also a problematic move, one that may well create as many difficulties as it solves. A refusal to experiment and a resistance to innovation can mark the rigidity and inflexibility of an imperialist culture that believes itself superior to those with which it comes into contact. Likewise, I recognize that an interest in novelty and a willingness to experiment are important aspects of a would-be food anticolonialist attitude—something I will pursue in part 4. For now, I wish to follow the trail where it has led us, from novelty and exoticism to authenticity—the second aspect of a food colonialist attitude I identified above and the one that will link the quest for novelty to the other as resource.

*Chapter 2*

# The Pursuit of Authenticity

For moderns, reality and authenticity are thought to be elsewhere: in other historical periods and other cultures, in purer, simpler lifestyles. In other words, the concern of moderns for 'naturalness,' their nostalgia and their search for authenticity are not merely casual and somewhat decadent, though harmless, attachments to the souvenirs of destroyed cultures and dead epochs. They are also components of the conquering spirit of modernity—the grounds of its unifying consciousness.

—Dean MacCannell,
*Tourist: A New Theory of the Leisure Class*

WHEN WE GO OUT INTO THE BIG, BIG WORLD OF EATING OPPORTUNITIES, AS FOOD adventurers we are usually looking for more than a novel or exotic eating experience. Adventurers want those experiences to be authentic. When we go out to eat, we are likely to report to each other that the food in a particular restaurant is or is not very authentic—and that we therefore should or shouldn't bother to go there. The National Restaurant Association notes this tendency in its study on ethnic dining. The study reports that "culture-oriented" consumers of ethnic foods (a.k.a. food adventurers) are particularly likely to seek out restaurants on the basis of authenticity rather than taste. Restaurants acknowledge the tendency as well; the word appears regularly on menus, outdoor signs, and advertisements.

Adventurers also tend to spend a lot of time trying to find out where They eat, on the assumption that if They eat there, the restaurant must be authentic. This is another practice so common that the National Restaurant Association included it in its laundry list of traits shared by culture-oriented consumers: "I like to go to restaurants where natives of that cuisine eat."[1]

Food adventurers tend to operate from the assumption that we really can sort out the authentic from the inauthentic—that we have clear, unambiguous criteria with which to do the sorting. Sure, there might be fuzzy cases once in awhile, but they are the exceptions. For the most part, we know just what we mean by the word authentic.

I don't believe this anymore. I've come to think that the very idea of authenticity is both confused and confusing. Food adventurers' overenthusiasm for it marks yet another way in which we participate in the appropriation and exploitation of the food of dominated cultures.

But wait: isn't it paradoxical for me to criticize authenticity? Isn't a respect for authenticity one of the only things standing between a cuisine and its destruction at the hands of the franchise machinery? Isn't my desire to eat only *authentic* Burmese food a desire I should foster, since it promotes the preservation of genuine cultures, and discourages the Taco Bell-ization of cuisines? The National Restaurant Association, for instance, associates the desire for authenticity with a *culture* orientation, an orientation that supposedly "transcends just the food and extends to the cultures that go along with ethnic food" (50). According to the National Restaurant Association then, if I'm interested in authenticity, I am interested in really learning about a culture. Surely it is Taco Bell that endangers Mexican cuisine—not me and my search for the world's most perfect chilaquiles. I'm protecting Mexican cuisine with my enthusiasm for authentic versions of it, am I not? To answer these questions—and to begin to unpack the sources of my suspicion about authenticity—let's consider what food adventurers mean when we describe food as authentic.

My discussion of culinary authenticity bears a number of connections to philosopher Peter Kivy's analysis of the philosophically more familiar concept of authentic musical performance. In *Authenticities: Philosophical Reflections on Musical Performance,* Kivy introduces a fourfold analysis of musical authenticity that will serve as a useful entry point into the culinary concept.

Kivy informs us that, in the world of music performance, the desire for authenticity has reached such a state that "those who find a musical performance to their liking, but unable to pass for authentic . . . must reach out for some new or distant sense of the term [authentic] in order to like what they like without losing their respectability."[2] "Authentic," he suggests, has come to be a synonym for "good." I don't think things have reached such a fever pitch in the world of ethnic cuisines, but the term has certainly achieved the status of an honorific.

Kivy both explicates and critiques four senses of the term "authentic" as it applies to a musical performance: "(1) faithfulness to the composer's performance intentions; (2) faithfulness to the performance practice of the composer's lifetime; (3) faithfulness to the sound of a performance during the composer's lifetime; and (4) faithfulness to the performer's own self, original, not derivative or an aping of someone else's way of playing" (6–7). He reveals the various inconsistencies and incoherencies embedded in each understanding of the concept, showing, in some cases, that it is impossible to achieve authenticity in the sense intended, and in other cases, that it is aesthetically undesirable to do so. I make similar arguments for the inconsistency of culinary authenticity, particularly in chapter 8.

Ultimately, Kivy argues that no global defense of authenticity is possible; its pursuit can be warranted only on a case-by-case basis. "I am a friend of any authenticity, or any mix of authenticities, that withstands the only relevant test there is: the test of listening" (285). The problem is not that some performers sometimes pursue authenticity in some form; the problem is when the pursuit of authenticity becomes a musical orthodoxy—the "single, solely justifiable ideology of musical performance" (286). What alternative does Kivy propose? He opts for a version of definition 4, which he labels "personal authenticity." The performer must attempt to realize their own version of the best possible performance of any given work—and the audience must in turn use its own (properly thoughtful) insights to evaluate that performance. That is the only *aesthetically* justifiable route to take—and perhaps the only ethically justifiable route as well.

In reaching this conclusion, Kivy rejects a linguistic model of music, on which the performer becomes a "messenger" who can, through his performance, "tell untruths" by distorting the composer's "message," which is contained in the composition. "The commitment of the musical performer has nothing to do with telling the truth, any more than does the commitment of the composer," Kivy notes. "That is not a misfortune. It is a liberation" (286). I explore the matter of truth-telling in cuisine briefly in chapter 8.

Cuisine and music both exist in the form of "performances." Just as a composition is not "the work of art" in the sense that the Mona Lisa is, neither is a written recipe "the dish." However, Kivy's analysis of authenticity specifically considers musical works composed by particular persons—not anonymous pieces. While "signed dishes" certainly do exist in cookery, I am primarily interested in dishes that have no authorship—the culinary equivalents of folk songs, perhaps. This marks one important difference between the domains we are discussing. It means, among other things, that I am unconcerned with authenticity as faithfulness to a creator's intentions—the first of his definitions.

Kivy is particularly interested in problems of authenticity that arise when performers attempt to reproduce performance practices of eras long gone. He convincingly points out that even if we can decide what it means to reproduce, precisely, the sound of an orchestra in Ludwig van Beethoven's time, there is no way that we can resituate ourselves as listeners in such a way as to be shocked by the beginning of his first symphony the way that his contemporaries would have been. This is another difference between Kivy's project and mine; I am considering the matter of cross-cultural authenticity. The problems Kivy identifies with authenticity understood as faithfulness to the performance practices and sound of an era other than one's own (his definitions 2 and 3) thus become problems about how to understand faithfulness to a culture not one's own. "How can I hear this work as if I were a nineteenth-century listener?" becomes "How can I experience this dish as if I were a member of a culture in which such a dish carries important religious meanings?" I don't taste what the cultural insider tastes—just as I don't hear what the nineteenth-century listener heard. The reasons for these gaps (historical versus cultural) are similar, but not identical. Thus, Kivy's criticism may not be as decisive in rejecting the search for cross-cultural authenticity as it is for historical authenticity.

Kivy's analysis is primarily an aesthetic one; mine, primarily ethical and political. The division between aesthetics and ethics is by no means hard and fast—indeed, I shall argue in part 4 that aesthetic and ethical judgments ought to inform each other more deeply than they often do—but it is nevertheless live. Perhaps because his emphasis is aesthetic, Kivy says, without question, that it is no *necessary* part of the performer's goal to attempt to achieve anything like fidelity to composer's intention; the performer's loyalty must always be to his own (well-considered) vision of the best possible way to perform a given work. When the question is reframed as an *ethical* one about the preservation of a still-living cultural practice, that answer will not necessarily suffice. (In the historical case, Kivy thinks it does; he believes our moral obligation to respect a composer's wishes is "far weaker in any given instance than our moral obligation to realize what we deem to be the best performance possible" [151].) My discussion in this book is my attempt to address the ethical/political questions as they arise for cuisines.

### Different = Authentic

*ok – this whitecentric ness is problematic*

As food adventurers we tend to see our own foods as having none of the interest of others'—and the more remote those others, the better. The foods of our childhood are flat, dull, monotonous compared to the fascinating, exciting food to be found in a new ethnic restaurant. Nevertheless, our interest in this new food is often quickly exhausted, as it, too, becomes familiar. This transformation from rich and exciting to dull and familiar never ceases to surprise us.

It surprises us, in part, because we don't realize the degree to which our interest in this new food is an interest in something simply *because* it is new, unfamiliar, and exotic. We mistake our interest in it for the discovery and appreciation of a truly authentic cuisine. What we identify as authentic in that culture is often simply what is new to us—which may or may not represent what insiders to that culture would identify as significant, traditional, or genuine elements of it. (Recall my misadventures in the Thai restaurant in Ireland, in which I used my completely parochial experiences in American Thai restaurants to decide which aspects of the restaurant were genuine and which were not.) In fact, our choices reflect our own experiences; whether or not they identify anything important about another culture is often an open question. However, in practice, what counts as an authentic aspect of a cuisine gets built around the expectations of the eater. What do *I* think I should find in this dish, in this cuisine, in this restaurant?[3]

What we food adventurers "expect," in the case of authentic food is, paradoxically enough, the unexpected and the unfamiliar; we expect the food of the other to be distinctly different from our own foods, and we tend flat-footedly to identify the unfamiliar elements *as* the authentic ones—

authentic in principle. But to build one's understanding of authentic cuisine upon a foundation of unfamiliarity is a quixotic move, to say the least.[4]

Why the deep fascination with authenticity—or with the surface level novelty we so frequently take for authenticity? Vine Deloria, a Native American political theorist, observes that "White people in this country are so alienated from their own lives and so hungry for some sort of real life that they'll grasp at any straw to save themselves. But high tech society has given them a taste for the 'quick fix.' They want their spirituality prepackaged in such a way as to provide *instant insight*, the more sensational and preposterous the better."[5] Deloria is speaking here about some white Americans' obsessive consumption of Native American religious practices, but the same words could be applied to our literal consumption of non-Euroamerican cultures' foods. Deloria understands Euroamericans' search for, and collection of, Others' cultures as motivated by our desire to fill an emptiness in ourselves—he calls it a hunger for something real. My obsessive search for the most authentic South Indian restaurant, then, ends up being a self-centered search. On Deloria's interpretation, lacking an authentic relationship to my own culinary roots, I seek to graft myself onto the roots of another cuisine, another culture, one whose authenticity seems palpably obvious to me—at least initially. Perhaps in the (properly preserved!) dishes of South India, I can find the deep, rich, meaningful relationship with food that is so sadly lacking in my own fast-frozen-junk-food culture.

In search of authenticity, we find our attention drawn by novelty. Disappointed when novelty quickly wears off and we feel no more authentic than we did before, we move on to try something else. We are not terribly interested in doing the work of coming to understand another cuisine; what we want is a quick fix meal that will give us an authentic relationship to an authentic tradition immediately—without any mundane, laborious effort.[6]

If authenticity is ever to be useful for challenging cultural food colonialism (and that is still a very big *if* at this point), we cannot understand it in terms of novelty and unfamiliarity. What is unfamiliar to me is in fact something of an accident; those elements of a cuisine that are unfamiliar to me may or may not be significant elements for those who eat from within its traditions. To understand another cuisine through the lens of my own unfamiliarity is at best a shallow approach and at worst a deep distortion of it, reducing the significance of the Other's cuisine to something about my own.

Collapsing authenticity into novelty is but one way to understand the concept—a way that many food adventurers would dismiss as shallow and unsophisticated. Sometimes food adventurers move beyond an appreciation of bare novelty and exoticism to become outsider *experts* on an ethnic cuisine, more knowledgeable than most insiders, and thus able to point out the inaccuracies in insiders' presentations of their own cuisines. Such adventurers seek to become the honorary insider, the outsider whose knowledge gives them the right to special treatment. Their desire for knowledge gives rise to another sense of authenticity.

## Authentic = Replicable

When we are somewhat knowledgeable about a cuisine, food adventurers tend to define "authentic" to mean "prepared the way it would be in its culture of origin—using the same methods and the same ingredients insiders would, substituting only when absolutely necessary, and then only if the substitution does not radically alter the original food." Jeffrey Steingarten, author of *The Man Who Ate Everything,* offers this working definition of authenticity in an essay on choucroute (an Alsatian dish involving fermented cabbage and various meats, including various cuts of pork): "If it *could* have been made in Alsace by a traditional cook, it is authentic."[7]

This model of authenticity tends to demand faithfulness to ingredients more than, say, fidelity to sources of heat or kitchen utensils used. One should not attempt to make pad thai unless one has access to nam pla, the fermented fish sauce that is a central ingredient in many Thai foods, but the pan in which one cooks it is not all that crucial. But one should not pretend to make tandoori dishes without a tandoori oven—it's certainly not that the source of heat is *never* relevant, just that it is often seen as less relevant to this form of authenticity than ingredients. Among food adventurers, arguments can—and do—regularly arise over the matter of whether some ingredient, pan, cooking technique, or presentation style does or does not preserve the authenticity in a particular dish. Can we place any faith in a *South* Indian restaurant that serves naan—a *North* Indian wheat bread? Should we authenticity seekers be taken in by the chapter title of one Singapori cookbook: "The Singapore kitchen: all modern appliances gratefully accepted?"[8] Would a Singapore kitchen bulging with modern appliances really be authentic?

Steingarten, a lawyer turned food writer (he was the food editor for *Vogue* magazine, of all the improbable publications), humorously reveals just how arduous are the demands placed on the home cook who seeks authenticity in the form of replicability. In his attempts to make an authentic choucroute at home in New York, he spent endless hours poring over diagrams of pig butchering in France and the United States, and more endless hours traveling all over the city to various ethnic butchers in hopes of finding the ones who would be willing to butcher a pig into the parts that an Alsatian cook would use—and then to cure or salt those pieces according to Alsatian specifications. It turns out that butchery is not simply a matter of "carving at the joints"—either that, or French and American pigs are differently jointed. In the end, Steingarten "lowered [his] sights a few millimeters," and contented himself to make choucroute with meats that could be procured in two hours' worth of shopping in New York City (246).

Defining authenticity as replicability may be the most obvious, common-sense meaning around—but there is still nothing necessary about it. The term could be defined radically differently, such that exact replication would not even be a criterion for it, let alone the primary criterion. An alternative definition might understand a cuisine as authentic only if it ingeniously adapts itself to the new conditions in which it finds itself—as when a refugee population finds itself uprooted and inserted into an utterly new culture in which its familiar foodstuffs are simply not available. Such was the experience of Hmong refugees to Minnesota, for example. They responded to a new climate by learning to grow and use all sorts of new vegetables, in addition to growing those vegetables from home that could adapt to Minnesota's climate. Adaptability has been an extremely important capacity for cuisines to develop throughout history; when a culture has been dislocated, its cooks have had to alter their cooking methods and ingredients in order to meet the conditions they have found in their new locale. Similarly, cultures that have remained in one location but have been overrun by an outside power have often found themselves confronted with new foodstuffs—and new demands on their cuisine from the colonizers. In response to such unwelcome incursions, cuisines have changed, often in remarkably resilient ways.[9] The example of the French occupation of Vietnam is illustrative here; the Vietnamese incorporated a variety of French ingredients into their cuisine, making them their own. Among these are coffee, asparagus, dairy prod-

*bank m*

ucts like butter and cream, and traditional French bread. Such a move represents an important form of resistance to colonialism—a case of using the master's tools, if not to dismantle the master's house, then at least to make one's own house much more interesting, in spite of the master's wishes.[10] I will have more to say about this issue in part 4.

If any general definition of authenticity is possible, it might make sense for it to emphasize adaptability instead of, or in addition to, replicability. After all, it is only with the emergence of the "global marketplace" that replicability has even been possible—that it has been possible to find foodstuffs *from* everywhere in the world *in* many places in the world. Now, persons of fairly modest economic means can expect that the pad thai they eat in Minneapolis, will be made with pretty much the same ingredients as a pad thai made in Bangkok. But such a pad thai could in fact be inauthentic—if adaptability has been an important part of Thai cuisine. A definition of authenticity that emphasizes replication at all costs may violate central organizing principles of a cuisine. In such a situation, to insist upon replicability may undermine the very quest for authenticity that motivates it.

What we as adventurers choose to do with this realization is up to us— we may decide that near-native replication is still an important quality to seek in an ethnic restaurant's menu, whether or not its proprietors consider it authenticity. What we cannot do, however, is continue to describe such replication as authentic in a way that pays no attention to the question "Authentic for *whom*? To what end?" Authenticity is not independent of context.

A few paragraphs ago, I breezily referred to the relevance of the "culture of origin" of a dish, as if such information were always readily available. "Where did this dish originate?" is often a question for the authenticity experts—and a question that brings to light another definition of authenticity.

## Native = Authenticity

Keith Floyd is a British restaurateur, television chef, and author of nearly two dozen cookbooks (companions to his various television series). In his book, *Far Flung Floyd*, a kind of travel cookbook on Southeast Asia, Floyd writes, "There are (in Malacca) great antique shops, dozens of street hawkers cooking noodles and rice and, of course, the ubiquitous satay—which isn't Malaysian at all; its origins are Arab."[11] With this "at all," Floyd weighs in with his opinion that a food cannot be authentically a part of a culture's cuisine if its *origins* are elsewhere; to be authentic means to be born-and-bred in a particular locale.

Obviously, meeting this criterion for authenticity is extremely difficult, the most difficult of all, given the crisscrossing ways in which cuisines develop, and the incompleteness of the records of that development. But the knowledgeable food adventurer is eager to hold onto it nonetheless, fearing that to give it up would result in the contamination and, worse, the homogenization of the cuisines of the world. (This fear is certainly not unfounded. I've been motivated to write this book in part because I believe that cuisines are harmed as a result of the ways in which they are co-opted. However, I don't believe that we can usefully combat those harms by enlisting the aid of authenticity, understood in terms of purity of lineage.) If foods cannot be said really to belong to one culture or another, but can be swapped around at will, then what is to prevent us from saying that ketchup is an authentic Thai ingredient?

I chose the example of ketchup intentionally, because in fact writers of Thai cookbooks discuss this very ingredient with considerable fervor. Thai cookbook author Jennifer Brennan (whose book I will discuss in detail in part 3) argues that ketchup is indeed an "authentically Thai" ingredient, and features it prominently in her recipe for pad thai, the so-called Thai national dish.[12] In other Thai cookbooks, ketchup, that quintessentially American sauce, is nowhere to be found. Food adventurers are often quite reluctant to believe that ingredients and foods of apparently American origin could become authentic parts of another culture's cuisine. If They borrow from Us, it is often evidence of the corruption of Their cuisine. (Not all foodstuffs are equally corrupting, though; the charge of corruption is more likely to be leveled if your culture decides to borrow ketchup or frozen biscuits-in-a-tube than if you borrow asparagus or heavy cream.) If We borrow from Them, food adventurers tend to see this as evidence of our cuisine's increasing sophistication—even when we regard the culture from which we borrow as less sophisticated than our own.

Naturally the case of ketchup ends up being even more complicated than Brennan or I imagined. Ketchup may now be a ubiquitous American sauce, but Mecke Nagel points out that it is hardly an authentic one in Floyd's sense. It seems that ketchup (kecap) started out as an Indonesian dipping sauce—

a dark sweet soy sauce, according to some accounts, and a fermented fish sauce according to others.[13] I bring up this example to show how tricky it is to authenticate foods in terms of countries of origin—when even ketchup ends up not being authentic, what can we believe in?—but it could equally well be the sort of example that food adventurers haul out to conquer their dining companion. "Ha! You think you know authentic! You don't know authentic! You probably think that ketchup is American!"[14] Playing this game with American foods cannot but lead to the conclusion that nothing is authentically American, since immigrants' foods obviously have *immigrant* origins, and Native Americans' foods are regarded by Euroamericans as outside the mainstream of the American diet, and thus obviously not authentic to it.

What if food adventurers could get our way, and all ethnic restaurants were to serve only authentic food, in all the senses I've described? Never mind, for the moment, that such a goal would be impossible. One consequence would be that ethnic cuisines would become rigid, unchanging bodies of recipes. Change, variation, and alteration tend to be objects of suspicion for the eater intent on an authentic experience. This suggests that the quest for authenticity is often a quest for the culinary essence of a cuisine, the pure elements that belong only to it. But cuisines have no essences in this sense. They possess aspects that at least temporarily set them apart from other cuisines, and also aspects that link them to other cuisines. They include many dishes that have deep and long roots in tradition—but even these dishes do not survive unchanged. So, to seek after some pure, unchanging, authentic essence in a cuisine is to look for something that does not exist. But the very search for it contributes to the essentializing of the Other that makes the search for authenticity part of the "conquering spirit of modernity" of which Dean MacCannell speaks in the epigraph for this chapter.

## The Strange but True Case of Curry

I want to render the problems with authenticity more three dimensional, by telling a story about curry. The story is "true," though it is certainly not the only true story to be told about it.

In many food adventurer circles, curry has come to stand as a kind of emblem of genuine inauthenticity; the origins of both the food and the word are understood to be rooted in deep ignorance about the real nature of the cuisine from which it supposedly emerged, and its current uses extend far beyond any legitimate referent it might ever have had. Curry seems to mean virtually anything, and thus nothing in particular. As such, it seems doomed to a life of being unavoidably, organically—*genuinely*—inauthentic, in at least two of the three senses I have described above. Curry is the unredeemable, morally bankrupt protagonist in this story. If curry were a person, it would be the sort of person your mother told you to avoid as a child; untrustworthy and slippery. A big phony.

## *In The Beginning*

The first chapter of this story of curry is an origins story. There exists considerable dispute over the etymology of the word "curry," although quite a number of sources say that the term is a variation of the Tamil word "kari," which means something like "sauce."[15] Actress Madhur Jaffrey is an authoritative writer on Indian cookery whose several cookbooks include the well-known and highly respected *Introduction to Indian Cookery,* a work she published at the very outset of the current fascination with ethnic food. She points out that others believe the word comes from the word "khari," a North Indian dish involving buttermilk and chick pea flour.[16] Jennifer Brennan points out that still others trace the term back to the word "kahari," a "wok-like metal implement in which curries are cooked in India . . ." (123). Then there is the kari leaf (or curry leaf, as it is often spelled in the United States), a leaf that is sometimes—but certainly not always—used in curry-type dishes (whichever they are) in South India and Sri Lanka. All of these etymologies trace the term back to either North or South India. Most of the sources I consulted do agree that curry (whatever it is) originated, in some sense of that word, in India.

Many foodwriters issue a disclaimer at this point: although it is likely of Indian inspiration, the word "curry," spelled as such, is in fact a British invention. Madhur Jaffrey points out that it is used in India *only* in English (5), and that it does not exist as a name for particular dishes or for a category of dishes in *any* of the indigenous languages of the country. There are, by Jaffrey's reckoning, no curries in India—a visit to a "real" Indian restaurant will prove it to you. (What is a real Indian restaurant? Well, among other things, it's the sort of place that would never try to fool its patrons into eating anything called a curry.) So, to suggest that curry is Indian in origin is tricky, be-cause most Indian cooking experts are not particularly inclined to claim it as their own.

Then where did it come from? Madhur Jaffrey accounts for the existence of curry with her own fabricated origin story—a story about curry powder, the stuff many American curry eaters regard as the essential ingredient in any "true" curry. In Jaffrey's tale, a British officer about to return home after several years in India, says to his cook as he departs "How I shall miss your delicious cooking. My good man, why don't you mix me a box of those wonderful spices that you have been using" (6). The scene changes; the cook is in the kitchen throwing together a bunch of spices, which he gives to the officer, with a promise to make more for his friends, if they like—for just two rupees each. Fast forward several years; the cook is now a success-ful exporter, shipping "best curry powder" overseas. All the boxes are marked "export only."[17] The moral of Jaffrey's story: if curry is Indian, it's a big In-dian joke on ignorant white people.

Recipes for curry have appeared in cookbooks in Britain and the United States since at least the 1850s. A cookbook published in 1859, titled *Breakfast, Dinner and Tea: Viewed Classically, Poetically, and Practically*, includes a descrip-tion of a "Hindoo meal." We read, "The favorite food of the Hindoo is rice and curry, which is prepared in the following manner: 'A quantity of rice is boiled in an earthen vessel. In another vessel of smaller dimensions, a chicken, fish or piece of mutton, is cooked in *ghee*, to which are added from two to five spoonsful of a powder composed of the following ingredients: ginger, saffron, cummin, coriander, aniseed, red pepper, tamarind, tumeric, garlic, made a liquid in cocoa-nut milk; the amount of the ingredients depending upon the taste of the person."[18] Note the relatively complicated spices called for. In con-trast, the 1896 *Boston Cooking-School Cookbook* includes an astounding recipe for "India Curry" that features veal—this is clearly not a "Hindoo meal"—and half a tablespoon of curry powder.[19]

R. A. P. Hare writes of curry in ways that provide substance for Jaffrey's claims. Hare, a British man stationed in India for some twenty-five years, compiled a cookbook of recipes regularly prepared by his personal cook. He includes a recipe for a curry powder containing approximately twenty ingre-dients. (So far, so good.) He then provides a list of curry "recipes" that basi-cally instruct you to put some vegetables into the curry (which has cooked slowly in ghee) and simmer the mixture. (Note that apparently one blend of curry spices will do for any recipe.) Curry, he notes, "may be the main dish of the meal. If not, then it must follow the meat course—it is never an entree [first course] as the meat following would have no taste."[20] Not only has curry been Anglicized here; so has the style of eating, divided into European-style courses.

Curry may be a big joke on the colonizer in India, but there exists a kind of "curry diaspora" in which the concept is in common, and respectable, usage. If you go into a restaurant featuring the cuisine of Sri Lanka, Burma, Thailand, Indonesia, Jamaica, or East Africa, you may well find on the menu at least one or two dishes with "curry" in their title. Cooks in this diaspora say the word "curry" regularly, with no particular embarrassment or apology, and often with a firm nod toward India as the origin of the dishes. I once spent a long time searching out a cafe in Mombassa, Kenya, which I understood to be named the "Swahili Carry Boil." In fact, its name was "Swahili Curry Bowl"—the kind of name an Indian restaurant in India would obviously never give itself. The restaurant had been recommended to me by a woman who had grown up in the city. She had carefully coached me on the proper way to pronounce her favorite foods in the restaurant—mahamri (small deep fried sweet breads) and mbaazi (coconut-flavored pigeon peas). However, she and I both had assumed—wrongly, as it turns out—that I was able to understand the English name of the restaurant! She no doubt assumed that the reference to curry would be obvious to me. The cafe presented a delicious version of coastal Kenyan food, one of whose principle influences is the cooking of its many Indian inhabitants—and it carried the word "curry" in its name with pride.

What is the moral of this origins story of curry? It seems to be that the food is at home everywhere except in its purported "home." And given the definitions of authenticity I outlined above, this fact is the source of at least part of its indelible inauthenticity. If a dish is authentic when it is located in its place of origin, and if curry has its origins in India but Indian cooks do not claim it, then this is truly a dish without a home, an inauthentic dish.

I have heard Jaffrey's officer-and-a-curry-powder story repeated as a genuine historical account. There is a not-so-subtle irony in the fact that her fabricated curry story is now taken to be an authentic history, when the curry powder—whose origins permanently mark it as "inauthentic"—has been taken up and used by cuisines all over the world.

What alternatives do we have for telling the story of the origin of curry? If we understood authenticity in a cuisine in terms of adaptability and flexibility, curry might turn out to be the ultimate example of an authentic contact food. This understanding would allow us to incorporate more pieces of the story of colonialism into the story of curry. For example, Heidi Haughy Cusick, in her book *Soul and Spice: African Cooking in the Americas*, notes that "a love of curry came to the West Indies first with the Dutch colonists and later with thousands of indentured East Indians. Because Arab traders had brought seasonings to West Africa, these flavors were not strange to the African-Caribbeans. . . ."[21] An origin story of curry should begin by acknowledging the pervasiveness of culinary exchanges, both forced and voluntary, both straightforward and sneaky.

*Curry Is . . .*

A curry story also requires a chapter on identity; just what *is* it, anyway? Foodwriters suggest that the term "curry," when it is used "properly," refers to any one of a wide variety of stewlike or soupy dishes. Jennifer Brennan, writing about Thai food, describes curry there as "a fashion of cooking" (123), and Madhur Jaffrey observes that, when Indians do use the word (in English, mind you), they use it to "distinguish dishes with a sauce, i.e. stewlike dishes" (5). Curries may be wet and soupy, or quite dry; they may contain meat and vegetables (or fruit), only meat, or only vegetables; and they are flavored with *some* combination of spices. These descriptions suggest that if you were to order a curry dish in a cuisine unfamiliar to you, you would be able to predict relatively little about the actual composition of that dish. The referent of the term is strikingly vast and fluid. (In some restaurants, for example, the reply to my question about the difference between the red and green curries on the menu has been "color," while in others, the answer is "spiciness.")

Indeed, one irony of the term is that, when "properly" used, it *is* so fluid, encompassing such a broad range of dishes from such a large number of regions of the world. Used "improperly," it refers only to Indian foods—where "Indian food" is understood to include only a tiny fraction of the foods actually prepared on the subcontinent, but most all of the foods that have (at least historically) been served in most Indian restaurants in the United States. (Indian food is only very recently beginning to undergo the sort of deho-

mogenization that Chinese food has been experiencing for several decades—
and then only in the largest and most cosmopolitan of U.S. cities.) Jaffrey
objects that Americans believe all of Indian food is curry—an assertion that
is less true now than when she made it in the 1970s, but is still nevertheless
heard with considerable frequency. To Jaffrey, the term "curry" is disrespect-
ful of Indian cuisines in the same way that the term "chop suey" degrades
the cuisines of China. By comparing curry to chop suey, Jaffrey underscores
the un-Indianness of curry; chop suey is a dish invented in American Chinese restaurants, probably at the time the railroad was built across the
United States.

*but do Chinese get credit for this?*

### Add One Tablespoon

What does curry powder have to do with the identity of curry—does it give it
its identity? Curry powder is a preground, premixed blend of spices that can
be purchased in most grocery stores in the United States and Britain. The mixture varies slightly from company to company, but it often contains cumin,
coriander, fenugreek, red peppers, and turmeric. We had a container of curry
powder on the shelf in our cupboard when I was growing up. I think my mom
told me she'd gotten it at a wedding shower in about 1950—not a popular
seasoning in our house. Despite its unpopularity with my mom, curry powder
is one of those things that appears in many American spice cupboards, and
can be used to flavor everything from deviled eggs to "real" curry dishes.

Curry powder, I've already suggested, is inauthentic by its very nature.
Madhur Jaffrey writes that "'curry powder' attempts to oversimplify (and
destroy) the cuisine itself. Curry powders are standard blends of several
spices . . . standard blends which Indians themselves never use" (6). Uma
Narayan concurs: "What we called curry in my vegetarian South Indian home
were some dishes of spiced mixed vegetable, eaten with rice, the spices
bearing little resemblance to curry powder."22 Curry powder, on this
account, is a shortcut attempt to duplicate the complicated—and highly
varied—process of spicing Indian foods.

Jaffrey admits that curry powders are "indeed manufactured [in Madras],
mixed in huge machines that look and sound like cement mixers, but they
are strictly for export. Not an ounce is for home consumption. [Really? Not
one ounce? What would happen if it were?] It never has been, even though
some families, over several generations, become wealthy on its sale to for-

eign nations" (175). "Foreign nations" include not only Britain and the United States—countries whose admittedly often ghastly contributions to the world of curries are the very illustrations of all that Jaffrey decries—but also Caribbean nations, whose cuisines we food adventurers regularly seek out. The author of one ethnic dining guide notes that "many Caribbean cooks use these prepared mixtures all the time and unabashedly."[23] "Authentic Caribbean cuisines" are thus dependent upon an ingredient that is scorned as inauthentic in its own purported homeland, a homeland to which these cuisines trace their roots. And in her book *Soul and Spice*, Heidi Haughy Cusick favorably reports on commercial curry spice blends from the Caribbean; according to her they "have their own distinctive flavor, one that seems more vibrant and alive than that of their East Indian counterparts" (28).

Obviously the world of curry powders has been enriched since Jaffrey wrote her original cookbook; at that time, only one mixture was available. Nevertheless, even in her most recent cookbooks, she argues that the use of premixed powders is not authentic to Indian cooking—and *ought not* be a part of other cuisines that seek to preserve their authenticity.[24] And in that regard, the *Africa News Cookbook* is wholly in agreement with her. The editors of that book note that the curries of South Africa, influenced by Malay and Indian cuisines, "rely on freshly pounded spices. You will notice that there is no curry powder in the ingredients, because authentic curries are made with different spice blends, depending on the type of food being prepared."[25]

Can curry ever be saved? Can it ever go home? Can it ever be legitimate? Genuine? Authentic? Well, of course it can; but not if we define it in terms of purity and lineage. Its supposedly sordid history leaves it doomed to the life of the mongrel, the outcast, if we take that route. An understanding of authenticity that recognizes the complex, complicated, less-than-ideal conditions under which cultures come into contact with each other and influence each other would enable us to appreciate curry as a dish with genuine, legitimate origins—in colonialism.

## Culinary Miscegenation

An anecdote will point us in that direction—though ultimately it can only take us a short distance toward a usefully retooled concept of authenticity. During a cocktail party at a conference I once attended, the talk turned to

ethnic restaurants. This sort of thing happens a lot at philosophy conferences; people start asking if there are any good ones within walking distance
of the hotel, any good ones in your home town, any good ones at the site of
the next conference. As this particular conversation progressed, one woman
described, with visible horror, a restaurant that served foods combining Indian and Italian cuisines, along with some third cuisine she could not even
recall (such was the depth of her dismay). "You just don't *do* that!" she ex-
claimed. (Obviously this exchange took place before fusion cuisine gripped
the culinary world.)

When I asked her to talk about why such "ethnic blending" bothered her
so much, she thought for quite some time before saying that it seemed un-
true to the original cuisines. She readily agreed that each of those original
cuisines already represented a blending of other cuisines. But this particular
blending seemed different to her—different in a troublesome way. She was
concerned that it was inauthentic to the original cuisines, not because they
were in some sense "pure," but because this mixing was artificial or forced—
not a "natural" occurrence. One may be willing to acknowledge—and even
welcome—the introduction of new ingredients, techniques, words, what have
you, without being committed to saying that *all* such introductions are good.
One might acknowledge with favor the transformative and resistant ways
that Vietnamese food displays the influence of French cooking (and its legacy
as a French colony), but still object to a restaurant in the United States that
attempts to combine Indian with Italian food. My fellow conferee wanted to
distinguish between legitimate and illegitimate mixings of cuisines—and
she wanted to do so on the basis of an appeal to authenticity.

Why might she have regarded this mixing as artificial in a way that the
adoption of elements of French cuisine by Vietnamese cooks was not? Part
of the answer surely lies in the fact that the Italian/Indian restaurant is a rare
species—perhaps even one of a kind—while the influence of French cuisine
on Vietnamese can be seen in a great number of restaurants. Thus, the Ital-
ian/Indian restaurant seems arbitrary and superficial in a way that French
Vietnamese food doesn't.

An even more significant reason this mixing seems forced is probably the
context in which the mixing takes place. In the case of Vietnam, members of
a culture adapt their own cuisine, in light of a colonialist incursion, whereas
in the case of the Indian/Italian restaurant, the mixing took place in a restaurant in a third country—the United States. In some sense, then, the latter

mixing was something chosen, rather than something that was suggested or dictated by the situation. If, furthermore, the restaurant were run by people who were neither Italian nor Indian, a further element of artificiality would be introduced. Rather than it being a case of members of a culture undertaking such a change out of necessity, or because circumstances encourage it, it would then appear to be a capricious act by outsiders. (Here is another way in which I think the ordinary uses of the culinary concept differ from the musical versions of authenticity; we are less likely to view a musical performance as authentic if a performer was somehow coerced into doing it *this* way rather than that. Certainly personal authenticity—Kivy's choice—would not be fulfilled in a case in which a performer was forced to play a piece according to someone else's prescription.)

In other words, on the view of my cocktail party companion, members of a culture do have privilege with respect to their own cultural productions. I think there is something sound about this response to food mixing, but I also think there is something fishy about it. What is sound is the impulse to respect the integrity and authority of a given culture, and to extend that respect even to its food. I will explore this important point in part 4, when I explore the strategic ways that authenticity can be used to resist colonialism.

My suspicions about this response arise from the fact that it renders the roles of restaurant diners invisible. Eaters become neutral observers, dispassionate spectators who are positioned to judge whether or not a culinary exchange is authentic. Diners thereby bracket their own role in that cuisine's transformation—a role that they inhabit simply by being in the restaurant in the first place.[26]

Consider the way in which white people often regard ourselves as having no race—of inhabiting the neutral state from which the race of others is clearly visible. Something similar is at work in eaters' discussions of the intermingling of cuisines, when those discussions do not acknowledge our presence as eaters-from-particular-cultures. The adventurer assumes that she occupies a position from which she can pass objective judgments about the legitimacy of a given borrowing, without factoring in her own perspective. It's the gastronomic equivalent of the Archimedean standpoint. *[this goes back to arguments about what counts as fusion,]*

Another way to say this is that if an adventurer were to interpret authenticity strictly along the lines that my conversation partner suggested, then her own activity would turn out to be "inauthentic" as well; for she is an outsider to a cuisine—an outsider whose cumulative requests and rejections surely will have an effect on the way that it is cooked in the future.

Perhaps this individual would respond that the authenticity of her eating practices depends upon the context in which she comes to eat a cuisine. If she is eating food prepared by a dislocated population—say, the Vietnamese in Minneapolis—then such an activity might be regarded as authentic, because it emerges from actual political events. Vietnamese restaurants in Minneapolis—and Euroamerican consumers of Vietnamese food—are an outgrowth of the war in Vietnam. But such an individual would, I think, have to agree that at least some of her eating adventures would count as inauthentic, given her notion of authenticity. An "eater's tour" of Thailand, for example—or perhaps even an "eater's tour" of Chinese restaurants catering to Chinese patrons in the United States—would, I believe, be inauthentic in just the same kinds of ways that she thinks an Indian-Italian restaurant run by a Euroamerican is.

But these examples show just how problematic is this notion of authenticity for making any sorts of judgments about the legitimacy or illegitimacy of various cooking and eating practices. It rests upon the assumption that cultures exist in isolation from each other. Like the conception held by the cuisine purist, it seems to assume that it is the *interactions* between cultures that must be accounted for and justified. Unlike the purist, adherents of this view may be more likely to justify certain interactions as legitimate. The French influence on Vietnam might turn out to be "legitimate" on this view of authenticity precisely *because* it was coerced; France's colonization of Vietnam forced the interaction between the two cuisines. In contrast, the lack of coercion—and the lack of any other sort of compelling reason for combining the cuisines, might explain the inauthenticity of the Italian-Indian restaurant.

Notice that this reading of authenticity produces a different result from the analysis of curry. Curry ended up being inauthentic in large part because of the coercive nature of the exchange between British and Indian cooks. In this case, my fellow conferee's view results in the conclusion that French-influenced Vietnamese food is authentic because of the coercion. While I appreciate the latter conclusion, I remain frustrated with the latent purism of this notion of authenticity—and also the disturbing possibility that such a conclusion could lead to the valorization of coercion.

To understand why and how food adventurers travel around the culinary world, gathering up the exotic-cum-authentic creations of Others' cultures with such remarkable ease and comfort, we need to consider one last piece of the cultural food colonialist attitude. Colonizers regard a colonized culture *not* as a culture in the full sense (whatever "full sense" might mean) but as a source of materials to be extracted and used to enhance our own cultures. We food adventurers regard the different-therefore-exotic Other as authentic in part because of that Otherness—and we regard the Other as someone from whom we are entitled to collect and extract portions of their culture, in order to adorn our own.

Cultural theorist Trinh Minh-ha, in her book *Woman Native Other: Writing Postcoloniality and Feminism*, helps to begin filling out the connection between exoticism, authenticity and otherness, and to move the discussion toward an examination of otherness specifically. In a chapter entitled "Difference: 'A Special Third World Women Issue'" she writes, "Now, I am not only given the permission to open up and talk, I am also encouraged to express my difference. My audience expects and demands it; otherwise people would feel as if they have been cheated: We did not come to hear a Third World member speak about the First World, we came to listen to that voice of difference likely to bring us what we can't have and to divert us from the monotony of sameness. They, like their anthropologists, whose specialty is to detect all the layers of my falseness and truthfulness, are in a position to decide what/who is 'authentic' and what/who is not."[27] Food adventurers are part of Trinh's "they": we do not come to a restaurant to eat a third-world member's cooking of first-world food; we come to eat what she might call a "cuisine of difference." Trinh points out that, whereas once we adventurers might have resisted her "difference," repulsed by it ("Why do they eat/dress/talk/think that way? It's not natural!"), now we are fascinated, enchanted by it. As she pointedly notes, it is her "difference" that now makes her an object of interest to us at all. We enter restaurants to experience that "difference." If we do not get enough of "it"—or if what we get of it strikes us as not being the genuine article, a real, authentic, capital-D *Difference*—then we leave disappointed, even angry, vowing never to come back.

Our yearning for difference—authentic difference—has its well-defined limits as well, however. Trinh continues, "Eager not to disappoint, I try my best to offer my benefactors and benefactresses what they most anxiously yearn for: the possibility of a difference, yet a difference or an otherness that will not go so far as to question the foundation of their beings and makings" (88). While we long for difference, for an encounter with the "exotic Other," we long for that difference primarily as a means of enforcing our notions of ourselves. The Other's difference, then, must fit into a premolded box, specially set aside for the purpose.[28]

How does Trinh characterize the "difference" to which the Western "authenticity specialist" is attracted? She points to the example of "the American tourists, who . . . strike out in search of what they believe to be the 'real' Japan—most likely shaped after the vision of Japan as handed to them and reflected in television films like 'Shogun'—or that of the anthropologists, whose conception of 'pure' anthropology induces them to concentrate on the study of 'primitive' . . . societies. Authenticity in such contexts turns out to be a product that one can buy, arrange to one's liking, and/or preserve" (88). The "authentic difference" Westerner colonizers believe they/we have found is that which Western colonizers have created. The Other (the oriental, the native, the primitive) regarded by Westerners as authentic is in fact an Other of Western design.[29] The authenticity of this Other (indeed, the very project of authenticating) is established against a standard constructed outside the Other's own culture, in the West, and for Western purposes. Not surprisingly then, given the consumerist proclivities of much of first-world Western cultures, the Other's authenticity turns out to be a commodity—a spirituality weekend, a meal, a jar of exotic seasonings, a piece of jewelry or an object for the coffee table. The next chapter continues this examination of the food adventurer's tendency to treat the Other as a resource for my use.

*Chapter 3*

# The Other as Resource

> Can one divide human reality . . . into clearly different
> cultures, histories, traditions, societies, even races,
> and survive the consequences humanly? By surviving
> the consequences humanly, I mean to ask whether
> there is any way of avoiding the hostility expressed by
> the division, say of men into "us" (Westerners) and
> "they" (Orientals). For such divisions are generalities
> whose use historically and actually has been to press
> the importance of the distinction between some men
> and some other men, usually towards not especially
> admirable ends.
>
> —Edward Said, *Orientalism*

AS FOOD ADVENTURERS, WE HAVE ONLY ACCOMPLISHED PART OF OUR TASK WHEN WE
have identified a cuisine as exotic and authentic. We must also see that cuisine as available to us—as something we are entitled to consume at will.
This step is vital; without it, we would leave ourselves with tantalizing but
utterly inaccessible ways to increase our cultural capital. So we must somehow define these exotic cuisines—and the people who create them—as
available to us *in principle*. We must make our access to them utterly legitimate, as *we* define "legitimate."

That this is a step in the cultural colonization process—and a necessary
step at that—tends to be invisible to adventurers, for a couple of reasons.
One is that we tend to see food as the sort of thing one would *always* have
access to, as a matter of course. Who would ever wonder if they have the
right to eat another culture's cuisine, for heaven's sake? While we might

think twice before trying on someone else's religious beliefs, or buying their archaeological treasures, or perhaps even playing their musical instruments, we tend to see food as just food—not the sort of thing that needs protecting, or that can be harmed in any way by someone else eating it or cooking it. We don't need to overcome any compunctions about eating the food of the Other, because, where food is concerned, no compunctions exist.

By now it's clear that I believe that thinking about a cuisine in this way— as either so tough or so superficial that it can't possibly be harmed—is wrong. In a sense, this entire book is my attempt to show why a cuisine *is* the sort of thing that can be harmed, in ways that bring harm to a culture. I can't, in a paragraph, dissolve this erroneous view. But I can contribute to its dissolution by suggesting that we look at food here slightly differently. Think not simply of eating someone else's food, but of walking into the middle of someone else's dining room or kitchen while their family is eating. Or into their meal of celebration or mourning. Deep and significant strands often connect a culture's foods and their customs and practices; practices central to the identity of a culture. (Think of wafer and wine in Christian commu- nion, of matzoh at the Jewish Passover seder). Given these connections, it is possible for the glib borrowing of foods engaged in by food colonizers to constitute a form of injury to another culture. Consider: it is generally rec- ognized that to treat another culture's social and cultural practices casually or disrespectfully can actually harm members of that culture. In the contem- porary American context it may seem hard to believe that food practices could ever be as sensitive or significant as religious practices or moral im- peratives, but it is still the case that they play important roles in cultures. (Indeed, they play an important role in mainstream American culture also; the largest demonstration I witnessed during my years in graduate school was a protest over the university's decision to change from Coke to Pepsi— or maybe Pepsi to Coke.) Recognizing that food is never just food, we may begin to realize that co-opting someone else's cuisine has the potential to af- fect another culture, just as does co-opting a spiritual practice.[1]

The other reason that this step—defining the Other as available in prin- ciple—tends to be invisible to adventurers is that availability is such a famil- iar element of so much of Western colonialist ideology that it has come to seem like a given, a fact of life. Western colonization has rested heavily upon the belief that the ethnic Other is a not part of a human culture in the full sense, but is a resource I may mine, harvest, develop, exploit or otherwise utilize. It also rests on the belief that Our interactions with Them are always to their benefit—even when that benefit is invisible to them. Many groups of Westerners have knowingly and unknowingly capitalized on this assumption.

Westerners invading indigenous African, Asian, and American cultures have often operated under the view that everything they found in the new setting was a resource available for them to take up and use. This view has extended not only to natural materials—minerals, timber, land—but also to people's very cultural products—art, music, stories, systems of governance, medicine, cooking. Explorers, artists, and entrepreneurs alike have treated the artistic and intellectual products of indigenous cultures—like their mineral deposits—as diamonds in the rough, raw materials awaiting refinement at the more capable hands and minds of colonizers.

In the process of "refinement," colonizers often tended to forget who originated these cultural products—even to forget that they *were already* cultural products before their so-called refinements. In the preface to *Marxism and Native Americans*, Ward Churchill addresses the ways in which Native American governance systems and agricultural practices were quarried, like so much iron ore, from the very peoples who had invented them. He writes, "The American Indian was rightly, if unwittingly, considered [by Europeans] as part and parcel of the natural order, a *thing* to be profitably surmounted. While proclaiming the land a wilderness to be brought under human control, the settlers relied upon the primeval richness of its soil to provide the basis of their agriculture; the pristine quality of its lakes and rivers to provide fish and fur; and its teeming wildlife to provide protein. In like fashion, while pronouncing the Indian as 'savage,' they lifted the form of the Iroquois Confederacy to organize their government and the crops of the Pequot and Pennobscott, Passamaquoddy and Wampanoag as the basis of their agriculture."[2] Europeans often made no distinction between a naturally occurring lake filled with fish and an agricultural system that produced abundant food; both were simply natural resources, there for the taking.

For the colonizer, resources have been regarded as developed or utilized if they are readily accessible to, and usable by, themselves—and particularly if those resources make a profit for them. Ethnic foods, on this definition, might be considered *fully* developed only when they are available in the frozen food section of a U.S. grocery store, or at the food court in a shopping mall—brought to you by a multinational food corporation. The fact that such utilization of cultural resources is not necessarily beneficial—and may well be harmful—to the lives, cultures, and eating habits of those who traditionally eat these foods tends to be regarded by its developers as beside the point.

But such commercial development would also be fairly unappealing to the food adventurer, who craves the novel and the exotic. By the time it hits the food court, an ethnic food has likely been purged of anything but its common denominators of salt, fat, and sugar; the partisans of authenticity will have lost interest in it (for anything other than its camp value). We are surely not to blame for the McDonaldization of Mexican food! We don't even (admit that we) eat in food courts!

So where do we food adventurers fit in, here? Why does *our* eating presume that the ethnic Other is a resource for our use?

The fact that we rebel against the sorts of development that homogenize and commercialize a cuisine should not leave food adventurers with any false senses of moral purity about our own activities. We may not hanker to set up—or even eat in—a chain of Burmese restaurants stretching from California to New York, but we have our own ways of conceiving of the Other as a consumer commodity; and, as I've observed before, the difference between food adventurers and other, less intrepid eaters is often one of degree, not kind. Adventurers transform the Other into a resource by means of two complementary tendencies: the tendency to regard the culture of the Other *not* as a culture in the full sense; and the tendency to regard ourselves as belonging everywhere. In short, we objectify the Other, in order that we may use them and their possessions (literal and figurative) to enhance our own lives—economically, culturally, socially.

For in the end, it is about *us*. The Other is interesting and important insofar as he or she serves to illuminate *me*, to render my life in the world more authentic.


## Mining the Other

In order for me to regard another human as someone from whose culture I am entitled to appropriate virtually anything I desire, I must first understand this human as radically unlike me. I do not regard myself as the sort of being who should be subject to such treatment, and so I must make sure that I understand those from whom I would appropriate to be radically different kinds of beings, beings not fully cultural. Edward Said suggests this is a defining characteristic of Western culture. He refers to "what Denys Hays has called the idea of Europe, a collective notion identifying 'us' Europeans as against all 'those' non-Europeans, and. . . the idea of European identity as a superior one in comparison with all the non-European peoples and cultures."[3] It is easy to see what tremendous influence such a belief could wield in a culture.

I separate myself from the Other, and render my culture superior to theirs, by a mechanism we've already seen in earlier chapters—namely, picking out aspects of their culture that are novel for me, and thus also exotic and authentic. As cultural theorist bell hooks puts it, in the commercial realm, "encounters with Otherness are clearly marked as more exciting, more intense, and more threatening."[4] Dangerous meats, seductive spices, sensuous fruits, alluring fragrances, authentic relationships with a culinary tradition; the food of the genuinely Other offers all this and more to the food adventurer weary of their own home cooking. Once I have isolated such features, I have, according to this logic, located the sources of their Otherness; it lies in those things most unfamiliar to me.

Food is a handy, readily available place to look for evidence of Otherness. If it is not a part of my experience—if I don't eat that food, if I don't cook in that style, if I don't order the courses in my meals thus—then it must be an authentic part of their cuisine. My unfamiliarity becomes the standard by which I define the true identity of the Other. And once I have defined the Other as radically Other, I have made them into the kind of being I can treat radically differently from the way I would treat any being like myself: "These people eat weird food/eat in an odd manner/use astonishing spices/don't seem at all interested in our food. They are definitely not like us." (What we choose to do with that "realization" is up for grabs. Identifying someone as radically other may result in a desire to consume them; it can also lead you to keep yourself at arm's length from them, and to refuse to let your children eat at their houses.)

It is certainly no coincidence that the cultures most likely to undergo this treatment at the hands of Euroamericans have been those we describe as third world, or of color. There is a complex interconnection in Euroamerican thinking between cultures we define as exotic and other, and those we

identify as third world. Such others, because we define them as radically
other, are not (so the logic goes) members of genuine, fully human, cultures.
Having undertaken to discover what it is that makes this society genuinely
unlike one's own, the food adventurer has in effect created a criterion by
which to rule it out of the category of culture in the full sense. If I am a
member of a culture in the full sense, and this society is radically unlike
mine, it cannot be a culture in the full sense.[5]

Because Others' cultures are not *genuine* cultures, adventurers can justify
appropriating not only their natural resources, but also their cultural productions—the sorts of things that would be off limits if this were a culture
like one's own. Food is just food (albeit exciting, novel, even vaguely dangerous food) to adventurers seeking a new experience. We ignore any attachments it may have to the social practices, religious traditions, economic
conditions of a culture—or else we treat these attachments simply as additional resources we may collect to give our acquisitions even more value,
not as things that might make us hesitate to barge in and borrow these
foods. (The consumer culture that surrounds us often makes this remarkably easy to do.) I may eat Thai food, but know little about the connections
that exist between Thai cuisine and other aspects of Thai culture; or I may
collect up information about the significance of Thai foods within Thai culture in order to acquire still more cultural capital.

We tend to believe that everything is for sale—or it will be, if the price is
right. Everything is a commodity (at least in principle), and commodities
can belong to whoever has the money to buy them. Food adventurers, for
example, often presume that a restaurant should offer all the foods with
which we are familiar, even if some of those dishes are rare and special holiday dishes, are from a different region of a country, or are not the specialties
of this chef. We wouldn't make the same assumption in a French haute cuisine restaurant; we'd never ask why such-and-such dish wasn't on the menu,
when we'd had it in another French haute cuisine restaurant a couple of
years earlier. We assume that chefs in French restaurants are artists, who
make individual artistic decisions about what they serve us. Ours is not to
question why—or to ask for something else. (Indeed, I received the equivalent of a public shaming in such a restaurant, when I asked if there wasn't
*some* vegetarian option available as an entree. "That would be an oxymoron,"
the host informed me.) In an ethnic restaurant, if I want a particular dish,
there should be nothing preventing me from having it, if I am willing to pay

for it. Notice that such a presumption may clash directly with our desire to experience a culture authentically; any random day is *not* a holiday in the real world, and if I want to act like it is, then I must forsake my commitment to authenticity, defined as "just the way they do it."

On the matter of money, consider the amount one pays for meals in many kinds of ethnic restaurants in the United States. Because money indicates value in a consumerist society (and indeed becomes one of the only measures of value in such a society), one equates fine cuisine with expensive cuisine. Thus the astronomical prices found in French haute cuisine restaurants are taken to indicate not just the price of ingredients, but also the elevated state of French cuisine, and French culture as a whole. In contrast, Americans *expect* most (non-European) ethnic foods to be inexpensive—as they often are. Why do we expect this? I suggest it's partly because at some level we believe that's what the cuisine (and the culture) are intrinsically worth; foods from South and Southeast Asia, Africa, and South America, *are not and cannot be* artistic cultural creations the way that French and other European foods are.

We also tend to treat Japanese cuisine and some parts of Chinese cuisine as artistic creations, but they may be the only non-European foods in this category. From the perspective of a hegemonic northern-European-American culture, certain foods are ethnic by nature, and some are more "ethnic" than others. German food is ethnic, but Italian food is more ethnic, and Greek food more ethnic still. Foods from any part of Asia are yet more ethnic, and African foods are the most ethnic of all. In part, this may be a function of the length of time that a cultural group has been present in the United States, and the degree to which its food has been assimilated into the mainstream— a fact that would explain why German food is less "ethnic" than Thai—but clearly time is not the only factor. Consider the example of soul food, one of the culinary traditions developed by African Americans. Soul food is regarded as some of the most ethnic of ethnic food, despite the very long time that peoples of African descent have been living on this continent. "Ethnic" functions as a code word for "Other"; if we were to map the foods of various groups, beginning with those regarded as least ethnic/most standard and moving to those regarded as most ethnic, this map would also identify the progression of peoples from least to most Other—seen from the perspective of the normal/neutral northern-European-American.

Ironically enough, I may use my knowledge of these supposedly less valuable, less sophisticated cuisines as a way to appear more sophisticated and worldly to others. These other cultures are raw materials that I can turn into cultural capital; their power to enhance my status is greater than the power they have to enhance their own. I can transform these ethnic raw materials into something important—just by virtue of paying attention to them. On their own, ethnic cooks cannot do that.

Food adventurers' ignorance about other cultures is not a passive lack of information. It is an active force with material and social consequences for the inhabitants of cultures whose foods we usurp. The same is true of our knowledge; the scattered things we do know about a culture will also have decided effects upon the ways we interact with members of that culture. Consider again that the foods that we in the United States are most likely to treat in this extractive manner are foods from economically and politically dominated nations—so-called third world nations. It is no coincidence that these cuisines are available to us in the United States. Citizens of many countries come to the United States to escape repressive, exploitive conditions in their own country—conditions sometimes created or exacerbated by U.S. government policies and corporate practices. Once they arrive here, the restaurant business may be one of few economic opportunities open to them. (And when social, political, or economic necessity forces you to peddle your culture, you do not do so freely; you may in fact do so at considerable personal and cultural expense.)

Yet we who eat in these restaurants often remain deliberately ignorant of those conditions—to say nothing of the historic and cultural conditions that surrounded the development of their cuisine. We happily pay the low bills—and give poor tips besides. In a piece in the anthology of Asian-American women's writings, *Making Waves*, Sucheta Mazumdar quotes a San Francisco man as saying, "Nearly everyone in the city goes down to Chinatown now and then for a cheap meal out. You just look around. Downtown, for any meal, you'll tip fifteen percent. In Chinatown, you tip ten percent. Nobody thinks twice about it. The meal is lower priced, so naturally the tip is lower too."[6] Naturally.

## What's Mined Is Mine and What's Yours Is Mine

So far, I've identified one aspect of food adventurers' tendency to treat ethnic Others as resources for use—the tendency to regard the culture of the

Other not as a culture in the full sense. Bluntly put, this means that the Other has no right in principle to deny access to it—only a true, full culture can deny outsiders the right to define it, borrow from it, reinterpret it. All that remains is for adventurers to see ourselves as entitled to *be* anywhere and everywhere—to believe that our access to the world should be unlimited. We need to see ourselves (or people like us in the appropriate senses) as just the people who ought to move in on the culture of the Other, and develop its creations as they properly ought to be developed.

For the food adventurer, "develop" may simply mean "appreciate in the way that no one within the culture can appreciate." Philosopher David Hume noted that "Laplanders" and "Negroes" cannot know the savor of wine, having never tasted it. Food adventurers may go one step further, and hold that Laplanders and Negroes cannot even fully comprehend the savor of their own foods, that only a member of a "sophisticated" culture such as our own could have the perspective and breadth of knowledge necessary for understanding the true delightfulness of a particular dish, the full possibilities of a particular preparation technique.[7] We adventurers *develop* a cuisine simply by *eating* it and *appreciating* it. In chapter 8, I'll also look at the way that adventurers develop the cuisine of the Other by writing about how to cook it.

Writers who analyze tourism and the collecting of cultural property identify the belief that one is entitled to be anywhere as a particularly modern, western notion. John Berger, writing about nature photography, notes, "In the windows of bookshops at Christmas, a third of the volumes on display are animal picture books. Baby owls or giraffes, the camera fixes them in a domain which, although entirely visible to the camera, will never be entered by the spectator." He quotes the introduction of one such book, which reads, "'Each of these pictures lasted in real time less than three hundredths of a second; they are far beyond the capacity of the human eye. What we see here is something never before seen, because it is totally invisible.'"[8] Nature photography represents one extreme, technology-intensive version of the view that "we" (however we define that we) ought to be able to be anywhere—even someplace *inaccessible to us in principle* due to our embodiment.

Other less striking examples of this belief abound. Many privileged inhabitants of the United States have come to expect a kind of unlimited access to our surroundings—we expect to be able to see behind, to go underneath, to enter the inner sanctum. Our fascination with this perspective has spawned a whole range of tourist activities that involve entering the site of the Other (who may be a human from another culture, an animal, or even an inanimate object) and getting a front row or (better yet) backstage seat to witness its goings-on. We imagine ourselves as bodyless, transparent, or infinitely malleable beings who can float into any sort of situation and be at home there—either by relying on our invisibility or by sufficiently assimilating to our surroundings so that our presence is unremarkable. The idea that there might be legitimate reasons we are not welcome everywhere is unfathomable to us—or at least irrelevant. Contrast this with the practice currently in vogue at exclusive restaurants, in which some lucky table of patrons gets to dine *in the kitchen*. These "kitchen tables" are often booked *years* in advance—and guests regard it as a tremendous honor to be allowed to sit in them and watch the chefs at work.[9]

One version of the belief that the world is an open book that I may peruse—and buy!—is manifested in the familiar caricature of the United States tourist abroad. While the portrait is indeed a caricature, many of us have nevertheless been witness to, and even participants in, scenes in which the caricature comes to full-blooded life. The American tourist (often with no malice or arrogance actively intended) believes that museums and restaurants should be open when she wants to visit them; that hotels should have vacancies; that nothing should be closed for repair the year she is abroad; that impassable roads will become passable for her; that "private" signs don't apply to people from the United States; and that anything *is* for sale—if you can offer enough money. The typical American tourist of this stereotype adopts the blustering attitude that "no one is going to tell me what I can and can't do," an air of bullheaded libertarianism that has provided material for countless jokes.

A stereotype? Yes, but I have found myself embodying it when, for example, I disregard the admonitions at the front of a travel book on East Africa and decide that somehow, miraculously, *I* will be able to travel on remote roads at 55 miles per hour, even though they are not paved and it is the rainy season. I find myself participating in it when I drool at being told that some place is off limits to me (because of my race, religion, whatever); even though I will respect the privacy of that place, I will indulge in a fantasy adventure in which I somehow sneak into that place, and behold the wonders never before seen by eyes such as mine.

Food adventurers manifest this belief in the universal legitimacy of our presence when we enter domains that are quite clearly designed with us *not* in mind—restaurants whose menus are only in Chinese, for example—and then express surprise when we are met with open hostility (or indifference) instead of open arms. "Outlaw Cook" John Thorne, co-author of a newsletter by that name and author of several iconoclastic books on food and cooking, describes an experience he had in such a place; the patrons "were almost entirely Chinese and the atmosphere was noisy and full of camaraderie. Every now and again, one of the chefs would strike a hanging pan cover with the back of his cleaver with a clang and the whole kitchen would break out into song. Waiters intercepted intruding 'foreign devils' at the door and attempted to dissuade them—me—from entering by reciting 'no spare rib, no chicken finger, no pork fried rice.'"[10] It seems not to occur to us that a restaurant might serve as a cultural gathering place for members of an ethnicity, and that the presence of outsiders (persons who also predominate in the culture outside the restaurant) would not always be welcome. Or, it occurs to us, but we are uncompelled by such exclusionary practices; good students of liberal individualism that we are, we believe that discrimination on the basis of race is always wrong. Never mind that there is an important difference between Blacks integrating a lunch counter in an all-white neighborhood in a white racist society, and white people "integrating" a Chinese restaurant located in the Chinese enclave of a larger white society.[11]

Thorne, as it happens, kept going back to that restaurant, because the food was so terrific. He notes, without rancor, that even his regular presence there was never more than "tolerated" and "little attempt was made at accommodation"—for example, the waiters did not speak any English to him (153).

## The Outsider with an In

The food adventurer often doesn't simply believe she has a right to be anywhere, despite the hostile stares from others. She also may believe she ought to be able to move in the Other's sphere as an insider—or, more precisely, as an insider whose outsider (read: superior) status is never entirely forgotten. The outsider who presumes that all foods are available to be eaten, and who attempts to become fluent in the cuisine of the insider, is often attempting to be respected by insiders as just like one of them, even while she wishes not to become a native (a move that the adventurer cannot but regard as a demotion). It is not enough to be tolerated in the world of the other; adventurers desire acceptance, but our own tricky brand of acceptance.

An incident in the movie *Wayne's World* illustrates both the desire and its fulfillment. The sleazy record producer character attempts to seduce Wayne's girlfriend (a singer whose native language is Cantonese). In order to insinuate himself into her life, the producer invites her and Wayne over for dinner, and then proceeds to call a Chinese restaurant and order food in idiomatically flawless Cantonese. He even tells jokes. The tactic works; the singer abandons her interest in Wayne, with his stumbling attempts to learn her language. (Okay, the abandonment is temporary: Wayne Gets the Girl in the end.) The message? The Other can never resist an outsider who can behave like an insider to her culture. The colonizer creates the conditions that make it legitimate to exert control over the Other. One way we may exercise that control is by coercing them into participating in our fantasy—the fantasy in which we actually belong in their culture as authentic members of it. When they participate in our fantasy, they prove that we have the right to be wherever we are.

The desire to be *like* an insider connects to the adventurer's desire to make the exotic into something familiar to oneself. To be an outsider with an in carries considerable cachet—just as does a casual familiarity with the exotic. But attaining either position is risky; the exotic ceases to be exotic (and can thus cease to hold any allure for us) once it is familiar. Similarly, it is possible to become too much of an insider, at which point I have lost that which separates me from the Other.

## Authenticity Redux

In a passage I quoted earlier, Vine Deloria notes white people's tendency to go for "quick fixes," in our quest for some "real life," instant spirituality, delivered in a weekend, for one low-low price. I think something similar is at work for many of us with food. Having cut ourselves off from our own eating traditions, we now look to other cultures for something to eat—especially to the other, nondominant cultures we consider more likely to have authentic food customs. But we are not really interested in becoming a part of another culture either; what we really want is the "quick fix" meal; the food that will enable us to have a kind of authentic relationship to a tradition immediately—without any of the mundane, laborious work of growing up in that tradition. And without the dangers of actually coming to be a part of that radically other tradition, with all the loss of status it entails.

I have noted before that hard-core food adventurers tend to regard ourselves as innocent of the colonialist project. We become uninterested in a food at the point at which the multinational profit makers enter the picture (the taco franchisers, the Mongolian barbecue chains); this fact gives us a heady sense of purity about our own actions. Our surgical strike interest in the cuisines of another country may seem to us remarkably unproblematic, especially given the sincerity of our interest in authenticity, and in comparison to the damage we see visited upon ethnic foods chosen for fast food chains.

But in fact, our obsessive interest in preserving the authenticity of the Other's cuisine (where authenticity is understood in terms of separation and purity) means that food adventurers play a direct and important role in the colonizing project. Trinh Minh-ha describes our role when she notes, "Today, planned authenticity is rife. . . . We [colonizers] no longer wish to erase your difference, We demand, on the contrary, that you remember and assert it. At least, to a certain extent."[12] Whereas once the forces of colonization demanded homogenization, and obliteration of all things different, today they call for a "celebration of difference." Difference can thus come to be another tool in the colonizer's tool kit, as when it "induces an attitude of temporary tolerance—as exemplified in the policy of 'separate development'—which serves to reassure the conscience of the liberal establishment and gives a touch of subversiveness to the discourse delivered" (89–90). Food adventurers, those on the first wave of Western exploration and appropriation of things exotic, are among the first to establish such a toleration for difference—indeed, even a respect for and celebration of it—all the while relishing the slightly subversive, on-the-edge quality to our celebration.

But so long as "difference" remains conceived of as the difference of an "authentic Other" from me-the-Westerner, any such tolerance, respect, or fascination is at best temporary, at most provisional. In the face of conflict—war, civil unrest—it can quickly be replaced by putting the different ones in their place. Trinh quotes Mitsuye Yamada as saying that " 'periodic conflicts involving Third World peoples can abruptly change white Americans' attitudes towards us. . . . We found our status as true-blooded Americans was only an illusion in 1942 when we were singled out to be imprisoned for the duration of the war by our own government. . . . When I hear my students say, "We're not against the Iranians here who are mindful of their own business. We're just against those ungrateful ones who overstep our hospitality by demonstrating and bad mouthing our government," I know they speak about me.' " (90).

So too, the fascination the Western food adventurer feels for the cuisine of another authentic culture can quickly be extinguished in a situation in which we perceive that culture as threatening the boundaries of the territory to which we have relegated them. For example, during the United States' war against Iraq, visits to Middle Eastern restaurants (Iraqi-owned and otherwise) in the United States plummeted. Similarly, in the aftermath of the September 11, 2001 attacks, Middle Eastern and even Indian restaurants were the target of numerous attacks, and at least one food worker was killed in a "retaliatory" act.[13] When I understand the authentic Other as different from me in kind, separate from me in principle, it only takes a small turn of the dial for that exotic and fascinating difference to become dangerous and hostile.

It can be wonderful to explore the wealth of foods the world has produced, to hop from cuisine to cuisine. But when all I know of a culture is what I learn from the inside of a restaurant, I have a very limited picture indeed. Out of this experience, I create a superficial image of a culture, an image that treats that culture as if it were designed for my use and pleasure. This way of eating is harmful both to colonizer and colonized, for it reifies and reduces colonized people, substitutes for authentic relations to food the exotic quick fix and normalizes colonialism, encouraging us to condone it in its other, more destructive economic and political forms.

Furthermore, in the midst of my colonizing eating and cooking, I miss my own tradition. And I think my missing it is something more than mere nostalgia for something that never was, that my desire to be tied to a food tradition is not simply a consequence of romanticizing the notions of tradition and authenticity. Knowing who I am means knowing where I come from—and that means, in part, knowing what people in my past cooked and ate. I cannot replace my own food traditions by stuffing others' into the place where my own could be. All this succeeds in doing is violating their integrity, and leaving me feeling like a wanna-be, someone who sees other traditions as rich, vibrant, interesting, and sees her own as at best boring, at worst, nonexistent.

In critically discussing this issue, I do not advocate some kind of hands-off policy for white people. Nor do I mean to suggest that ethnic groups are always utterly justified when they install roadblocks to their cultures. I mean only to question the *absoluteness* with which Euroamerican adventurers presume our right to explore whatever we want, and our concomitant belief that others have no legitimate right to deny our access. Sorting out how respectful culinary interchanges ought to take place is a difficult challenge—one I will take up in part 4. Suffice it to say here that I do not believe the solution lies in isolationism.

# PART TWO

# How I Ate Civet Cat and Lived to Tell the Tale

I'M AN AMATEUR FOOD ADVENTURER. I LIKE TO EAT OUT, BUT I DON'T DO IT ALL THAT OFTEN, and I certainly don't do it for a living. I like to cook, but no one pays me to do it, or to write about it. I know a few things about a few cuisines, but certainly not enough to make me a valuable or sought-after figure on the food scene. However, even we amateurs have our standards to maintain. In my continual quest for cultural capital, I'm always trying to learn more, acquire more familiarity, become more savvy about ethnic foods. Fortunately for me, and for the ever-growing ranks of amateur adventurers, there is an entire food-writing industry devoted to serving our desires. Virtually every large U.S. newspaper publishes restaurant reviews. Glossy magazines feature travel-and-food articles about locating the world's best quality cinnamon, or where to go to experience a real Jamaican goat barbecue. Television shows take us to culinary nooks and crannies around the world to enjoy (vicariously) dining experiences we'll never experience firsthand; their celebrity hosts produce best-selling books about their adventures. A large and growing body of scholarly and semischolarly works explores food and culture; the audience for them extends well beyond the typical academic one.

Food writers who write specifically about ethnic foods contribute significantly to the care and feeding of a culture of food colonialism. They do considerable work to identify, codify (and thereby rigidify) the exotically authentic elements of an ethnic cuisine, and to create and shore up an unbridgeable separation between the consuming Western self and the consumable ethnic other. And they do so in a great variety of ways, sometimes intentionally, and sometimes quite unintentionally.

Rena Diamond makes this point in her essay, "Become Spoiled Moroccan Royalty for an Evening: The Allure of Ethnic Eateries." She writes,

In restaurant reviews, as in colonialism, the non-dominant culture is exoti-
cized, fetishized, and consumed. The rituals of the "other" are appropriated
for "our" use. The reviewers produce images of the group in question which
perpetuate ideas its members had no intention of advocating. . . . What gets
represented is seemingly the "truth" about the food and culture in question. . . . In this way, the reviews provide a confirmation of an "other" whose
life, language, and customs are indeed radically different from the reader.
This "other" must be represented in a suitably exotic yet simultaneously re-
alistic manner, one which continually reasserts justification for unequal
power relations: between reviewer/patron and proprietor, and by extension,
between America and the country or group in question.[1]

Diamond focuses her critique on restaurant reviews in newspapers and magazines, detailing the language that reviewers use to create this aura of exotic authenticity, and separation between the eating self and the ethnic other. The result? Among
other things, ethnic restaurant reviewing concretely contributes to "the perpetual
marginalization of immigrant groups in America" (2).

How does it do so? Chapters 4 and 5 of this volume explore the ways in which
food writing creates and encourages a quest for the exotic, a zest for authenticity,
and a tendency to treat the ethnic Other as a commodity I may exploit as I choose.
Before turning to those tasks, however, I sketch a schema for cataloging food writers
that will help to sort out the various ways in which they contribute to the food adventuring project.

## Aristocrats and Democrats: Varieties of Food Writers

"No matter how often one dines out . . . one always has questions about foreign cuisines. In fact, that's part of the excitement of exploring unfamiliar
foods. . . . Unfortunately, that adventure can be a little intimidating, given
the uninformative nature of most menus, coupled with the fact that most of
us do not speak the languages associated with the cuisines we are sampling.
But it needn't be that way."[2]

"Eating in the East. Did I eat the last giant catfish of the Mekong? My
companion, Alan Davidson, had long feared it was extinct. What did it taste
like? *I* certainly don't know: it was served in one of those Thai soups redo-
lent of lemon grass, and with so much chili that your eyes sting. . . .

"Then this April . . . Willy Mark, the almost official gastronome of Hong Kong, arranged a marathon lunch, at which everything was aphrodisiac."[3]

"Whereas the travelogue as an autobiographical discourse often constructs its narrative around the general experience of its heroic traveler, expecting the reader to fill in the narrative gaps through a kind of identification with the narrator, the discourse of [tourist guides] is obsessed with ways of specifying the knowledge it provides, thus attempting to cover every possible point of information about the Orient"[4]

The autobiographical travelogues and the information-packed tourist guides of which Ali Behdad writes in his book *Belated Travelers* have their counterparts in the world of food writing as well—as the above excerpts from the *Restaurant Lover's Companion* by Steve Ettlinger and *Out to Lunch* by Paul Levy suggest.

Philosophically trained Paul Levy (he holds a Ph.D. from Harvard University and has published a book on G. E. Moore) is a multiple-prize-winning food writer for the *London Observer* and numerous other publications, and the self-described member of the world's "Foodie first eleven."[5] Such autobiographical writers regale us with stories of their dining exploits and invite us to imagine (but *just* imagine) what it must be like to be them. Food aristocrat Levy does not aim in his essays to prepare his readers for our culinary jaunts to China, but even if we were to make such journeys, they would be under far different circumstances from those in which he travels—a fact of which he enjoys reminding us. The "almost official gastronome of Hong Kong" will not be organizing any special meals on my behalf.

Levy plumbs the depths of a cuisine, in order to understand it at a level that even very few native eaters achieve. Levy is like the author of a travelogue Behdad describes who wishes to "see beyond the obscure appearances, searching for more 'authentic' aspects" out of a "Cartesian desire" for "epistemological mastery" (22,23). An illustration of this desire to acquire more—and more esoteric—knowledge, occurs in Levy's description of eating bear paws at a reenactment of a Chinese imperial banquet. Levy notes "I am pleased to think I have eaten bear's paw at last, and can now refuse it without feeling ignorant" (94). By eating bear paw, the ignorance of which Levy unburdened himself was an ignorance of the flavor and mouth feel of bear paw. It was not an ignorance of where bear paw comes from, or of what happens to the bear whose paw it was, or even of how bear paw was or is usually prepared and served. All of this is information that was at Levy's disposal independently of his consuming any actual paw. Nevertheless, the knowledge of the taste and texture of bear's paw was something Levy believed he needed.

Why? According to Levy (whose tongue must be at least partly in his cheek when he makes the claim), only eating bear paw gives him the knowledge he needs to refuse it in the future without feeling ignorant. Only by tasting it does he win the credential needed to make his future refusals something more than squeamish—or even principled—rejections. "No thank you," Levy can now say, "I've eaten my bear paw." Levy now has access to knowledge available only to a handful of people in the world—knowledge of the way bear paw actually tastes. And that, after all, is what it's really about.

Of course the pleasure of food is, to a significant degree, wrapped up in its taste. But in the case of a food one has no intentions of eating again, of what importance is that taste?[6]

Once he has uncovered the authentic and/or esoteric features of a cuisine, Levy, like the travelogue author, wishes, according to Behdad "to expose what he finds hidden" (22)—to write it down for the rest of us. More accurately, he writes it down for the rest of us *Westerners*. For, in true Cartesian fashion, Levy, like the travelogue author, keeps himself aloof from the object of his examination—the culture whose cuisine he consumes. Levy "eats like a native" but remains always at one remove from a cuisine and its culture in order to evaluate it (objectively) for his fortunate European and American readers.

In contrast to Levy, who writes of experiences his readers can never duplicate, Steve Ettlinger set out to write the *Restaurant Lover's Companion* with the goal of arming readers of his dining guide with all the information they need to "eat ethnic." "To avoid incompleteness," the dining guide, like the tourist guide Behdad describes, "packs layers of information in ways that leave no space for interpretation or possible misunderstanding" (45). In Behdad's nineteenth-century tourist guides, this means including countless maps, charts and tables, and information on everything from the character of the natives to the road conditions in the rainy season. In dining guides such as Ettlinger's or the *Unofficial Guide to Ethnic Cuisine and Dining in America* by Eve Zibart, Muriel Stevens, and Terrell Vermont, the layers of information include maps; lessons on geography and history; glossaries; notes on eating utensils; discussions of key ingredients, flavors, and nutritional values of the cuisine; lists of specific dishes; recipes for home cooking; and information on how to "order and eat like a native."[7] Dining guides aim to help their readers avoid awkward situations such as Ettlinger's embarrassing thali incident, which I quoted in chapter 1. If Levy is a kind of food aristocrat who enables his readers to eat like a pro *vicariously*, by reading about his exclusive dining exploits, then Ettlinger plays the role of food democrat, giving his readers the information to eat like natives for real.

The dining guide also democratizes the knowledge-acquiring process itself, inviting its readers to collect information about a cuisine for themselves—to make collecting information part of the very activity of eating ethnic food. Behdad notes that the tourist guide "encourages its consumer—making the tourist feel almost morally obligated—to become an information collector." The result is that "information gathering [becomes] a touristic activity (Behdad, 44)." Ettlinger similarly makes information gathering a part of the dining, by inviting us to write to him "if [we] find alternative names or other information that pertains to the dishes listed here."[8] If we work on this together, maybe, just maybe, we can crack the Thai menu code![9] Levy, in contrast, expresses no desire for input from his readers; he has access to more—and more esoteric information—than any but the other members of the "first eleven" could ever have. He presents Us with the objective facts about Them.

The democratizing impulse in dining guides does not extend to include the participation of those Others whose cuisines we are mapping, however. Just as Levy ultimately preserves a separation between himself and the Others whose cuisines he studies, so too does a dining guide shore up a separation between the food adventuring selves to whom this guide is written, and the Other cooks who are feeding us.

Behdad argues that "the guidebook encourages the notion that the Orient just happens to be there for the use of the tourist-consumer" (47). It does so in part by refusing to discuss the political and social climate the tourist will find. The tourist guide stops its discussion of social and political structures well in the past—and discusses the present in terms of geography. In the nineteenth-century tourist guide, for instance, the tourist is never confronted with the fact of colonialism. According to Behdad, "History here is provided so as to distance the Other, not to bring him or her closer to the European tourist" (47). A similar distancing mechanism works in the dining guides. For instance, in the brief history sections usually included in these books, there is little or no discussion of the circumstances that brought immigrants to the United States, and led them to open restaurants here. We may learn of the ancient origins of Chinese cuisine, or even of the more recent colonial history that brought various culinary influences to bear on the cooking of Vietnam, but the history stops abruptly—and without exception—well before any discussion of, for instance, the recent waves of war, decolonization, and displacement that brought Vietnamese people to the United States. (In fact, the *Unofficial Dining Guide* simply dispenses with history altogether in its section on Vietnamese food. Every other section includes something between a paragraph and three pages of history about the region in question.[10])

Frequently, the history presented has a potted quality to it, or a whimsical tone, suggesting that all of this isn't particularly important, because these people are really rather silly, after all. For instance, in the *Restaurant Lover's Companion*, the section on Caribbean food notes that "Before the arrival of Columbus, two main tribes of Native Americans occupied the islands of the Caribbean. These tribes were the peaceful Arawaks and the fierce Caribs. The Caribs were voracious meat lovers and frequently added an Arawak along with wild boars to their cookpots" (4–5). Har har. The *Unofficial Dining Guide* finesses the discussion of the British occupation of India, noting that "the British eventually dominated [over the French and Dutch, mind you]; but it was not until the mid-eighteenth century, when repeated Persian and Afghani insurrections weakened the Moghul rulers, that the British Empire actually claimed the entire territory. Britain's withdrawal reignited the historical Mulim-Hindu struggle, and an estimated 50,000 people died in the riots that accompanied the partitioning of Pakistan" (169). Moral of the story? Much safer to have let the British continue their rule.

The dining guide, like the tourist guide, is "on the side of amnesia" (to paraphrase Behdad), obliterating the events by which the ethnic Other became available to the Western diner. These others become unreal, static archetypes whose cooking remains unchanged for centuries. One notable exception to this tendency is the introduction to the *Unofficial Guide*, written by Zibart. It is strikingly forthright about the fact that many immigrants who open restaurants in the United States are victims of political upheaval, poverty, and violence in their own countries. She admonishes diners not to make assumptions about a culture based upon our first experiences of its ethnic restaurants, and she reminds us that diners' choices have a tremendous impact upon the kinds of food that a restaurant serves. "The quality and variety of a foreign cuisine . . . [reflects] the economic stability that [an] immigrant community has achieved in our society." I only wish Zibart had found ways to infuse this way of approaching ethnic restaurants throughout the rest of the book, instead of closing her introduction by assuring us that "there is little preaching in the text that follows" (viii).

Both autobiographical food writers and authors of dining guides give their readers a funny kind of insider status, a sense of being in the know about a cuisine in a way that normally only a native would be. With someone like Levy, I've suggested that the pleasure is very much a vicarious one—we get to hear about what it is like to be such an insider—whereas Ettlinger wants us to have that pleasure for ourselves. But just what pleasure is it? It isn't the pleasure of passing (or watching someone else pass) for a native; indeed, part of the pleasure comes from never being taken for Chinese or Vietnamese or Indian, but from having the knowledge that only such a genuine insider would normally have. I cannot treat another culture as an exotic commodity intended for my amusement if I come to be a member of it. As a food adventurer, I seek only to *act as if* I were a member of the culture of the Other. The Other must remain, ultimately, Other.

*Chapter 4*

# And Reader, We Ate It

THERE'S NOTHING A FOOD ADVENTURER LOVES BETTER THAN A GOOD STORY—
preferably one we ourselves tell about the amazing, otherworldly, delicious,
weird, utterly unfamiliar food we just had at a little place that no one knows
about yet. Lacking any recent dining adventures of our own, we'll settle for a
story from another food adventurer—preferably an adventurer with more
cachet than we have, so we can add a few tidbits to our stock of esoteric ethnic food knowledge. Nothing fills that bill better in writing than a tale from
a food aristocrat—someone who experiences the novel and exotic on a daily
basis. The more an aristocratic author impresses us with the exoticism of the
experience, the more we like it (even as we may grind our teeth with envy at
the experiences we will never have).

Perhaps there is one thing that food adventurers like almost as much as
a good story, and that is knowing how the story ends. As much as food adventurers love experimenting, exploring, and discovering new dishes, new
restaurants, and new cuisines, many of us at heart also appreciate a certain
degree of familiarity in our dining experiences. (We are not, after all, so very
different from those "restaurant-oriented" and "preparation-oriented" diners
next to us in the ethnic restaurant.) If we can be familiar where others are
unfamiliar—the exotic-by-extension—so much the better. Here is where the
dining guide comes in handy. While we might well resent the democratizing
intentions of dining-guide writers (and while we might secretly hope that
this particularly *thorough* guide doesn't sell many copies, so that its information might remain at least a bit esoteric), we nevertheless appreciate the
soothing prose in which these guides explain to us everything we need in order
to act suave and well composed when we enter that Burmese or Ethiopian
or Salvadoran restaurant for the first time.

"Soothing" is indeed a good word to describe these guides. They com-
miserate with their readers about how intimidating it can be to walk into an

ethnic restaurant and confront a completely unfamiliar menu, perhaps only partially translated into English; to smell aromas that, while they may be tantalizing, are nevertheless new to us; and to contemplate the possibility that we will order something that we find completely inedible. These guides set as their task the familiarizing of their readers with every possible aspect of an ethnic cuisine—or at least every possible aspect they are likely to encounter in a relatively authentic restaurant in the United States.

Given their task, it is no surprise that words like "novel" and "exotic" do not appear often in these guides. In fact, the guides make somewhat tedious reading for the food adventurer—the equivalent of grammar exercises that we must do before we can safely go out to dinner. They give us a good sense of how to make the exotic familiar, but not a particularly good sense of how to keep the exotic exotic. And indeed, these are not really works of or for food adventurers. Like the travel guides of which Ali Behdad writes, they are for diners "belatedly searching for the disappearing exotic"[1]—an exotic whose dimensions have already been measured out for us.

In contrast, the tales of food aristocrats tend to be gripping page turners, filled with one wild story after another. Exoticism, mystique, and novelty are served up on every page, in heaping portions. If we amateurs cannot live these dashing experiences *really*, at least we can do so vicariously.

## Another Slice of Komodo Dragon? Eating Exotic Animals

Among the activities in which food adventurers delight, and about which adventuring food writers write with great frequency, perhaps none makes their blood run quicker than the quest for exotic meat. Obviously it doesn't appeal to all food colonizers; vegetarianism, interest in the welfare of at least some animals, squeamishness about eating animals other than those familiar from one's childhood, and other apprehensions combine to make this activity unattractive to many otherwise intrepid diners. Despite—and in part because of—such misgivings on the part of some, eating exotic animals holds tremendous allure for many food adventurers.

What exactly do I mean by "exotic" animals? When I use the term, I include at least the following: uncustomary parts of customary animals (i.e. the parts of cows, pigs, or chickens not often eaten by Euroamericans); animals that are familiar to food colonizers, but not normally eaten by them (e.g. cats, dogs, bear); and unfamiliar wild or game animals (antelope, zebra, civet). Two significant subcategories categories of exotic animals are those whose consumption involves some form of danger (the fugu fish, which can poison its eater if it is not prepared properly); and rare or endangered animals.[2] Readers may regard this last category as quite beyond the pale; surely no one can approve eating endangered animals! But in fact the hyper-rare can have tremendous allure for some food adventurers, as I shall discuss momentarily.

"Exotic," then, covers considerable ground. What definition of the term can hold all these various animals and animal parts together? I think that a standard dictionary definition in fact does. Euroamerican food adventurers tend to describe animals and/or animal parts as exotic if we don't eat them—if consuming them is foreign, alien, not native, to us. In this respect, the spinal cord of a steer is as exotic as a poisonous Southeast Asian snake. And while for some such unfamiliarity breeds disgust or horror, for food adventurers, the prospect of eating strange and unfamiliar meat excites them in a way virtually no other food can.[3]

Sometimes food adventurers come upon the opportunity to consume an animal traditionally eaten by a particular ethnic group that is itself regarded as exotic. (The Venezuelans who feast on roasted capybaras [giant rodents] at Easter time, for instance.) The animal may be consumed as part of a tradition no longer practiced—and thus a doubly exotic food—or it may be a tradition still in use. In some cases, the animal may traditionally be eaten only on very special occasions, or by a certain very select (or very marginalized) segment of the population.

In still other cases, there may in fact *be* no tradition of eating the animal within the culture in question, but for one reason or another, often having to do with attracting tourists who believe that this *is* the sort of thing People Like Them eat, it comes to be prepared and eaten there. Such is the case with the Carnivore, a Kenyan restaurant that is a regular stop on the tourist safari circuit. At the Carnivore, Kenyan-animals-not-normally-eaten-by-Kenyans are the restaurant's daily fare.

Endangered animals are exotically alluring precisely because they *are* endangered. Their endangered status makes such animals exotic everywhere—

even where they once were plentiful. In the case of a rare animal, its appearance is always unexpected, even on its former turf; thus it is always out of place.

Why does meat so particularly capture the essence of the exotic, such that eating it distinguishes the real food adventurer from the mere dabbler? My answer to this question contains several strands—cultural, nutritional, and physical. Furthermore, the answer entwines an understanding of the exotic with issues about bravery and intrepidness—important attributes for any would-be food colonizer.

Surely part of the reason for meat's status as exotic food par excellence is wrapped up with the significance meat holds in the cuisine of many cultures, including many segments of Euroamerican culture. And Western cultures are not unique in ascribing great significance to meat. On almost every continent are people for whom meat was or is virtually the only food in their diet; the Ihalmiut of North America and the Hua of New Guinea are just two examples. In many other cultures, while meat does not comprise a large portion of the diet, it comprises a symbolically central part of it.[4]

Among its many meanings, meat is macho food, food for men most of all. What is so macho about meat? First, eating meat requires killing animals. Killing is often dangerous business, filled with the possibility of injury to oneself. (This remains true for slaughterhouse workers today, working under modern, and thus supposedly safer, industrial conditions.[5]) Thus, killing animals is man's work—a belief that comes to us in various forms, from potted archaeological accounts of "man the hunter" to contemporary images of male slaughterhouse workers and deer hunters. In Euroamerican cultures, if we imagine women involved in the process of making meat at all, we tend to envision rather romantic, even bucolic jobs for them; gathering eggs, killing chickens, or stuffing sausages; anything bigger or more dangerous than that is left for men.

Furthermore, once the animal has been killed, prepared, and placed on one's plate, some of that danger remains—symbolically, at least—in the animal's very flesh. This seems to be especially true in the case of carnivorous animals; eating an animal that eats animals holds especially powerful symbolic value, because that animal sits on the top of the food chain. By consuming it one partakes of or subdues the power—literal and symbolic—that animal possesses. Thus, it requires yet another kind of bravery to taste the flesh of an unfamiliar animal. It may be considered polite, and thus womanly, to try a new, unfamiliar meat dish if one is a guest in someone's home. But it is brave, daring, and manly to order it intentionally in a restaurant.[6] Such bravery is generally not necessary to taste a new root vegetable or berry. Exceptions obviously exist. One notorious exception is durian, a fruit popular in South and Southeast Asia, whose smell is so pungent that it is literally forbidden on airlines and in many enclosed places such as hotel elevators. But notably, the smell is likened to excrement, vomit—or rotting flesh. So even in a case where bravery is required to try a new fruit, the reason it is required links back to meat.

Eating meat also marks a particularly bold move into the realm of the exotic because of the fact that meat does, after all, consist of animals. And, despite the fact that many persons eat their accustomed chicken, steer, pig, lamb, or fish every day without qualms, once they move beyond this familiar farm, they find eating animals much more discomfiting. If the animal is one they might have enjoyed watching in a zoo, or especially if it is one they might have owned as a pet, the idea of eating it may be quite repugnant to them.[7] If the animal eats things that one finds disgusting (vermin, muck from the bottom of a river), the thought of eating it may be revolting as well. Overcoming this repugnance can be a move to embrace the exotic.

Furthermore, we treat meats as especially exotic because meats often seem to have the strongest flavors, the most pronounced textures; meats seem to us strikingly (and often unpleasantly) different from our own foods. It seems unlikely that this is true in some objective sense—that animals always have stranger flavors than plant foods. Nevertheless (no doubt partially as a consequence of their other characteristics), we tend to perceive meats to be the most different-tasting things we could eat. This perception contributes to the hyperexoticism they hold for Euroamericans.[8]

It is also worth noting that meat is the centerpiece of a meal in the tradition of much of European and Euroamerican cooking. Vegetarian feminist theorist Carol Adams likens it to the plot of a story.[9] Adam Gopnik describes both French haute cuisine and nouvelle cuisine as "formulaic" in their treatment of meat: "a disk of meat, disk of complement, a sauce on top."[10] To skip or avoid meat is to skip the main point of a meal. This sense of meat's importance often holds for people even if meat is *not* the main point of the meal in the ethnic cuisine being consumed—even if it is only a peripheral or complementary element of it.[11] (Indeed, the tendency of Euroamerican food colonizers to see meat as the focal point of their meal has had the effect of inducing many ethnic restaurant owners to construct menus in which meat plays a far more prominent role than it would on a menu in their home country.) The food colonizer who balks at tasting the flesh of unfamiliar animals thus misses the whole point of the meal. They are ignoring the plot, focusing on the setting and the character development.

### But I Thought It Was Extinct!

Paul Levy writes about eating animals in virtually every one of the categories of exotic I've described. He has dined on duck's tongue, frog's ovaries, and dog. One of the most spectacular adventures he recounts in writing featured a three-day-long banquet, a reconstruction of a Chinese imperial banquet of the sort served to Emperor Kang-hsi between 1684 and 1707. The reenactment Levy attended was hosted by the Mandarin Hotel in Hong Kong, and of it, Levy observes, "The outstanding dishes, though, were not necessarily the ones that tasted best, but the ones we are more likely to remember because they are bizarre, or because they are made from endangered species. Thus, tonight we had shredded turtle with bamboo shoots and black mushrooms, which Harry Rolnick (author of the as yet unpublished *Endangered Species Cookbook*) said he could not eat, even though he knew this particular turtle was farmed. . . . But . . . it was the 'Braised Civet Imperial Court Style' that none of us will ever forget, alas. . . . [I]t was served with its head on the platter, and its little face stared at us with reproach."[12]

Levy ponders the nature of the civet; is it a fox, as he has heard, or is it in fact really a relative of the cat? He hopes not, "as I do not relish the thought of having eaten a pussycat. . ." (93). Whatever his reservations about its genealogy, Levy can report that he ate it, as well as every other dish placed before him, no matter how "bizarre" (his word) or rare its ingredients.

Levy engages in this activity with a curious mixture of excitement, modesty, braggadocio and regret, blended in varying proportions and displayed with varying degrees of persuasiveness. He seems to approach the eating of endangered animals similarly to the way he approached the bear's paw in the episode I described earlier: I'll do anything—once. But with the case of an endangered animal, the meaning of "once" takes on an entirely new tone.

Levy seems to relish the delicious agony of the idea that his last taste of an animal may be one of the last tastes *anyone* has of it. For the food aristocrat Levy, this is the ultimate way to set his experiences apart from those of the ordinary food adventuring Joes and Janes reading his book.

In one adventure, Levy accompanied Alan Davidson, world-renowned expert on fish cookery and former member of Britain's diplomatic corps, on a trip to Southeast Asia. While in Thailand they spent a night at an American resettlement camp on the Mekong River across from Laos—this opportunity courtesy of Davidson's former career. They had dinner in a large, nearly empty restaurant, curfew requiring all but foreigners and their drivers to be in after sundown. Their dinner was a soup made with pla beuk, known to English speakers as the Giant Catfish of the Mekong, an exceedingly rare fish thought by the Lao to bring good luck to those who eat it. Levy's report on the meal warrants a direct quotation:

> We huddled over the pot, staring reverently at its contents. *Pla beuk*, announced our furiously grinning Thai driver. And so it was. That is how we became probably the last people of European descent to taste the Giant Catfish of the Mekong—though the amount of chili pepper in the soup prevented me from forming any clear idea of what the taste *was*.
>
> It occurs to me that, touching though the scene was, it does not prove that the *pla beuk* is not extinct. Certainly, a local fisherman did catch one of the huge creatures some time that week. It's a horrible thought, but it could have been the last one. And, reader, we ate it. (190)

Many of the details Levy provides contribute to the exclusivity of this adventure. It isn't only the fish that is rare here; virtually every feature of the trip is. He travels with one of the world's great fish experts (who is the author of several cookbooks, one of which is "so rare that [it] can scarcely be consulted outside the British Library . . ." [186]); they visit a spot that foreigners cannot visit without special permission; they are among the only persons allowed out after dark; and they are the only patrons in the restaurant. All these details contribute to the event, which culminates in the eating of a kind of fish so rare that it may have gone out of existence with this specimen. (Certainly it would have been possible for Levy to gather at least some information about the likely truth of this last claim; he regularly reports on the investigations he carries out to check the veracity of someone else's claims. However, in this particular case, to attempt to check the facts would disrupt a mystery, the existence of which only serves to increase the value of Levy's experience in the eyes of his readers.)

Levy's enjoyment of the consumption of endangered animals is not at all straightforward; as the passage above shows, he does not express anything so crude or vulgar as glee at the thought that he has just consumed the last Giant Catfish of the Mekong. He tempers his expressions of enjoyment with sober reflections, and sometimes even expressions of regret; he doesn't delight in impending extinction per se. Nevertheless, his attitude does seem to be, "Well, if it's going to become extinct, I want to taste it once before it goes, so I can say I've done it, and so I can tell people what it was like." Levy, like an Orientalist expert or a travelogue writer, gathers every bit of information he can about a cuisine—the more esoteric the better.

Levy's approach also bears more than a passing resemblance to that of travelers who rush to visit landscapes that are in the process of being destroyed, or societies that are just becoming open to outsiders and are rapidly changing as a result of the encounters. The approach combines fatalism with opportunism; they assume that the destruction or transformation of the animal, land, or people in question will go on, ineluctably, with no chance of its being stopped or diverted. However, they also recognize that if destruction or transformation continues, experiences of the animal/land/people will become increasingly rare, and thus increasingly valuable *to have had*.

Levy also plays the role of the manly man in these escapades. Here is a man who is not only not afraid to eat weird, ucky animals, he is also not afraid to suffer the slings and arrows of public censure for eating *rare* weird, ucky animals. Part of Levy's fascination with the information he gathers seems to be precisely that it is somewhat morally tainted.

Levy stands to garner considerable cachet, so as long as he reports his escapades afterward in such a way that he doesn't risk being condemned for them. By circumscribing the moral significance of this event—by stressing the obvious fact that his consumption of a single animal hardly brought about the destruction of an entire species—he can avoid a good deal of moral opprobrium, *and* capitalize on the allure of having had a nearly unrepeatable experience at the same time. In this light, consider Levy's closing words regarding the imperial banquet: "I am relieved that this sort of thing can only happen once in a lifetime; but I am awfully glad that it happened in mine. . . . I feel wildly honoured and flattered that the Mandarin [Hotel] asked me, and am swanking with pride that I knew enough about Chinese food and etiquette to be able to appreciate it. And dismayed: the menu practically amounted to a list of endangered species. It is comforting to think that this event is unlikely to be repeated" (94–95).

Levy seems to enjoy the tricky mix of emotions required for participating in, and subsequently reporting on, this sort of event. He expresses his dismay at the death of endangered animals eaten in the extravaganza—but at the same time lets his readers know that he's tremendously glad the extravaganza happened and that he got invited. He even manages to throw in some humility—the passage about feeling "wildly honoured"—thereby inviting his readers (presumably lots of people whose stations in life do not present them with invitations to three-day Chinese banquets) to identify with him just a bit in the bargain.

In the end, however, I'm not sure how successfully Levy finesses this mix of emotions. His modesty never seems quite genuine or heartfelt, coming as it so often does on the heels of a boast. Thus, while he reports feeling honored to have been invited to a three-day-long Chinese banquet in Hong Kong, he reminds us that he was invited to the banquet because he is one of the "world Foodie first eleven" (95)—no ordinary chap, despite having grown up in Kentucky. Levy knows that he is witnessing the end of an era as, for example, he huddles over that hot pot in Vietnam; he's read up on the symbolic significance of the pla beuk. This opportunity is not lost on *him*, the way it might be on some poor ignoramus who didn't know Giant Catfish from your ordinary bullhead. Levy, the knowledgeable outsider, assures us that he is just the sort of person you would want to eat the last of a species.

In this regard, Levy bears a certain resemblance to an art collector, a specialist in pre-Columbian art named Lowell Collins, who is quoted as saying in regard to the removal of artifacts from their countries of origin, "What the hell! As long as U.S. laws are not broken, it's all right. After all, these things are not appreciated in those countries. They're brought here and given a home. Now cultured people can see them."[13] In other words, better that a knowledgeable outsider—the travelogue writer, the pre-Columbian art expert, the food critic—scoop up the treasures of a country than that they languish in the hands of ignorants whose only claim to these treasures is their residence inside the same borders.

Levy seems to operate his professional life as if it were sharply separated from the world around him—and as if his actions did not reflect, or have consequences for, that world. True, he welcomes the cessation of activities that he recognizes are harmful—but not until he's had an opportunity to partake of them (thus, incidentally, giving his experience even more value than it would otherwise have had; much more prestige to be the *last* European to eat pla beuk than to be one of the last hundred). His writings do not suggest that he in any way actively campaigns against such things as imperial banquets or eating rare fish; indeed, his disapproval of them seems confined to a certain amount of after-the-fact hand-wringing, accompanied by a firm declaration of "no more of that for me!" In his writing, Levy doesn't explore the connection between his choosing to participate in these activities and any large-scale consequences—social, environmental, economic—they may have.

Indeed, Levy says as much, though in a context quite unrelated to the issue of eating endangered animals. In describing a session with a hypnotist whose aid he enlisted to help change his eating habits, Levy reports that the hypnotist "tried to get me to understand subconsciously what I have jolly well consciously known to be the truth since the age of four: that the problem of starving children in foreign countries is to do with the world-wide distribution of food and is not affected one jot by the disposition of the food on my plate" (51–52). With one neat, swift slice, Levy completely severs his own plate of food from worldwide food distribution systems, thereby foiling any attempts that world might make to pin responsibility upon him. His plate cannot be implicated in the world food problem.

It would surely be ludicrous to suggest that there is any simple connection between Levy's cleaning or not cleaning his plate and the malnutrition that children elsewhere do or do not experience. But the countless parents who have urged their children to "think of the starving children in . . ." have never thought there was a simple connection between the two acts either. Consider the almost unlimited mileage that seems to be gotten out of the joke about the child who responds, "Well, then, let's send it to them!" when their parent reminds them that there are starving children elsewhere who would love to eat the food on their plate; the joke is amusing because it reveals what we all already know—namely, that the child's eating or not eating this particular plateful will not produce any direct effects on any other human beings. Levy is not the only person to have figured this out by age four. Parents who have used this tactic to get a child to eat are trying, however crudely, to get them to appreciate what they have, not to waste it, and not to be ungrateful for it.

But in reflecting on this parental ploy, Levy goes farther than simply rejecting straightforward and silly causal connections between his plate and starving children; he rejects any sort of connection at all between starving children and "the disposition of the food on my plate." (The latter phrase conjures in my mind the image of three lone peas, arranged in a row on an otherwise empty plate, and a father saying "You won't leave the table till that plate is empty.") What is responsible for the problem of starving children, according to Levy? World food distribution inequities, which are completely unconnected to the food he leaves uneaten at the end of the meal.

I commend Levy for working to overcome the urge to eat everything on his plate, mechanically, just for the sake of having done so. (Consider the phrase "clean your plate," which suggests not a gastronomic activity so much as one properly performed by a dishwasher.) Nevertheless, I cannot support Levy's efforts on his own behalf when they take the form of denying the real connections between his plate and the plates of others around the world.

What are some of those connections? The very fact that his plate is so full that he can leave food on it and still be satisfied illustrates the fact that he stands in a highly privileged position in that world distribution system. The fact that the foods are of unbelievable variety and quality further speaks to his privilege in that system, as does the fact that they come from all over the world. In short, while there is no miraculous link between Paul Levy and any hungry individual or group of individuals, there are all sorts of ways in which his making different choices about what to eat could have small, but concrete effects on the world food system. This would be true for anyone standing in such a position of relative privilege in the system, but it is more particularly true for someone like Levy, whose writings about food are read by many people.

Choosing to eat less, or to stop eating particular foods, or to eat more of other foods, can make dents in the ways that foods are produced, distributed, and consumed in the world, especially when the one doing the choosing is a food critic whose choices are assiduously followed by his readers. This is particularly true when one makes such choices in concert with others, and when one couples such choices with other sorts of actions—for example, working for organizations aimed at creating more equitable, just, and healthy food systems. The power Levy has to encourage such choices in others is significant. Instead, however, he chooses to write in ways that deny or minimize that power. In the end, I think Levy's discussion of his plate connects disturbingly to his discussions about eating endangered and otherwise exotic animals.[14]

Taken together, his comments reveal an unpleasant opportunism—and a resistance to seeing himself as part of a larger system—enlisted in the service of his palate, a palate that has a deep and constant craving for new, unusual, exotic, extreme tastes, and for the adventures that go with them. Levy attempts to render innocuous the activities he must engage in to satisfy the cravings of that palate. But one cannot taste rare animals without contributing in some way (direct or indirect) to their increasing rarity. One cannot eat sumptuous three-day banquets filled with such animals, without registering at least tacit consent for a world food system that leaves you bloated while a significant percentage of others in that same city are chronically malnourished.

This discussion began as an elucidation of one concrete form that the quest for the exotic can take among cultural food colonizers—namely, as a quest for exotic animals, and specifically rare species. It has progressed to a discussion of the justice of pursuing such a quest. Before leaving the topic, I wish to take one final look at it, focusing this time more narrowly on the question of how this activity is colonialist. I do this because I want to make it clear that the problems I see with the activity that Levy describes are not simply and straightforwardly moral problems arising from killing and eating representatives of species that are in danger of being annihilated. They are also specifically the problems of a colonialist activity, an activity caught up in the quest for the exotic.

Endangered animals are *especially* animals that We don't eat. By this I mean not only that Western food colonizers do not eat members of specific endangered species, but also that endangered species, as a class, are off limits. In many countries of the world—including the United States—laws stipulate penalties for those who harm members of such species. In Thailand, and in Hong Kong, Levy thus engages in an activity that he could not engage in without penalty were he in the United States.

For the sake of letting out his foodie belt another notch, it also makes Levy parasitic on these other cultures for his exoticism fix. Levy takes advantage of a situation in which he engages in activity that may not be illegal in the country in question, but is morally questionable at best.

Animals this rare provide the exploring colonizer the opportunity to have an experience that is nearly unrepeatable by virtue of the convenient fact that only limited numbers of animals exist. Thus, the colonizer is almost guaranteed of attaining tremendous amounts of cultural capital from the experience, because it cannot become a common experience. It cannot be mass-marketed. Its value lives on in perpetuity—so long as it doesn't become horribly unfashionable. In many ways, there could be no more perfect exotic eating experience.

That this is so is illustrated, to great comic effect, in the movie *The Freshman*. Matthew Broderick plays a college freshman who gets tangled up with a mobster (Marlon Brando) and is forced to work for him as a result. The mobster's racket is hosting endangered species dinners, at which guests pay thousands of dollars for the opportunity to eat the last of a species. Broderick is charged with picking up the rare animal of the week—a komodo dragon, a type of lizard—and bringing it to the banquet hall, where it is paraded before all the guests before being taken to the kitchen where, presumably, it will be killed and prepared. But in fact what the kitchen prepares for the guests is chicken—the flesh to which all other unfamiliar flesh is compared. The guests leave, satisfied that they have witnessed the end of an era. And the komodo dragon walks away from the deal.

## The Food on the Wall: In Search of Authentic Cuisines

"Clientele is also judged with respect to 'authenticity.' The quotes that illustrate this are particularly jarring, as they are replete with negative and reductionist stereotypes. A Japanese restaurant is described as 'excellent and authentic . . . the clientele is overwhelmingly Japanese.'. . . A Chinese restaurant is said to have 'ethnic color' because 'one's fellow diners here are authentic enough.'. . . The implication is that an inauthentic diner in this case would be any non-Chinese."[15]

Food writers of all sorts worry in print about whether or not they are getting the real thing in a given restaurant. They assess the table settings, the music, the servers' dress, the decor, the order of service, and the food itself, trying to determine if this restaurant's offerings are authentic. As Rena Diamond points out in her analysis of restaurant reviews, what reviewers identify as evidence of authenticity is often a static portrayal of a culture, created precisely with the outsider in mind, and having little to do with any insiders' understandings of their own culture (2). Such reviewers are attracted to cultural differences that they can comprehend—exotic differences that have been sufficiently domesticated to make them accessible to us.

But many foodwriters seek to move beyond the level of the familiarly exotic, the predictably authentic—beyond the restaurants that feature all the little decorator touches that we "nonethnics" have come to see as marks of authenticity. These writers aren't impressed by native dress or traditional music; they are interested in finding the Real thing, the food They really eat—not just the food that they *tell us* they really eat.

Journalist Calvin Trillin wrote three well-known books detailing the food adventures he had while traveling around the country writing his "U.S. Journal" for the *New Yorker*. He later said of these books, "I wrote about eating rather than food, and I wrote as a reporter who was enjoying his work rather than as an expert. If there was a unifying proposition in what I wrote on the subject, it was that Americans should celebrate rather than apologize for the local specialties that they actually enjoyed. . . ."[16]

While he claims no expertise for himself, Trillin's works were among the first to celebrate local foods in the United States—crayfish in Louisiana, barbecued mutton in Kentucky, chili in Cincinnati—and thus, for his readers, he became a kind of expert. Does that make him a food aristocrat in the style of Paul Levy? Despite his obvious expertise, and despite the fact that his tales are autobiographical ones, Trillin can't really be labeled a food aristocrat for at least one important reason: he isn't particularly interested in separating himself from either his readers or his research subjects (who are often one and the same). Like the writers of dining guides, he regularly lets his readers in on the secrets he has discovered for finding good local food, because he wants to preserve local foods, and he recognizes that the way to do this is by inviting his readers to eat them. He also regularly complains about being kept away from the *real* best restaurants in town, because the local folks want to treat him like visiting royalty. You don't serve visiting royalty boiled crayfish—even if boiled crayfish happen to be the best food in town.

In order to carry out his local-food adventuring, the dry-witted Trillin must therefore employ a variety of methods to extract from the locals the information that will enable him to eat at a really good restaurant (the one serving pan-fried chicken), instead of the restaurant the local Chamber of Commerce president wants him to visit (the one serving "Duck a l'Orange Soda Pop," the kind of restaurant Trillin names "La Maison de la Casa House"). The locals, however, are often shy or even embarrassed about admitting to a visiting New York reporter that the best restaurant in town is a barbecue joint that doesn't even use plates. In a kind of parody of participant-observer research, Trillin carefully develops a set of techniques designed to divert the locals' attention away from his New-York-reporter identity, and to endear himself to them, so that they will tell him where he'll really be able to get a decent meal.

I have long loved Trillin's writing—he was one of the first food writers I read, as a high schooler. There's something wonderful about his efforts to get people around the United States to admit the existence of, and to feel proud about, their less-than-glamorous food traditions, especially in the face of creeping (galloping!) McDonaldism. I owe a debt of gratitude to people like Trillin, and Jane and Michael Stern (authors of *Road Food* and *Good Food*[17]) for their writings in celebration of home foods; I've eaten well (and put a little money into local economies as well) as a result of their work. Their love of local food—and their willingness to work hard to find it, and to show their unabashed admiration for the people who make it—undoubtedly make important contributions to its continued existence.

Furthermore, it's not hard to imagine myself *as* a "local" of the sort whose town might get visited by Trillin. I try to imagine what they would admire about the local joints in which *I* hang out—*my* joints. I'm proud to imagine Trillin visiting these places, proud to think of him working hard to find out where folks in south central Minnesota go when we want a *really* good meal.

Something different happens for me, however, when Trillin turns his investigative skills in the direction of Chinese restaurants. Whereas I find endearing his persistent, insistent efforts to get the locals to spill the beans about the best pan-fried chicken in town, I find myself losing patience when he concentrates his efforts on trying to make Chinese restaurant waiters let him in on the secret of what their Chinese diners are eating. His zest for the real thing, the authentic local food, takes on a different caste when the locals in question are the Chinese patrons of their neighborhood restaurant.

Trillin loves the vast variety of regional Chinese foods he can order from the menus of restaurants in cities like London, New York, and Chicago. But he's convinced that, even more than the food listed in English on the menu, he would love the food that isn't on the menu—the special dishes advertised on the walls of those restaurants—if he could just get his hands on it. As Trillin explains, Chinese diners in Chinese restaurants don't order off the printed, English menu; they order off the wall, and the signs on the wall are only in Chinese. These dishes—the dishes to which he has no access—are of course just the ones Trillin craves. They look so delicious and the (Chinese) people eating them are so obviously enjoying themselves—enjoying themselves more, he's convinced, than he ever can by ordering off the English-language menu alone. For Trillin, the dishes on the wall represent the real Chinese cooking, not "some chop-suey equivalent put on the menu to pacify the passing meter reader or paper-supply salesman who happened to drop by because he suddenly got hungry while on his rounds" (283). *They* are Authentic Chinese Cuisine. The printed menu is a mere cover story for outsiders.

Throughout the course of the three books, Trillin concocts, or reports on, various (hilarious) schemes that will allow him to find out what They are eating, and to get some of it for himself. Each scheme fails for one reason or another. For example, when he tries simply asking servers for translations, they tend to tell him something incomplete (like "Shredded Three Kinds" [277]), or something utterly unsatisfactory ("you no like" [284]). Unlike the folks in Kentucky or Cincinnati or Louisiana, who will eventually break down and admit that there's this great little place down the road that makes barbecued mutton, or five-way chili, or crawfish étouffée, the servers in Chinese restaurants refuse to comply with Trillin's increasingly desperate requests. It drives him to distraction. Like the scholar convinced that the subject of her research left all the most important works in a set of unpublished esoteric texts that are now held by a private collector who will not allow them to be viewed by the public, Trillin is certain that he is only being given access to a watered-down version of the truth—dishes that may be good enough in their own way, but that do not get to the heart of Chinese cuisine. (Similarly, folklorist Lucy Long reports that she has regularly been refused her menu selections in Korean restaurants, because "Several dishes in particular are thought to be unpalatable to anyone except Koreans."[18])

Trillin tries to persuade his wife, Alice, a teacher of English as a foreign language, to enlist her Chinese students in a menu translating exercise as a way of improving their English (85). He reports on a man in his acquaintance who carries in his wallet a slip of paper on which is written, in Mandarin, "Please bring me some of what that man at the next table is eating." He eventually locates James McCawley, a linguist at the University of Chicago, who produced a booklet entitled "The Eater's Guide to Chinese Characters." McCawley takes him on a Chicago eating tour, gives him a short course in menu reading, and presents him with a copy of his guide. Reading it on the plane trip home Trillin concludes that, even with the guide (which includes a 140-page glossary), the task of translating from Chinese characters is too complex (the guide doesn't cover script, nor does it cover the modifications in Chinese characters that occurred after World War II) and too fraught with risks (misinterpret a slang term and you end up with fish stomach instead of wonton) to make it feasible. He opts for the slip of paper in the wallet instead.

Is Trillin's pursuit of Chinese food really any different from his pursuit of any of the dozens of local specialties he obsessively seeks out? I think it is. When he seeks out local specialties, Trillin begins by asking persons in the know—local eaters—where the good food is. In contrast, in the case of Chinese restaurants, he begins with the *assumption* that the good food (or real food, or authentically Chinese food) is what's advertised on the walls. Consider: when it comes to local food, Trillin's technique typically involves arriving in a region noted for a particular food (country ham in Kentucky, ribs in Kansas City), and then asking people where a great example of that food can be had. Sometimes he may be unaware of a regional specialty, so his questioning has to be more general: What's good to eat around here, anyway? Eventually, this line of questioning will net him the name of some obscure place not advertised in the Yellow Pages, and with no sign out front, but with terrific pan-fried chicken. And off he goes.

When it comes to Chinese food, Trillin arrives in a restaurant, spots a dish being consumed by a Chinese person, or sees a row of signs on the wall, and decides that these are the dishes that he must have, these *are* the best dishes in the house. He doesn't, for example, ask the server "What's good here?" because he's convinced that the server won't tell him—or won't tell him what he really wants to know. She'll tell him what she wants him to know. Chinese servers, in Trillin's picture of them, are at best paternalistic (deciding for him that he won't like something, because he's not Chinese) and at worst deliberately deceptive (keeping from him the information that would allow him the greatest gastronomic pleasure he's ever experienced). So there is no sense in asking servers what's good; they'll just give him some answer-for-Westerners.

All this is not to say that his treatment of American regional food could never take on the same character as his treatment of Chinese cuisine; it certainly could, particularly when he takes on American ethnic cultures that have themselves been the site of much opportunistic plundering. Part of the reason that Trillin's investigative efforts are disturbing when the topic is Chinese food, but charming when the subject is country ham, is that, in the first case, Trillin stands as yet one more in a long line of Westerners who have attempted to pry their way into Chinese culture—sometimes, as in Trillin's case, innocently and amusingly, but sometimes also savagely. Trillin's forays should be read against that backdrop of centuries of imperialism. Many American ethnic cultures have also experienced significant cultural exploitation, and they too might put up barriers to the appropriation of their cuisines. Trillin's efforts to scale those barriers would be equally disturbing, given that context. If Trillin were to write about his quest for authentic African American, Native American, or Mexican American cuisines the way he has written about Chinese food, similar criticisms might indeed come his way.[19]

There is another aspect of Trillin's zeal for the food on the walls that also contributes to its colonizing character—namely, his tendency to act as if he is entitled to whatever information he desires. While Trillin's irritation at not being able to read the wall signs is always good natured and more tongue-in-cheek than not, it is, nevertheless, irritation; those pesky Chinese just keep making it unnecessarily difficult for him. And we laugh along, some of us food adventurers, because we have been irritated in just the same ways ourselves once or twice. Trillin doesn't really consider (at least in writing) the reasons they make it difficult; he doesn't, for example, give much thought to why the signs are written only in Chinese in the first place, and he only very briefly admits that, when a waiter tells him "you no like," he is frequently correct—that, for whatever reasons, Euroamerican palates do not find these foods to their liking. (Perhaps a case in which the exotic has not yet been sufficiently domesticated? An instance in which the Other remains stubbornly and unconsumably Other?) But for Trillin, the issue is that he *should* be able to find out what Chinese people are eating, and order it himself. He can see no good reasons this information is being withheld—and every good reason why he should have it—and this is a free country, so cough it up.

Trillin's quest for the food on the wall manifests the tendency Trinh Minh-ha has noted for Western colonizers' quest for authenticity to focus on the remote and hard to attain—the "'unspoiled' parts of Japan," the "unspoiled African, Asian, or Native American." This is so because "the less accessible the product 'made-in-Japan,' the more trustworthy it is, and the greater the desire to acquire and protect it."[20] The foods on the wall are the ones to be trusted; these are the foods They eat, not the ones they make to throw us off the scent. They will allow access to the culinary culture as it truly is.

Calvin Trillin presents the comic version of the view that I, as an American, am entitled to go anywhere I want, and have access to anything that I want. For a much less amusing, and much more invasive, manifestation of this belief, consider that, in the southwest United States, various Pueblo communities have found their traditional festivals overrun by tourists, academic researchers, and other Euroamerican outsiders intent on getting a look. Several pueblos have finally closed their festivals to outsiders, because of the disruptions those outsiders caused. Certainly the various cuisines of China—practiced, as they are, by literally millions of people all over the world—are not vulnerable in the ways that the traditions of these tiny pueblos are. However, for any given restaurant, the disruption may feel similar in magnitude. For Chinese people living in the United States and surrounded by Euroamerican culture, restaurants may be one of the most important places in which to hang out and live, without having to translate or explain themselves.[21] For Euroamericans to demand complete access to even such spaces may well feel like the last straw.

Christy Hohman-Caine, writing about the practices of art collectors, observes, "The notion that all things (realms, values, objects) must necessarily, by right, be open to examination and, thus, possession (whether physical or perceptual), is a strong Western value which lies, unquestioned, at the basis of many conflicts ranging from reburial of human remains and study of sacred artifacts, to conservation and repatriation."[22] I think that it might also be found to lie—albeit in a much milder form—at the base of Trillin's conviction that he should be able to ferret out the information on the wall.

But surely he's right, isn't he? Surely he should be able to order whatever he wants in a restaurant! Taken from the perspective of a modern Western thinker in the tradition of liberal individualism, the obvious answer is "Sure!" But taken from the perspective of a culture that is constantly being encroached upon, it may not be so obvious. It may be that, in this small act of refusing information, a Chinese restaurant attempts to keep yet one more feature of their culture from becoming the object of fascination for outsiders.

Do I think Trillin is bad or wrong for attempting to get this information? No—I don't think moral opprobrium is particularly appropriate or useful here. Nevertheless, his writing about Chinese restaurants leaves an unpleasant taste in my mouth. While the Westerner in me keeps agreeing that of course he should be able to find out what's written on the wall, another part of me keeps wanting to ask, "but why should *they* have to translate it for you?"

## Chapter 5

# What Do You Mean We Can't Film the Market Sequence Here?

"Knowledge of the Orient, because generated out of strength, in a sense *creates* the Orient, the Oriental, and his world. . . . The Oriental is depicted as something one judges (as in a court of law), something one studies and depicts (as in a curriculum), something one disciplines (as in a school or prison), something one illustrates (as in a zoological manual)."

—Edward Said, *Orientalism*

## Consult a Pro: Food Writer as Objective Expert

THE ORIENTALIST IS A PROFESSIONAL WHO INTERPRETS THE ORIENT FOR HIS READER and, in the process, quite literally makes the Orient (as object of the West) come into existence. The Orientalist helps to make the Oriental other available to Westerners by explaining and interpreting the Orient for them. In the process, the Orientalist comes to have authority about what counts as the Orient, an authority so great that even direct, firsthand experience that contradicts it can be regarded with suspicion.

Like Edward Said's Orientalist scholars, restaurant reviewers interpret ethnic foods for their readers. Their explanations of the food used, and the ways that food is prepared, served, and eaten, make these strange or unknown cuisines visible and accessible to Western diners. The restaurant critic, occupying a position of cultural strength and aloofness (read: neutrality and objectivity) relative to the ethnic Other, identifies, explains, and critiques the food of this Other, and thereby helps to make the ethnic Other come into existence (for us diners), as "something one consumes."

Furthermore, restaurant critics shape the menus of restaurants both directly, by the remarks they make about the food at a particular restaurant, and indirectly, via their readers, who come to make particular demands on restaurants as a result of reading restaurant reviews. Diners who have read or heard about special occasion meals want to experience them ourselves—and we assume that we ought to be able to, at any time, and in any restaurant of the "right" ethnicity. Restaurant owners, eager to please customers' demands in order to stay in business, come to serve whatever the customers ask for—never mind about cultural practices. So, am I calling for the abolition of restaurant reviews? Not at all; but I do nevertheless think it is worthwhile to examine the influences that such food professionals have upon their readers.

Food critics, like the Orientalists Said describes, come to have the authority to define what is and is not authentic, what is and is not genuinely representative of the Other's cuisine—and thus what is and is not worthy of the attention of Euroamerican food adventurers. The food expert invents (by defining, by setting up expectations) the authentic cuisine much as the Orientalist invents this thing called the Orient. The result is that the ordinary diner who goes into a Cantonese restaurant and finds something different from what Paul Levy has described to her may well reach the conclusion that her experience is not authentic and that this restaurant must be doing it wrong—not that Levy's experience is incomplete, inaccurate, or idiosyncratic, or that a cuisine is responding (in authentic ways) to the context in which it finds itself. By extension, Ms. Ordinary Diner becomes a kind of food expert herself; by reading the critic's column faithfully, she too can possess the knowledge that would justify her in giving her stamp of approval or disapproval to a restaurant's offerings.

### Can I Be a Pro Too?

While I've sometimes played food critic when dining out, I know that I am *not* really a food critic, and that a gap will always remain between me and the person who gets paid to give restaurants two stars or three chef's toques. As I've already noted, many food critics write in ways that guarantee that their readers never mistake themselves for the real expert. The case is different with dining guides, however; the authors of these books write with the intention of making their readers into confident, self-assured, *expert* diners, who can "eat Szechwan" tonight, Cajun tomorrow night, and Ethiopian the night after that.

This effort at inclusion takes the form of explaining everything from the more familiar aspects of a cuisine or a style of dining (how to hold chopsticks, or how to say thank you in Spanish), to its more esoteric and arcane aspects (the fact that buttermilk is the traditional drink with couscous, even though you won't find it in most U.S. restaurants serving North African food, or that calves' feet are particularly admired in Peruvian, Argentinean, and Brazilian cookery). Dining guides give every kind of eater—including the daredevil, the timid, the easily embarrassed, and the fussy—enough information to ensure that, at any moment during the meal, we will have some knowledge of how to proceed. Read *The Restaurant Lover's Guide* and you'll know how to order (make sure you ask if raita is included with the meal at an Indian restaurant), how to serve and eat (don't use chopsticks—except with noodle dishes—in a Thai restaurant), what things in the bowl not to eat (star anise and sticks of lemon grass in a Vietnamese restaurant), and how to signal or thank a server (tap your fingers on the tablecloth without making eye contact to say thanks for tea water in a dim sum restaurant).

If the information you acquire from one of these guides doesn't quite leave you in danger of being mistaken for the *New York Times* restaurant reviewer, at least you won't embarrass yourself (and lose that major business deal!) the first time you visit a new kind of restaurant; you won't order anything you hate (because you will already know that menudo is tripe), and, if all goes well, you'll enjoy yourself! Why? Because you had the confidence that comes with Knowing Enough, with having enough information to act like you've been there a dozen times before. Knowing enough to act confident is, particularly for mainstream Euroamericans, extremely important; it's part of our identity. We don't want to find ourselves in the position of being ignorant, because ignorance means vulnerability.

### Hmmm . . . Why Are All the Pros White Guys?

Experts possesses a power to grant legitimacy to a cuisine; we, their readers, let them tell us where to eat. Their authority is not simply a product of the knowledge they possess—after all, possessing knowledge never guarantees that one will be taken seriously. In the case of food writing, the expert's authority also derives in part from their purported neutrality and objectivity, which, in turn, are functions of their aloofness from the culture and cuisine they are examining. It is in part *because* they are outsiders to a culture that we believe they are to be trusted; insiders cannot be objective—precisely because they are insiders. They have no perspective because they are too invested (emotionally, culturally, or otherwise) in the cuisine. Furthermore, insiders often have nothing with which to compare their own cuisine—this is the only cuisine they've experienced. Only outsiders can ultimately be reliable authorities; only they have the proper distance on the knowledge they possess—the distance that is essential for objectivity.[1]

But the critic, far from occupying a neutral-and-therefore-objective position vis à vis the cuisine he critiques, in fact occupies a position deeply shaped by his privilege—racial, class, and often gender privilege. Virtually all of the writers I discuss are white European or American men who also occupy a privileged economic, social or educational class. These are the persons who have traditionally been defined as neutral-thus-objective, *because* they are (or at least are able to be perceived as) male, white, and middle class—because, that is, they are not burdened with a race, a gender, or a class. Only women have a gender, only people of color have a race, goes the familiar story; to be white, male, and middle class is to have no relevant class, race, or gender. But in fact a middle-class white man occupies a position of considerable privilege, and against a background of Western colonialism, that privilege takes on a particular flavor.

Consider, first, the matters of race and ethnicity; the food writers I discuss are white Europeans or Americans, while the ethnic foods they eat and write about are most often the foods of formerly colonized peoples—generally people of color. (Not entirely; dining guides usually include sections on various European cuisines, and sometimes American regional cuisines as well—though in that latter category, the most notable examples are often the cuisines of racial minorities.) What is the significance of the fact that food reviewers are almost always in the position of racially privileged outsiders when they walk into an ethnic restaurant? How do structures of race and racism shape their food adventuring? How do they shape the ways that they write about those adventures?

What about gender? If cooking is women's work, writing reviews of it appears to be men's. How does the construction of masculinity figure into the construction of the food adventurer? Is food adventuring a particularly manly activity? Do you have to be brave (a masculine virtue) to be a real food adventurer? Is doing it and then writing about it (bragging in print?) particularly manly? How do women food writers prove their worthiness as adventurers?

Then there is the issue of class. Restaurant reviewers may not make much money, but their positions often present them with opportunities to visit exotic locales and to try rare, unusual foods specially prepared for them—opportunities ordinary folks never have. Their expert status empowers them to speak with authority on a topic, and to make truth (the Orientalist again) about it. Thus, while food writers may not have economic class privilege in a simple monetary sense, they do have significant class privilege—privilege that derives from education and occupation. How does this privilege shape the relationship between them and their readers? And how does this privilege shape the relations between them and the culture they are discussing? How, for example, is authenticity parasitic on class—that is, does the critic tend to define the authentic foods of a culture to be only those enjoyed by middle-class or wealthier people? (Or perhaps only by poor people, who are sometimes romantically cast as the "only real people" in a marginalized culture?) These are not questions for which I have answers, but rather questions I invite you to keep in mind as you think through the stories I describe.

## The Other as Backdrop

In *Far Flung Floyd*, television chef Keith Floyd lets his readers know from the outset that, even compared to the average Brit, he is a privileged man.[2] When he makes a trip to Southeast Asia in the early 1990s to film his television show, we learn that he flies in the "first class cabin (naturally)," and that, during the flight, he goes to see "the poor people—by that I mean my director and cameraman etc." (8). Floyd invites his readers to experience the adventures from his seat—which remains first class for his entire trip. (I sometimes wonder if Floyd pronounces his first-class-all-the-way status so often and so vociferously precisely because he lacks confidence in its legitimacy.) Readers learn what Floyd thinks, what he eats, what he cooks. As with Paul Levy, however, readers are never invited to imagine fully *occupying* the seat of privilege; rather, Floyd invites us to adopt something like a fly on the lapel perspective. He frequently reminds the reader that he is treated regally on this trip because he is Floyd; he is given the best whiskey, the best rooms, the most exquisite food (whether or not he wants it). He is humored and cajoled by his crew—and by staff members on location—who do everything in their power to make sure that everyone he encounters will also do his bidding. The photos in his book may show him palling around with his worker bees, but the division between him and them nevertheless is firmly and deeply etched.

Floyd's privilege is also deeply colonialist. In his descriptions of his travels in Southeast Asia, the "natives" enlisted to serve him are always either naive, available and eager to please, or—if they fail to do his bidding—unreliable, intransigent, and uncooperative. (The word "sullen" is present, if unspoken, in many of his descriptions.) Their virtues and vices as humans are summed up in the quality of their service to him. On the first day of the first leg of his trip, Floyd goes to an open-air market in Terengganu, Malaysia, accompanied by Awi, the local man hired to drive his car. When he was done shopping, "I seemed to have lost Awi and I couldn't remember where the car was. I reached for the endless flimsy polythene bags full of the produce we had bought, only to find them snatched out of my hand by Awi—who materialised, rather like Jeeves, from absolutely nowhere" (19). The good native is invisible but utterly reliable—and he *always* carries your bags, heavy with the fruits of the region.

Floyd's appropriative attitude toward local people does not even restrict itself to those actually employed to work for him; he seems to regard everyone in Southeast Asia as someone in his service. The colonized should be accessible at all times and in all contexts to the colonizer; that is part of what it means to be colonized. One incident is particularly illustrative in this regard:

> We had asked our interpreter from the Hong Kong Tourist Board . . . to obtain permission for us to film. It was refused. We had never, in the seven or eight years of making these programmes, been refused permission to film, anywhere. We were all amazed. And filming market scenes before the cooking sequences is an important part of the make-up of the programme. Finally, somebody gave permission. We bought our fish and set up the portable wok at the end of the jetty, having taken great care to keep out of the way of the odd porter who trundled by, or the odd passenger climbing on to the ferries—brightly painted sampans with coloured awnings and driven by decorative gnarled old ladies, not one under the age of eighty.

Suddenly there was a crowd around us as there usually is, often curious, often amused, often surprised and frequently amazed by this motley clan of Brits. . . . But this crowd was hostile, they wanted money. But they had no right to ask for money. As we started to film and the argument grew louder, the ringleader took off his jacket and held it in front of the camera, like a cockerel in a farmyard protecting his territory—and this man was impotent with rage.

We told the tourist guide to sort out the crowd, but he was no match for this wily old gangster. It was here I did one of these pieces to camera which I hope to God will never be shown, on which I vented a whole lot of anti-Chinese feelings. We had come, of course, to praise the place, not to bury it. (47)

Several aspects of this encounter and of the way Floyd reports it merit attention. There is Floyd's shock at the resistance with which their request to film was greeted. Floyd's response to and analysis of the situation reveal no small measure of the belief that the Western visitor is entitled to virtually unlimited access to a culture, especially if he perceives such access as being necessary to his needs. "Filming market scenes before the cooking sequences is an important part of the make-up of the programme," Floyd explains. And because these scenes are important (to whom? for what?), Floyd implies that the tourist board and marketplace workers should simply agree to the presence of his cameras. What possible reason can they have for not making themselves available as colorful background? It's free advertising for them, after all!

Floyd becomes even more outraged when workers in the marketplace begin to demand money in exchange for the filming: "they had no right to ask for money." Floyd presumes his right not only to be in a particular place, but to record images of that place—images he will later go on to use for his own financial gain. However, he regards the persons whose images he captures as having "no right" to demand money of him. In the narrow, legalistic sense they probably don't have a right; there is likely no law in Hong Kong requiring tourists to pay the locals for taking their picture. But Floyd seems to claim they have no right *even to ask*; they are presumptuous to suggest that the thing he is taking from them by filming them is something they own, something they can withhold or offer at their discretion. Conversely, he assumes he has an *absolute* right to collect their images for his own use.

Floyd attempts to soften the edges of his presumptuousness in this passage by suggesting how reasonable and accommodating he and the crew were. No doubt he intends to create a contrast with the unreasonable natives who were thwarting his plans, and also to show that what his crew was asking to do was really a small thing indeed, something that did not in any way interrupt the flow of commerce or conversation in the marketplace. Thus he describes the care they took to stay out of people's way in a tone that is at once self-deprecating and self-aggrandizing; he and the crew are a "motley clan," yes . . . but British.

Floyd reduces the locals in this scene to props, useful for the color they add to a camera shot or a written phrase, but carefully relegated to the background—literally. We are presented with the odd porter, the gnarled old ladies. They become objects, interesting textures against which to create the real story. Only one of these characters refuses to remain in the background—the old man—and so Floyd must use another technique to reduce his humanity. He turns him into a rooster, and an "impotent" rooster at that. Roosters are generally regarded as having two abilities: strutting around making noise, and inseminating hens. A rooster who can only make noise is probably not long for this world.

Floyd responds to the encounter by unleashing his anti-Chinese racism—and by telling us about it in print.[3] *His* thwarted desires serve as evidence of the inferiority of the Chinese.[4] In contrast, when his desires are met by a member of any particular ethnic group, that fact becomes evidence of the general wonderfulness of that group. A good native is an agreeable, accommodating native, whereas a good gastronome is resourceful but uncompromising in his quest for excellence.

## From Biology to Fine Art

Floyd writes of the people of Southeast Asia as a resource—a kind of ready labor pool he can enlist at will in order to pull together his television show. For Jean-François Revel in his book *Culture and Cuisine,* cuisines themselves becomes resources, raw materials that must be refined if they are to be elevated above their primitive origins to become genuine Art. Revel is a political theorist, as well as an avocational food historian. His is a scholarly project: to develop a theory of the emergence and development of cuisine in history.

On his model, certain cuisines stand as a kind of primitive stuff out of which genuine culture is created.

The theory Revel develops makes a hierarchical division between two kinds of cuisines, international and regional. International cuisine—he also uses the term "international culinary art"—constitutes "a body of *methods*, of *principles* amenable to *variations*. . . ."[5] In contrast, regional cuisines consist simply of particular dishes comprised of particular foods indigenous to a region. The international is universal; the regional is particular.

International cuisine—also known as Grand Cuisine—merits the modifier "international" not only because it rests upon universal principles, but also because it is rooted in creativity and inventiveness: "[I]t alone is capable of comprehending the creative principle behind this or that local knack . . . and of applying consciously what was executed unconsciously and mechanically. For international cuisine has curiosity as its motivating force . . ." (246). In contrast, regional cuisines are deeply rooted (mired?) in tradition, in repetition: "regional cuisine . . . is *obliged* to remain routine and exclusive, finding its salvation purely and simply in the refusal to take into consideration any other register of flavors than its own" (246; emphasis in the original).

Regional cuisine, in short, is uncreative, but this lack of creativity has its own kind of integrity—so long as it is adhered to rigorously. One can almost hear here the missionary, or the development specialist, complaining about the intractable locals: "No matter how many times we show them other alternatives, they just can't seem to do it any other way. It's palm oil or nothing. And yet, in their stubbornness, there *is* something somehow admirable."

International cuisine, because it is rooted in universal principles, is a *genuine* art.[6] Regional cuisine, on the other hand, is "ethnology, or a mixture of biology and ethnology" (246). In contrasting "art" with "biology/ethnology," Revel invokes a nature/culture division on which international cuisine represents culture—*high* culture. Regional foods, however, are natural (biological); they are tasty but primitive. They are, in short, raw materials awaiting refinement and development.

Indeed, Revel suggests that much international cuisine uses regional cuisine as its natural resource: "it has the capacity to integrate, to adapt, to rethink, I will say almost to rewrite the recipes of all countries and all regions, or at least those that are amenable to such treatment" (245). The resultant international dishes are typically superior to the regional dishes that inspired them (245–46). The principles of international cuisine operate like a kind of development agency for regional cuisines, lifting dishes up from the provincial (primordial?) soup in which they languish, and realizing their genuine potential. Revel's explanation of this process calls to mind Picasso, who took so-called primitive creations and made them into genuine art by incorporating them into his own art works, and by displaying them in museums. Picasso transformed the primitive, instinctual creations of the native, using the universal principles of Art. So too does the international chef transform regional cookery.

Not all regional dishes admit of such rewriting, Revel admits; some are inextricably woven into the region in which they emerged, and to internationalize them is to destroy them. Such dishes, Revel is quick to point out, still have their own rustic charm. All *art* food is international—but not all *good* food is. The fact that some resources just cannot be developed does not mean we can't enjoy them where they are found—some gems are lovely in the rough.

Can everyone participate in the creation of international cuisine? Alas, no: international cooks are always professional chefs; this despite the fact that the distinction between international and regional cuisines is not a distinction "between the complicated and the simple" (248).[7] While Revel offers no specific argument for why Grand Cuisine must be practiced by professionals in restaurants, it is probably safe to assume that he would point to the fact that it uses general principles—principles that must be studied long and carefully in order to be understood. The chef must be theoretical; the regional cook can operate by instinct (biology again!), "unconsciously and mechanically" (246). One cannot learn *international* cuisine at home, from Mom. But for that matter, one probably cannot *learn* regional cuisine from her either; one rather imbibes it, absorbs it. (This notion that certain kinds of cooking are instinctual crops up with some frequency in ethnic cookbooks as well—most notably, in cookbooks written about African American cooking styles.)

It will probably be unsurprising to learn that Revel describes international cuisine as French cuisine (245). By this he does not mean that French regional cuisine has taken over the world; rather, he means that the principles on which international cuisine rests were developed in France in the eighteenth and nineteenth centuries, and it is French regional cuisines that were first refined and came to be a part of a cosmopolitan, international art.

France *happens* to be the site at which these refinements took place; it is the accidental birthplace of international cuisine, not the necessary one. (And yet, one wonders how much of an accident he actually believes it to be. Where else, I want to ask him, do you think this could have happened? What conditions were necessary and sufficient for such a birth to take place? Could it have happened in one of these places with a rich but supposedly instinctual regional cuisine? When did the French stop cooking by instinct and start cooking by theory and why? How can you tell the difference between the two?)

If we acknowledge that Revel has undoubtedly gotten his history right, then he is certainly justified in describing this set of culinary practices as French. Let us also reckon that he is correct that the principles on which this practice rests do allow one to modify and transform dishes from all over the world. Such capacity and flexibility may well be desirable. What makes it international, however? Why does Revel leap from a set of principles developed in France and applied to dishes from many other regions, to the assertion that this set of principles is somehow universal?

This is the word that really lies behind Revel's international/regional distinction; international cuisine is actually universal cuisine. Its principles are objective—that is, applicable—in all cases and in all contexts. To describe this cuisine as international in Revel's sense is really to say that its principles underlie all other cuisines; it is the foundation on which these others are built. What the international chef does by refining a regional recipe is to strip away superfluities in order to reveal the underlying structure—or, in the case of dishes that cannot be exported, to reveal that there *is* no underlying universal structure.

I understand that Revel says nothing the least bit quirky here; if we took a poll among chefs in the world, his view of international cuisine would likely find much favor. That his view of the world of food dominates, however, is beside the point. The fact that certain principles can be applied to many regional dishes does not, in and of itself, count as evidence that these principles constitute the universal foundations of those dishes. Just because international cuisine has developed these flexible principles does not show that they constitute underlying truths of cuisine-in-general. To claim that it does—and to claim that regional dishes somehow come into their own when they are transformed through these (French) principles, sounds suspiciously like the claim that a colonized culture's natural resources must be properly developed—along lines dictated by the colonizer.[8] No coercion may be involved in the case of a cuisine—no chefs wresting control of regional dishes away from the home cooks—but nevertheless, there is the presumption that such dishes can and should be developed, and the view that only those trained outside of the culture are in a position to know best how to develop them. The natives don't always recognize their own gems in the rough, and even when they do, they often don't know how to cut and polish them. They just don't have the (international culinary) skills.

PART THREE

# Let's Cook Thai

JENNIFER BRENNAN BEGINS *THE ORIGINAL THAI COOKBOOK* WITH THESE LINES: "IT IS DUSK in Bangkok and you are going out to dinner. The chauffeured Mercedes 280 sweeps you from your luxury hotel through streets lined with large, spreading trees and picturesque tile-roofed wooden shops and houses." She goes on to describe your arrival at an elegant Thai home—where you are greeted by an "exquisite, delicately boned Thai woman, youthful but of indeterminate age"—and also your meal—a "parade of unfamiliar and exotic dishes."[1]

Renato Rosaldo has coined the phrase "imperialist nostalgia" to describe the longing of the colonizer for that which he perceives to be destroyed by imperialism. Brennan here evokes what might be called "nostalgia *for* imperialism" when she invites her readers to imagine themselves as wealthy and privileged visitors in a culture not their own, and in which they are treated with great deference and respect by some of the wealthiest and most important people in the culture. (To complete the picture, Brennan also invites them to imagine that they are "tall and angular" (5), a description that not only draws a contrast between the average heights of Thais and Euroamericans, but also appeals to Euroamerican standards of beauty, and flatters the many white people who do not fit this description.) Brennan's description effectively reduces the identity of the Thai hostess to her relationship to her guests; she seems to exist just to provide you pleasure, visual and gustatory. Brennan, an American who has spent much of her life in South and Southeast Asia, invites her reader to *be* the protagonist of this colonialist story. Her descriptions invite us to luxuriate in the fantasy of wealth, and although she eventually gets down to the business of telling you how to cook your own food (a detail that acknowledges that you do not in fact have a Thai cook of your own), she never completely dismisses the colonialist fantasy she has created.

This is the sort of scene that one might expect to find in a British novel set in occupied India. But this is a cookbook published in 1981, and Thailand is not a colony. Its introduction illustrates just one of the ways that ethnic cookbooks may contribute to a culture of colonialism—in this case, by perpetuating a view of the Other as existing to serve and please the colonizer.

Taking up the topic of cookbooks—the focus of part 3—moves my discussion from consumption to production, a move that will illuminate the three aspects of the cultural food colonialist attitude in different ways. For example: cookbook writers, like other writers, have the task of familiarizing their readers with ethnic foods, while at the same time not destroying those foods' exotic allure. I've suggested, though, that the view that a food is exotic tends to rest quite heavily on its novelty, unfamiliarity, and differentness. When one learns to cook a particular cuisine, one loses the sense of novelty and with it, potentially, the allure of the cuisine. Cookbook writers and adventuring cooks must devise ways to preserve the food's exoticism—to make it turn on something other than unfamiliarity—or to compensate for the loss of this exoticism.

Cookbook writers must also balance another tension, this one involving the authenticity of recipes. There exists a tension between saying that a recipe has been developed—for example, for use by Westerners—and saying that it is authentic, meaning prepared just as They would do it. If a writer places too much emphasis on the claim that she has *developed* recipes she runs the risk of losing credibility as a purveyor of authentic ethnic recipes. However, there is the risk that if they are developed too little, they will remain too completely Other, too far outside Our experience to be even recognizable (let alone desirable) to us.

European and Euroamerican cookbook authors have been recording recipes from cultures other than their own for centuries—probably for as long as both cookbooks and colonial activity have existed. A 1655 cookbook published in London included recipes for "A Persian Dish" and "A Turkish Dish," as well as recipes from Italian, Spanish, and French traditions.[2] In the chapters that follow, I explore some of the ways that ethnic cookbooks create and reinforce the food adventurer's colonizing attitude.[3] I focus on cookbooks that claim to emphasize the authenticity of the cuisines they discuss, and bracket off cookbooks that intentionally and explicitly offer Americanized versions of some ethnic cuisine. An entry in the latter category is *Betty Crocker's Good and Easy Cookbook*. The first edition of this book, published in 1954, included the following "ethnic" choices for lunch and dinner: "Noodles Cantonese" (pork, noodles, celery, green beans, onion, and soy sauce); "Mexican Green Bean Salad" (green beans marinated in French dressing and garnished with grated cheese); "Sub Gum" (mushrooms, onions, pork, celery, bean sprouts, soy sauce and canned gravy!); and "Chinese Chicken Goulash." In this book potatoes are still listed as "Irish."[4] Food adventurers are generally drawn to the former sorts of books; if we are going to cook Their food, we want to do it as much like They would as is humanly possible.

In chapter 6 I discuss the significance of cookbook authors' status as insiders or outsiders to the cuisines they present, and examine some of the ways that insider/outsider status is used to assess the authenticity of a cookbook. Chapter 7 explores the ways that ethnic cookbooks attempt to satisfy their adventuring readers' desire for the exotic, and in chapter 8 I examine several ways in which cookbooks make their subjects into resources-for-use.

## Chapter 6

# Can the Doughboy Be an Insider?

IN INVESTIGATING THE WAYS THAT ETHNIC COOKBOOKS CREATE AND SUPPORT cultural colonialism, it is useful to develop some categories in which to classify these books. I've chosen to construct categories based on the question, in what relations do the cookbook author and its intended audience stand with respect to the culture whose cuisine is being described? Is the author or presumed audience an insider to that culture or an outsider, or is their position a more complicated hybrid of insider and outsider, a position that perhaps challenges the very meaning of those terms?

The categories "insider" and "outsider" play an important role in assessing the question of whether or not a recipe or cookbook is authentic, and so I will conclude this chapter by exploring some of the ways that authenticity plays out in cookbooks.

## Insiders and Outsiders

Reading the questions I posed in the first paragraph, some readers may immediately object that such questions are simplistic and distorting, because people's identities are far too complicated to be reduced to a simple in-or-out dichotomy. I agree that these categories reduce complicated identities in ways that distort them; many persons stand as members of several ethnic communities, for example, and their memberships in some of them may be highly contested. But many persons are at least regarded by others as unambiguously belonging or not belonging to particular cultures. For example, I am not Thai, or Thai-American, but I am German-American. My nonmembership and membership in those groups is uncontested and, for the time being at least, pretty incontestable. When I read a Thai cookbook, I unquestionably read it as an outsider.

Furthermore, despite the fact that such a dichotomy does distort people's identities, it is also one of the most common ways that a cookbook author

identifies her- or himself—in the introduction, if not already on the cover of
the book. Identifying as an insider gives one almost immediate authority in
the eyes of an outsider audience (sometimes regardless of the amount of relevant cooking experience one has had), while being an outsider means that
one must bolster one's credentials, and establish one's authority and legitimacy as a chronicler of the cuisine. The fact that an insider author may have
less knowledge of a cuisine than an outsider is beside the point; the insider
will tend to be regarded as having a privileged access to the cuisine.

Finally, the designations of insider and outsider shore up colonizing relationships in important ways. For this reason, if no other, it is important to
address them here.

Using the insider/outsider distinction, I can sort cookbooks into several
categories. Some are written by insiders to a culture and its cuisine for other
insiders. In the early twentieth century, (primarily European) immigrants to
the United States wrote cookbooks for other members of their community.
There were probably hundreds of such immigrant cookbooks.[1] Some of them
would have been altogether new phenomena within cultures in which recipe
creation and dissemination had been oral practices, and in which girls had
learned to cook by helping their mothers.

More recent examples of this genre also exist. They include works such
as Joan Nathan's *The Jewish Holiday Kitchen*,[2] written for Jewish cooks who
did not grow up learning how to cook the foods of their heritage; and also
books written for the most recent waves of immigrants to the United States.
Such cookbooks can strengthen ties to the old country or the old set of traditions, and ensure that the next generation of (usually) women will still
know how to cook the foods of their mothers, even if they didn't learn how
in their mothers' kitchens. Jewish cookbooks such as Nathan's might be good
examples of the way that "insider-to-insider" cookbooks function to strengthen
community ties, and to ensure that younger cooks will still know how to
cook their important "heritage foods." I've been at several Passover seders at
which someone, upon being complimented on their Passover cake or their
tsimmes has announced, "It's Joan Nathan's." At the same time, cookbooks
might be sad evidence that, while the recipes live on, a cuisine has not necessarily done so. John Thorne argues that a cuisine, in the fullest sense, is
best understood as a "complex amalgam of tradition, prejudice, shared skills,
and that ultimate common denominator—available ingredients. What is
dangerous is when the use of recipes becomes so prevalent that this co-

herency is lost—because recipe cooking cannot bring it back."[3] So if subsequent generations are left to carry on cooking traditions aided only with the recipes they find in cookbooks, those traditions will not survive—or they will survive, but in seriously attenuated forms.

Works by and for insiders generally have not made their way into the hands of food adventurers, whose access to them was often restricted by language differences, limited availability of the books, and the difficulty of following recipes that originated within another cooking tradition and have not been modified for persons outside that tradition.[4] When adventuring cooks do find a way into such a cookbook, we tend to regard it as the mother lode—the most authenticity one could hope to find in a cookbook. Like ordering off the menu on the Chinese restaurant wall, cooking out of a book written by *and for* Them allows the adventurer to claim a kind of unmediated access to the authentic Other, the other (allegedly) untouched by encounters with our culture. Nevertheless, I will not further explore cookbooks written by and for ethnic insiders, precisely because I, as an outsider, have a great deal of difficulty doing so. Furthermore, I'm interested in looking at the ways in which ethnic cookbook writers specifically contribute to cultural food colonialism through the ways in which they address outsider cooks—and this sort of cookbook doesn't set out to address outsiders.

So, I confine my attention in this chapter to ethnic cookbooks written primarily for outsiders. In particular, I consider cookbooks that address a mainstream American audience, where that audience is implicitly understood, though rarely explicitly described, as white and (aspiring to or passing as) middle class, and generally female—persons who are outsiders not only to particular ethnic cuisines, but to all cuisines defined as ethnic. This is the audience of the generic white people I described in my introduction; people who believe that we are ordinary, that our speech is unaccented, and that we have no real ethnicity of our own—and people with the wherewithal to stock our kitchens with at least a modest assortment of rarely-used specialty ingredients and single-use pans.

## Insiders

Among cookbooks written by insiders for outsiders, some represent insiders' attempts to shore up the authenticity of a cuisine they believe is being misrepresented or eroded in ethnic restaurants in the United States. Madhur

Jaffrey writes that she wrote her first cookbook, *An Invitation to Indian Cooking*, "as a gradual maneuver in self defense" because she was appalled by the quality of Indian restaurants in the United States at the time, and tired of having to cook real Indian food for everyone who wanted to taste the genuine article.[5] Jaffrey wrote those words in 1973. In 1997, I came across the following message on a food-related e-mail forum: "I am an Indian . . . embarking on a crusade against the term 'Indian food' (no such thing) and the characterisation of the cuisines of my country as the junk one finds in Tandoori restaurants all over the world. The correct term for that obnoxious food is 'Punjabi-Moghlai' and I want to let the food lovers of the world know that India has a lot more to offer."[6] And more than half a century earlier, Ardashes H. Keoleian describes a similar aim for his *Oriental Cookbook*, and of his personal sacrifice to bring that aim to fruition: "Being of Oriental origin, but knowing quite thoroughly the characteristic taste of Western peoples in certain of the fine arts . . . we have taken the pains, at the original suggestion and because of the incessant requests of some intimate American friends, to prepare this book. It has cost us many of the best years of our life and many expensive trips to the Orient, in order to secure at first hand right, positive, tested and authoritative information. . . ."[7]

As I've already suggested, insider cookbooks often are regarded as automatically authentic, by virtue of the "authenticity" of the author's heritage. When an author's ethnicity "matches" the cuisine she discusses, food adventurers may tend to ignore the question of whether the individual knows very much about cookery in general, or the cooking of her own culture in particular. She *must* have insider knowledge—she grew up there, after all!

In this regard, it is worth noting that some of the most highly regarded insider-to-outsider cookbooks currently available have been written by economically privileged women who did not learn to cook until they left their home country and moved to Europe or the United States. Both Madhur Jaffrey and Claudia Roden, author of *A Book of Middle Eastern Food*,[8] note that they began to learn to cook because they were homesick for the flavors of their childhood. Jaffrey reports that she learned her cooking by mail, in recipe letters from her mother. Neither Roden nor Jaffrey had been encouraged (let alone required) to learn to cook as a child; they grew up in the sorts of households in which kitchen work was done by servants. Jaffrey's and Roden's accounts are likely to be tinged with a kind of nostalgia (for their homes and their childhood, as well as their food) that may serve as a fitting complement to the longing for exoticism felt by many Euroamerican food adventurers. Obviously, insiders such as they will tend to have a substantially different relationship to their cuisine than would, say, the child of a cook in either of their childhood homes, who has grown up watching her mother cook this food for people who could satisfy their desires for flavors without having to know how to do it themselves. I do not mean to suggest that somehow Jaffrey's or Roden's experiences are artificial or ungenuine, but only that their love of their cuisine no doubt has a different quality than it would, had they spent their early childhoods standing in a hot kitchen chopping vegetables for someone else's dinner.

### Outsiders

Among cookbooks written by outsiders, some are the accounts of cooks who have taken a brief trip to a region and gathered up a collection of tasty and unusual culinary souvenirs, amusing anecdotes, and traveler's tales. Keith Floyd's *Far Flung Floyd* is an example in this category.[9] This surgical strike cookbook dispenses with any historical or cultural context for its recipes, focusing instead on the author's experiences while collecting them. In no way does it attempt to represent a cuisine; instead, it presents a series of *dishes* that suggest or intimate a cuisine.

Some outsider cookbooks assume something of the tone of detective novels; their authors reveal the secrets of a cuisine they've discovered through diligence, long hours of work, and stealth. Jennifer Brennan's *Original Thai Cookbook* is such a cookbook.[10] The outsider author makes her way into the natives' kitchens and reports the secrets she coyly or cunningly prized out of her household cook; the patience with which that cook explained particular techniques; the many hours they spent together talking over recipes; and the difficulty of getting the cook to give her exact measurements of ingredients. Her ability to engage companionably with her cook stands as proof that she has produced a reliable and authentic cookbook. Sometimes the kitchens into which the author has sneaked are the kitchens of friends, or members of the family into which she has married, the relationship adding another layer of credibility to the resultant recipes.

Some outsiders accompany their cooking instructions with erudite pieces of information about the relevant cultures, and with accounts of the origins of the recipes they provide. Paul Levy and his coauthor Ann Barr speak with approval—indeed with reverence—in their *Foodie Handbook* of a group of women whom they call "anthropologist cooks."[11] Writers in this category, who include Elizabeth David, Paula Wolfert, and (insider) Claudia Roden, are characterized by the care with which they research recipes on location, and the contextual detail they include in their cookbooks.

To the food adventurer, cookbooks written for outsiders already represent diluted access to the food of the Other—diluted, in a sense, by the fact of their, the adventurer's, own presence. I worry that I do not *really* learn how They cook when the cookbook is written *to me*. When, on top of that, the cookbook writer herself is an outsider, the resultant effort seems even more diluted. Outsider cookbook writers who wish to appeal to food adventurers must work to prove the genuineness, the authenticity of their recipes.

Sometimes they do so by acquiring a stamp of approval from an insider to the culture. Heidi Haughy Cusick, a Euroamerican, begins her book *Soul and Spice: African Cooking in the Americas*, with a foreword by Jessica B. Harris, an African-American cookbook author. Harris notes that "Heidi Cusick's culinary voyage is doubly fascinating because she was not born into the heritage of African cooking in the hemisphere." This book gets Harris's stamp of approval because it "begins a second phase of the exploration of the heritage of African cooking in the hemisphere, one that takes it from the hands of those who created it and transports it gently and with affection and respect to the tables of all those who love to eat well."[12]

Another way for an outsider to establish legitimacy is to show how one has learned at the shoulder of an insider. I will discuss this further when I examine Jennifer Brennan's *Original Thai Cookbook* in the next section. Not only outsiders establish their credentials in this way; some cookbooks written by economically privileged insiders include the story of how they finessed the opportunity to learn at the shoulder of the family cook. Mimie Ouei, in *The Art of Chinese Cooking*, notes that, "in a typical [wealthy!] Chinese house, the kitchen was many courtyards away," and "no one intruded into . . . the cook's empire."[13] Ouei learned to cook because she was the child of a diplomat, often living outside of the country under conditions in which she had more access to the cook. "Our very own chef who traveled with us all over the world was Ah Hing. He was a good friend as well as a marvelous *Ta Shih Fu* [chief cook]. He accepted my frequent invasions of the kitchen with incomparable patience. . . . From Ah Hing I learned the art of cooking . . ." (x).

Similarly, Carmen Aboy Valldejuli, the author of *Puerto Rican Cookery*, notes that "when I was a girl in Puerto Rico, most of the young women I knew were taught in the Spanish tradition that proper young ladies never performed menial household chores. Cooking was one of those chores. Servants were plentiful in those days. . . ."[14] It was only through her marriage to a man interested in food that she was "launched on a lifetime adventure—collecting recipes of dishes which are representative of Puerto Rican cookery" (x). When economic privilege, with its attendant strictures and rules of behavior, has kept a cultural insider out of the kitchen as a child, she too may have to prove her credentials when she sets out to write a cookbook—just the way an outsider must. For indeed, she is a kind of outsider—an outsider to the working-class kitchen culture of her own world.

Yet another form of credential flashing for the outsider comes in the claim to having produced the first noninsider—or the first *authentic* noninsider—cookbook for a particular cuisine. In the 1958 work *Classic Chinese and Japanese Cooking*, Janet and Charles Richards write that the earlier edition of this book, entitled *Basic Chinese and Japanese Recipes*, was "the first of its kind by an American publisher, at a time when hardly anything authentic had been written in English on this ancient subject."[15] Being the first to introduce members of a culture to a "new" cuisine gives one a status similar (in kind, if not in degree) to that of explorers who return from their journeys loaded down with unusual and alluring stories, artifacts, and maps of the region they've explored, all of them all the more alluring for their striking unfamiliarity. Being the first to render a cuisine in the English language (for example) makes one a kind of expert by default, simply by virtue of knowing more than most any other English-speaker.[16] This knowledge can give one the authority needed to overcome the obstacle of being an outsider, because it makes one indispensable to all the other outsiders who want access to a culture's cuisine.

## Insider-Outsiders

Among those who do not neatly count as either insider or outsider, some are "former insiders" who have lived in another culture for so long that their understanding of their home culture is deeply mediated by the culture in which they now live (and who were in some cases always outsiders to the kitchen culture they now describe). Claudia Roden and Madhur Jaffrey may exemplify this position—although they may well reject the suggestion that they do. (They might well resent this label, and particularly object to my giving it to them, given my own ignorance about their cultures and their places in them. In my defense, I would repeat that I do not think such distinctions accurately carve up the world—but that they are regularly used as if they do. I'm reporting on usage, not sanctioning it.) Others may be outsiders to the culture about which they write, but Euroamericans may nevertheless regard them as coming from a culture much closer to it than to our own cultures. Such individuals are thus treated not quite as insiders, but not as outsiders either. Dorinda Hafner is a Ghanaian who writes about the foods of a number of different African nations. She is an outsider when writing about the coastal cuisines of Kenya; nevertheless, in the white Australian context in which she writes, she also ends up being seen as an insider, simply by virtue of being African. To people of European descent, it may come as a surprise that East and West African cuisines differ dramatically from each other, such that Hafner would know less about the cuisines of Kenya than would someone from India (a country whose cuisine dramatically influenced the coastal cooking of that part of the continent).

## Who's Authentic? What's Authentic?

My discussion of insiders and outsiders has led me to some questions—worries—about authenticity. I've claimed that whether or not a recipe or a cookbook is deemed authentic often is predicated upon the status of the individual supplying it. Is she unquestionably an insider to the cuisine in question? If not, what other credentials does she bring? Does she, for instance, speak with the blessings of some insider or insiders? Can she point to years spent in an insider's kitchen? I've also noted that establishing insiderhood is not always sufficient to stamp one's cookbook as certified authentic—as when an insider only begins to learn to cook upon moving to another culture.

When we think of authenticity in terms of the problematic categories of insider and outsider, we quite clearly help to shore up the colonizing quality of the relation between adventuring cook and ethnic cuisine. Fortunately—for those of us who are interested in challenging the colonizing character of such relationships—such a notion of authenticity will also dissolve into inconsistency, even incoherence, something I shall discuss at the end of this section.[17]

Worries about authenticity arise in several forms for both cookbook writers and cooks. I examine two of these worries in some detail—one here, and one in chapter 8. The first is the matter of authentic preparation. Both cookbook writers and cookbook readers frequently raise concerns about whether or not the foods they are describing or preparing are the way they are supposed to be, the way they would be if made by an insider cook. The second worry is related: When and how, and at whose hands, is recipe variation justified? How flexible is a recipe, and when does variation make it cease to be an authentic representative of a dish?

### Authenticity Worry #1: How Would They Do It?

Cooks who are themselves on a quest for authentic foods become suspicious of a book in which the author goes to pains to explain that the recipes have been "scientifically" standardized or simplified, or—what is cause for even more consternation—modified to include only ingredients readily available in this country. The claim to authenticity, for the cookbook writer, often rests on the assertion that one has substituted ingredients only when the original ingredient is absolutely not available. (I would note, however, that, whatever one's convictions regarding authenticity, one is likely to be struck by the utter improbability of the substitution suggestions one finds in many of these books. In one 1950s-era recipe I found, the writer suggested using beer if you couldn't find soy sauce.)

The worry about authenticity I describe is obviously not one shared to the same degree by everyone in the American cooking population; it primarily affects those of us who look to acquire cultural capital by learning as much as possible about an exotic cuisine, including learning how to prepare it. But many others will share this goal to at least some degree; even the most conventional cook generally cannot resist the allure of producing some unusual ethnic dish, and serving it to her friends with studied casualness ("Oh, yes, I learned how to make this when we were on vacation in Mexico last year. The guy in the bar said this is *exactly* the way his mother does it").

This worry rests on a particular understanding of the term "authentic," one already encountered in chapter 1. The chief characteristic of an authentic food, on this reading, is that it be prepared identically to the way it is prepared in its native region—meaning everything from which ingredients are used, to the way the ingredients are measured, to the tools used to prepare them, and the names given to the resultant dish (how exactly should that be spelled?). An authentic dish should look the same when cooked in Keokuk as in Kuala Lumpur—or at least as similar as is possible, given Keokuk's grocery scene and the cook's budget and schedule.

I am reminded of performances of period music, in which the performers use period instruments and period conducting and performance techniques. The problems of authenticity that arise in the two activities bear some interesting similarities to each other: How far must we go in our attempts to be faithful to the original? What counts as enough? Do the musicians have to sit in the same sorts of chairs they would have three centuries ago? Does a cook have to build a fire using twigs from trees that actually grew in the country from which the dish originated? Just what level of fidelity is sufficient?[18]

This understanding of authenticity leaves unexamined—or at least unspecified—the role of context, and the right of insider cooks to determine what elements of a dish actually are important to her. The adventuring cook who, reading a cookbook, assumes that authenticity demands that a recipe be transplanted in its exact form ignores, first of all, the degree to which that recipe has already evolved in response to elements of its prior context(s)—elements that may include environmental conditions, cultural practices of the people who eat the dish, the types of cooking equipment and fuels used in the area, and other factors. Being authentic may sometimes require that a food first and foremost be reflective of and responsive to its context—a context that obviously changes once a dish is exported. Not all dishes are deeply responsive to all (or even many) aspects of their contexts. But cuisines do tend to reflect their natural and cultural environments; to ignore this fact in an attempt to be authentic at one level (the level of identical reproduction) is already to fail to be authentic on another—the level of attentiveness to environment.

Consider one example from a cookbook in which the question "Authentic to what?" arises for me. Keith Floyd, in writing about the Malay tendency to temper the sourness in their foods with a bit of sweetness, writes, "if you want gastronomic authenticity, you should try and obtain palm sugar. In Malaysia and throughout south-east Asia, you will find discs of palm sugar. . . .

I have seen it in plenty of shops in the UK, but if you are unable to find it, then a strong demerara would be an acceptable substitute" (18). Floyd explains to his readers what authenticity would demand, but also provides a substitute. The substitute, we must understand, is not authentic. But perhaps substituting for what is available is an *authentic* Malay practice, such that any self-respecting Malay cook living in London would never dream of spending extra time and money searching for palm sugar when it simply isn't readily available or of the quality she is used to at home. Perhaps in the case of this ingredient, she would; my point is that, for colonizing cooks and cookbook writers, there often seems to be only one road to authenticity—the road of exact replication.[19]

Another issue that arises here has to do with intentionality—in this case, the role of an insider cook's intentions or motives. How would insider cooks decide to transplant their own recipes to a completely different context? Which aspects of their cuisine would be important to them, and which would they disregard? (And should their intentions be the ones to govern our actions as outsiders? Can we just adopt whatever practices they would use, even though our relationship to the cuisine is fundamentally different from theirs?) When confronted with different kinds of equipment and/or the different indigenous foods they would find in a new country, an insider to a cuisine might *authentically* decide to make changes to her traditional recipes in order to take advantage of new things rather than laboriously attempting to do things just the way she did at home. ("Authentic" is a concept about which insiders are often far less romantic than outsiders.)

Often in such situations, change goes in both directions. The most obvious example of such mutual transformation in the United States is that which grew out of the centuries of enslavement of Africans and African Americans. Slave cooks created entire new cuisines—for both themselves and their enslavers—with the foods they were handed. These cuisines bore the mark of their African heritage, but also the imprint of ingredients and cooking techniques from the United States. Slaves also figured out how to grow foods from Africa in their new locales, and introduced them into the local diet. More recently, Hmong people who now make their homes in Minnesota raise some of their home vegetables in Minnesota and sell them to European Americans at the summer farmers' markets. They also have come to make use of local Minnesota foods in preparing their own cuisines. On this point, a cookbook such as *Cooking Thai Food in American Kitchens* is illustrative.

Malulee Pinsuvana, author of the bilingual *Cooking Thai Food,* writes that she has attempted to use ingredients "that can be found readily in any supermarket," though some few are available only in Asian groceries; she has also modified cooking techniques to be "simple enough for any new housewife or students with little time to spend in the kitchen" (unpag. introduction). In her eyes, these modifications do not diminish the authenticity of the recipes that she offers; rather, they speak to the conditions of those people—Thai and American—who will be using her recipes.

Pinsuvana's recipes are authentic Thai recipes—when one is cooking Thai food in the United States. Regarding vegetable substitutions, Pinsuvana notes simply that "they worked very well" (1). In the recipe in which Pinsuvana calls for Pillsbury buttermilk biscuits ("instead of preparing the flour in the Chinese way" [92]), she matter-of-factly presents the substitution; why wouldn't a busy Thai student use an American convenience food, if it served the same purpose as the more time-consuming homemade version? In contrast to Pinsuvana's casualness about using ingredients of American origin, consider Brennan's anxious assurances about the Thai use of ketchup, which I discussed in chapter 2 (Yes, it's authentic! Even bottled locally!). Brennan (because she is an outsider and thus sees herself on tenuous footing?) seems compelled to verify that this American ingredient is "really Thai"—that is, really used in Thailand—whereas for Pinsuvana, the question of what is used in Thailand is not the relevant issue; Pillsbury biscuits don't (or at least didn't) exist in Thailand, but they do in the United States, and they serve the purpose, so why not use them?

When colonizing cooks, in their desire for authenticity, ignore the roles of insiders' intentions and of context in order to reproduce dishes identically, these dishes may fail to be authentic at another, perhaps more relevant, level—the level of appropriateness to place. Notably, the cook who chooses to be authentic by attempting to prepare foods exactly as they are prepared in his home context is likely choosing the definition of authenticity that is the most dependent upon the global market structure. It typically requires the purchase of large numbers of imported ingredients and equipment. (It is likely that this definition requires the most purchases, period; one can never substitute a cooking dish one owns for the dish that one is supposed to use;

authenticity-as-replication requires that you purchase the proper pan.) The pursuit of such authenticity tends to be a luxury activity, restricted to those of considerable means.

What if instead our primary notion of authenticity were predicated upon how members of a cultural group might make their food if they were suddenly transplanted to the United States? Immigrant populations, even when they are intent on preserving the ways of the old country, often change their foodways in response to the new conditions they find. Naturally, immigrants do not always and wholeheartedly regard such changes as positive. But sometimes they do—and they often see them as necessary. But what if this practice of adapting to context were taken as the—or a—paradigm of authenticity?

*The Africa News Cookbook* includes a discussion relevant to this kind of authenticity. In the introduction, editor Tami Hultman writes, "In its original conception, this book was to be a collection of *authentic* recipes, a guide to cooking as Africans do. It didn't take long for us to recognize how simplistic that aim was." Among other factors, "urbanization has given rise to a greater variety of cooking methods, a larger reliance on semi-processed foods, and—like everywhere else in the world—to foreign influences in eating habits."[20] Hultman reports that she and the other editors at Africa News Service "came to understand a society's way of eating as a living, evolving process, [and] we also recognized the need to adapt the common dishes of rural Africa to the ingredients, kitchens and schedules of this book's likely users. What we have produced, therefore, is not a set of instructions for replicating what Africans eat. But it is an introduction to the cuisine of Africa that tries to reflect the spirit—and respect the skills—of those who create it" (xiv). As such, it might be termed authentic in the sense I described above; it is reflective of and responsive to the context in which it will be used, while also attempting to be faithful to what they call the "spirit" of various African cuisines.

Consider one other cookbook that might be said to illustrate this adaptive model of authenticity—this time one written by a Euroamerican about cooking his own foods in a new context. The book is *Mythology and Meatballs: A Greek Island Diary/Cookbook*, by Daniel Spoerri.[21] Of it, food writer John Thorne observes, "Spoerri is not interested in becoming a Symiote [an inhabitant of the island on which he is living]. What makes this book unique is that he does *not* set out to master Greek or even Symiotic cooking, but continues to be his own cook, while learning to take advantage of what Symi has to offer. His Greek friends are as puzzled as they are appreciative of his efforts, for he takes their ingredients and their dishes and works them to his own taste, after his own manner."[22]

Viewed from this direction, the approach becomes clearer, if also somewhat scandalous for the adventuring food colonizer to comprehend ("Go to Greece and *not* cook like a Greek?).

## Which Authenticity?

The examples I've explored here have begun to reveal some incoherence at the heart of the notion of authenticity. The question, "Which kind of authenticity is most authentic?" is an open one. To assume that it is answerable—and that it may be decided by outsider cooks, passing judgment on the authenticity of an insider's cookbook—is to place the answer outside of the culture in question. Frequently, colonizing cultures have established rules for deciding who counts as an authentic member of a culture, or for deciding which practices count as authentic, and thus permissible. Even for outsiders to place the determination in the hands of insiders is to make a decision about who counts as an insider, and who counts as the most reliable insider—and to assume that it is that person or group of persons who are most entitled to speak for an entire culture.

I will return to the issue of authenticity in chapter 8, when I examine some of the ways that cookbooks reinforce the view of the Other as resource-for-use. In chapter 7 I turn to a discussion of exoticism in cookbook writing. Adventuring food colonizers' desires for exotic eating experiences also extend to the domain of cooking; I explore several ways that cookbooks fulfill these desires.

*Chapter 7*

# How to Stuff a Wild Zucchini

TO COOK INVITES ONE TO DEVELOP A RELATIONSHIP TO FOODS QUITE DIFFERENT from the sort that develops if one only eats them. When I first began work on this book, I tended to regard that relationship as a kind of magic bullet that would serve to prevent the cook from ever being a food colonizer. As I conceived it then, the knowledge that was required of a cook—knowledge of foods and cooking techniques—immunized one from the kind of ignorant acquisitiveness that characterized food colonizers, who never left the table to enter the kitchen. On that earlier view, colonization came about because of distance and disconnection from the food one eats, ignorance about how it is made. I've abandoned the belief that learning to cook will make one an automatic anticolonialist; I've come to understand that close proximity to, and intimate knowledge of, a cuisine can in fact serve as vehicles for even more zealous food adventuring, as I shall show in this chapter. Nevertheless, I continue to believe that cooking can also become a part of a food anticolonialist strategy—something I'll discuss in part 4.

One does not necessarily know more about a food just because one has cooked it, but cooking foods does require one to understand their temperaments in ways not required in order to eat them. This familiarity presents an interesting problem for the food adventurer, because it can destroy the much-prized novelty and exoticism of a cuisine. Cookbook writers who wish to preserve the exotic qualities of foods for their adventuring readers must approach their task in a way quite different from that used by adventuring food writers such as those discussed in part 2. Their roles differ because they attempt to engender different responses in their readers.

Whereas food adventure writers (particularly food aristocrats) often emphasize the strangeness of the foods they consume, ethnic cookbook writers teach their readers how to replicate particular dishes—to make the strange familiar, in a sense. Thus the dishes they describe are already likely to be more prosaic, because most cookbook authors at least *intend* for their recipes to be usable.[1] Some cookbooks explicitly mention the recipes they do not include. Pearl Buck includes a long introduction to each section of her cookbook, *Pearl Buck's Oriental Cookbook*,[2] mentioning many dishes for which she provides no recipes, because crucial ingredients were simply not available for them.

How can the cookbook writer present usable recipes without sacrificing the exoticism of the dishes she presents—a crucial aspect of their allure and the source of considerable cultural capital for the food adventurer? Why would the adventurer ever be interested in learning to cook, if it means giving up the most immediate source of exoticism in a food, its novelty?

The first answer to this question I've suggested already in part 1, where I noted that being casually familiar with a cuisine that is still radically unfamiliar to most Euroamericans represents its own culturally valuable relationship to the exotic. A person who holds such a relationship in a sense *becomes* the exotic, or at least the exotic-once-removed. Learning to cook an ethnic cuisine enables me to create authentic examples of that cuisine, and also to recognize authenticity in restaurant food—to become a kind of expert, able to pass judgment on the legitimacy of a restaurant's efforts. Jennifer Brennan takes this approach to exoticism in *The Original Thai Cookbook*.[3]

A second way to answer the question, Why learn to cook if it means giving up exoticism? is to reject its premise and assert that learning to cook does *not* require sacrificing the strangeness of a cuisine, and thus certainly does not destroy that cuisine's exoticism. A cuisine can retain its novelty if one remains on its surface, never learning too much about it even as one selectively learns to cook certain of its dishes. Keith Floyd takes this sort of approach to cooking in *Far Flung Floyd*, a text that keeps the ethnic Other always at least an arm's length away—even during dinner.[4]

I'll explore both Brennan's and Floyd's strategies in some detail here.

## The Exotic as Familiar

Some cookbooks encourage cooks to make their recipes a part of the cook's ordinary weekly menu—not just something to make on special occasions. They may stress the fact that dishes and ingredients that seem exotic are actually quite familiar and available—or will come to seem familiar and essential once one has tasted them. Heidi Haughy Cusick, in *Soul and Spice,* stresses the fact that virtually all the ingredients for recipes in her book are readily available in U.S. supermarkets. She acknowledges that "some of the Bahian, Caribbean, and African recipes may sound exotic or formidable to U.S. cooks if they haven't tasted them at the source," but insists that unusual ingredients "are worth making the special effort to obtain."[5]

The practice of making the exotic familiar may not be as counterintuitive as it sounds; as literary theorist Graham Huggan suggests, part of what makes the exotic exotic is proximity: "exotic artifacts from other cultures circulate as commodities within the global economy—it is precisely their availability that renders them exotic."[6] I understand Huggan to be saying not that *anything* proximate to me can be exotic, but that we are most able to exoticize those features of the Other's culture to which we have most access. Possessing even a rudimentary knowledge about another cuisine (even possessing a cookbook or two) can give one the kind of access to the exotic of which he writes. (I find that guests in my home often credit me with having knowledge of cuisines far beyond my wildest imaginations, simply because they see the collection of ethnic cookbooks I have acquired. I was once taken to an enormous, well-stocked Chinese grocery in Washington, D.C., precisely because the friends I was visiting were convinced that I would be able to shop there and cook them a wonderful regional Chinese meal.)

In order to make the novel/exotic into the familiar in a way that continues to satisfy the food adventurer's desire for exoticism, some cookbook writers first reassure the would-be cook that she is indeed confronting something strange; it's different, hard to pronounce, mysterious to use, and often difficult to obtain. Jennifer Brennan, in the preface to *The Original Thai Cookbook,*[7] writes that, although there are now Oriental and Thai markets in "nearly every town" they are filled with "a dazzling and, sometimes, baffling array of foodstuffs: native herbs and spices . . . . unusual species of fish; unlabeled cuts of meat; vegetables you might consider weeding from your garden; assortments of strange canned foods and sauces—all with exotic names, sometimes foreign language labels—all purveyed by shopkeepers unfamiliar with English" (unpaginated preface).

Brennan seems to say that, even though the exotic has come to a grocery store near you, it still remains utterly remote from you. Walking into a grocery store can be just as alienating and confusing as picking up a cookbook

written by insiders for insiders; there are no helpful pronunciation or con-
version guides, no store hostesses asking if you have questions about how to
use a particular spice. In the stores that Brennan describes, Euroamericans
catch a tiny glimpse of what it is like to be decentered, for our needs to go
unmet.[8]

(It bears mentioning that the situation with respect to Thai foods has
changed dramatically since Brennan published this book in 1981. Now, not
only are there more Asian groceries than ever before, featuring products labeled in two or more languages, but also one can buy many of the ingredients
for Thai foods in food co-ops and upscale supermarkets in many cities and
towns in the United States. One can even buy various premixed "Thai spices"
in foil packets and glass jars, with directions clearly labeled in idiomatically
flawless American English. While they are considerably more expensive—and
still less accessible—than the ubiquitous taco seasoning packets that sit on the
shelves of even the tiniest grocery stores in the Midwest, I have little doubt
that they will one day be every bit as common, as Thai food becomes more
and more a part of the mainstream U.S. consumer diet.)

In her introduction Brennan invites her readers to imagine themselves
visiting an elegant Thai home and being served a banquet of "unfamiliar and
exotic dishes" (5). Her lengthy description of this imaginary banquet highlights the glamorous novelty of everything from the street scenes to the
clothing to the way in which the foods are presented at banquet. *Cooking
Hawaiian Style*, written two years earlier, uses a similar technique; its introduction capitalizes on the "lilting strands of song, floating on a tropical night,"
the "brown skinned girls swaying gracefully in the hula," and, in general, the
Hawaiians' "joy and satisfaction in being alive."[9]

Indeed, ethnic cookbooks have long relied on stock descriptions of the
mystery, allure, and exoticism of a land and its people to describe a cuisine.
*Pearl Buck's Oriental Cookbook*, published in 1972, describes Indonesia as
consisting of "three thousand islands, lying languorously along the equa-
tor. . . . It is musical, exotic Bali; it is sultry, exciting Java; it is Sumatra, Bor-
neo, Sulawesi (Celebes) and West Irian, the western half of still near-savage
New Guinea. . . ." (13). Many cookbooks take you on an imaginary tour of
the country or countries in question, attempting to create in words the experiences the traveler allegedly experiences firsthand. These descriptions almost invariably founder in cliches and stereotypes.

Contrast this approach to exotic ingredients with that of a cookbook writer in 1930s Palestine, attempting to persuade her readers, Jewish immigrants to the land, to try the odd vegetables they find in their new homeland. As food theorist Yael Raviv notes, "what is highlighted is not the mystic [sic] of the ingredients, their unique and new flavor or aroma, or how they can contribute to a greater variety in the reader's cooking." Instead, the author seeks to help her readers learn how to "make do" with ingredients they'd really rather not be eating; "The attitude here is not of a new adventure, but of having to learn to use these foreign products for lack of an alternative."[10]

The reassurances of exoticism that cookbook writers like Brennan employ can serve two related purposes: they may confirm for the cook that the food she will learn to make is, in some objective sense, exotic and that even familiarity with it cannot alter that purported fact. Its exoticism means that a cook will definitely gain that particular kind of stature if she serves it to her dinner guests, for whom home-cooked Thai food is still likely to be a novelty. Second, they assure the cook that she is not simply naive, ignorant, or overly cautious. (This food really is strange! You don't have to be embarrassed about your finding it so, because it really is! But I, the cookbook writer, will demystify it for you so that you can serve it to your guests—and mystify them!)

Another example illustrates both purposes. It comes from a cookbook published twenty years before Brennan's, entitled *Japanese Food and Cooking*. In the foreword to it, author Stuart Griffin describes the respective experiences of "Mrs. American Housewife" and "Mr. American Husband," upon landing in Japan. Mr. American Husband's arrival predates that of his wife, so he has time to explore Japanese cuisine, and to determine that he "could leave a lot of Japanese food alone," specifically the "big, briny tubs of pickles, the fish stands where every species eyed him, and the small stool-and-counter shops with the stomach-turning cooking-oil smells. . . . But he found lots of things that he wanted to eat and did like."[11] When Mrs. American Housewife arrives, her husband and her Japanese cook (every American in Japan has a cook, of course) enter into a conspiracy to get her to try Japanese dishes. By the end of the foreword, Mrs. American Housewife is hosting dinner parties for her (American) friends, featuring an "entirely Japanese" menu (xiv). In doing so, she becomes to her friends a kind of exotic herself—an American familiar with, and conversant in, Japanese food.

When Brennan and Griffin describe food as "strange" and "stomach-turning," to whom are they speaking? Brennan identifies her audience as English-speaking people in the United States. Griffin writes at least in part for expatriate Americans trying to get along in Japan. But in emphasizing the unfamiliarity of the foods, Brennan actually specifies her audience much further. Presumably, English-speaking Thai Americans would find many of the ingredients in Thai food quite familiar, since their cooking likely would use many of them as well. The same would likely be true of many Vietnamese Americans, Chinese Americans, Indian Americans, and Malaysian Americans—any people whose heritage foods have interacted with Thai cuisine. The ingredients Brennan describes would in fact be deeply unfamiliar only to certain English speakers in the United States. But Brennan's description of the Asian grocery recognizes no such distinctions; you, English Speaker, will find things strange in such a store. "Strange," like "exotic," comes to mean strange-in-principle because strange-to-Us. The Euroamerican experience remains squarely in the center of things, and others' experiences are to be understood and described through it.

Even insider cookbook authors come to use these ways of describing their own cuisines. Claudia Roden evokes notions of the exotic Middle East when she variously describes certain salads as "rich and exotic," baba ghanoush as "exciting and vulgarly seductive," and Turkish Delight as a food "no harem film scene could be without."[12] Many foods she describes as "exciting," a word that evokes adventure: meat soups, for example, "can be exciting and delicious served at a late party with Arab bread, or *pitta*" (125). (One can't help but wonder if such soups would be described as "exciting" in Cairo.) And many of them appeal to stock American images of the Middle East as a place where steamy sex lurks just beneath the surface—images that remind us that the term "exotic" also often refers to nude women dancers.

In the face of all this strangeness, Brennan offers her cookbook as a guide to the perplexed, a way into the strangeness that will reveal it as being not so strange after all, but something that can be mastered and can become a part of one's everyday life. She writes, "I have attempted to bridge the gap that occurs when one tries to reproduce the cuisine of a distant, unfamiliar country in a Western kitchen" (unpaginated preface). Later on, in a section entitled "Memo to the Cook," Brennan elaborates this reassurance, saying, "While, at first, the recipes herein seem difficult because of the number of ingredients and their unusual names, you will find that familiarity breeds affection. After a few attempts at the exotic, you will become friendly with methods, ingredients and dishes" (62). Your dinner guests, however, will probably still be *un*familiar with them, so you'll be able to score big points off them.

Similarly, Roden comments frequently on the ease with which the dishes she describes can be prepared; she notes that "Middle Eastern cooking, though sometimes elaborate, is easy" (5). Later on, in a chapter on desserts, she suggests that "every housewife who tries will be able to make [specialty sweets] easily and successfully . . ." (375). Furthermore, she emphasizes that the foods of the Middle East are economical due to their frugal use of meat and the absence of alcohol (6). In other words, despite its being exciting, seductive, rich and exotic, and so on, Middle Eastern cuisine can be prepared by Mrs. American Housewife in Nebraska with great success and at low cost.

This "on the one hand exotic, on the other hand economical (or practical, or easy)" description appears in countless ethnic cookbooks spanning many decades. On the back cover of *Dinner at Omar Khayyam's*, an Armenian cookbook from 1944, we read that "The dishes described are exotic and different, but thrifty, healthful and easy. . . . Nearly all the recipes call for simple ingredients which can be bought in the neighborhood grocery store."[13] A 1956 advertisement (in a cookbook by Cora and Bob Brown) for *Recipes of All Nations* notes that the book "is as practical as it is authentic," an attempt to reassure the home cook that these recipes have not been watered down for her use.[14] And in her introduction to the 1963 *Tia Victoria's Spanish Kitchen*, Elizabeth Gili writes, "However complicated the richer and more exotic recipes appear to be, the instructions for their preparation are straightforward and can be followed by those with only a little experience of cooking. At first sight, some of the ingredients may be unfamiliar, but there can be few towns that do not claim at least one good delicatessen shop which provides a wide selection of continental sausages and exotic foods."[15]

In other words, all that separates me and my southern Minnesota kitchen from those of cooks in Kuala Lumpur or Cairo or Cochin are a *really* good grocery store and some practice. A cuisine is really a collection of ingredients and a set of recipes. Give me those things and the time to practice them, and I can become an ethnic cook—an *exotic* cook—too.

## The Exotic as Weird

The other approach I suggested for resolving the tension between exoticism and familiarity is to reject altogether the presumption that learning to cook engenders familiarity with a cuisine. Some ethnic cookbooks are written in such a way as to make the foods they describe *remain* strange and unfamiliar; they never move to the level of familiarity.

Many cookbooks that emphasize their authentic representations of a cuisine nevertheless exclude entire aspects of that cuisine as simply being *too* exotic—too far beyond the experience of Euroamerican eaters to be considered seriously. (The most hard-core food adventurer will probably tend to shy away from such books, since they seem to make decisions for us that we'd rather make for ourselves.)[16] It is not simply that we cannot get the ingredients here (though this may often be the case); but even if we *could* get them, this is simply not a food for Us. These cookbooks may tell you about a given dish, but refuse to provide a recipe for it, or they may provide a recipe, but for what appear to be purely encyclopedic purposes. Roana and Gene Schindler write that in their *Hawaii Kai Cookbook*, while most recipes are practical for the mainland cook and have popular taste appeal, "Several recipes such as poi are so representative of Hawaiian cookery that to exclude them would be unthinkable, but we have cautioned the reader that mainland diners often find them unpalatable."[17] Notably, this "unpalatable" food was the staple of indigenous Hawaiians. To exclude it from a discussion of Hawaiian cookery would indeed be an odd omission.

A historical example of this genre is the 1859 *Breakfast, Dinner and Tea: Viewed Classically, Poetically, and Practically*. The title page goes on: *Containing Numerous Curious Dishes and Feasts of All Times and All Countries Besides Three Hundred Modern Receipts*. Did it not have so many subtitles already, I would suggest that it could have been given another—*Those Crazy Foreigners*—for here is a work that simply catalogs the peculiar (to the author) foods of civilizations all over the world: ant eggs in Siam; birds' nests, sea slugs, and rat soup in China; putrid (his word) seal in Greenland. The recipes, by contrast, are quite prosaic—including the familiarly British-sounding recipe for curry I mentioned in chapter 3.

Keith Floyd's cookbook-cum-travelogue *Far Flung Floyd* is an example of a work in which authentic recipes are presented in a context of unrelenting exoticism—an exoticism that shades into dangerous weirdness. And indeed there is a danger in this approach, a danger that in emphasizing the exoticism of a food the writer will move it too far out of our world. A cookbook that renders a cuisine unappetizing-sounding is not a successful cookbook. This challenge is the opposite of the one faced by cookbooks that invite their readers in by showing them how familiar everything is about a cuisine. In between the too-exotic and the too-familiar (a location that itself constantly changes) is an area that is just right—just far enough beyond the pack to be rewarding, but not so far as to be incomprehensible.

Floyd's is a cook-and-tell adventure, filled with stories of his dining exploits, photos of the natives, and recipes and pictures of the foods of the regions. His book makes only the thinnest attempts at mapping the region he surveys—and it is a tremendously large region. Floyd spent a bare two months in "far flung" Southeast Asia, during which time he visited—and cooked "native" in—Malaysia, Hong Kong, Vietnam, and Thailand. Rather than an atlas, his book might best be thought of as a scrapbook filled with items clipped from a newspaper. Reading this scrapbook, one comes away with a few sample recipes from each of several different cuisines, such as one might find in the newspaper's Wednesday food section, and also with some new adventure stories, clipped, perhaps, from the Sunday travel section. Through these accompanying stories (rather than through descriptions of the food itself) Floyd promotes his sense that the cuisines of Southeast Asia are exotic and strange—and sometimes just plain disgusting.

Floyd is most interested in experiences of the exotic that involve animals—a familiar interest by now. His is the interest of the fascinated-but-horrified adventure traveler who cannot quite believe the ghastly practices in which the natives indulge. The exotic, for Floyd, becomes evidence of the (moral) inferiority of Those People—evidence that Floyd seems to use, in turn, to justify his belief that all of Southeast Asia is filled with people who should do his bidding.

In one adventure, constructed for his television show, Floyd visits a well-known Saigon snake restaurant, where a cobra is killed, cooked, and served to him. The restaurant kitchen in which the cobra is prepared, a dark "lean-to" with a slippery floor, rudimentary washing facilities, and the "wonderful smell of ginger, garlic and lemon grass" (58), is also a "ghastly gastronomic menagerie" (58), filled with cages containing snakes of various kinds, bats, and "assorted rodents . . . I couldn't identify" (58). (It is interesting that, despite his inability to identify the animals, he knows they are rodents, a word that for Westerners often conjures up the rat, one of the most despised animals in existence—definitely not one we regard as edible.) Floyd reports that the sight of the animals in cages was "sickening" (58), even to him, a man who "feels no compunction" in killing animals for food. His description of the kitchen establishes it as a kind of torture chamber for weird and dangerous animals.[18]

Note that the snake Floyd was invited to consume was poisonous, and that its fangs had not been removed—it could still inflict a poisonous bite. Overcoming danger, I've noted before, is often a step in the process of exoticization. Floyd, interestingly enough, takes no apparent pride in partaking of this danger. He notes with disdain that the young boy working in the kitchen "dexterously, proudly, arrogantly" removed the snake from its cage and flourished it about a bit—no doubt acquiring for himself some cultural capital with his own peers, whether or not Floyd the outsider was willing to grant any.

The boy kills the snake and slits open its stomach. (Floyd averts his eyes.) The cook then blanches it, scales it, chops it into pieces and stir-fries it with vegetables, noodles and spices. Floyd, waiting in "desperate anticipation" (59), is presented with a plate of this stir-fry, a glass of snake's blood, and a glass of raw snake organs. He is saved from having to eat the organs by a waiter "who wanted to show off his prowess," by eating them himself. (Floyd, who should be grateful to this man, nevertheless takes the opportunity to mock him for his "foolish" beliefs about the powers of snake organs.) A member of his own crew graciously drinks off the blood, and Floyd is left only to tackle the snake. He reports that it tasted like frog's legs.

Whereas Paul Levy tends to emphasize the "specialness" of the events in which he is served exotic animals (the imperial banquet, the foreigners-only restaurant), Floyd focuses on the horror he feels throughout the experience, beginning with his shock at the living conditions of the animals and ending with his revulsion at being offered a glass of snake's blood. Needless to say, he includes no recipes for snake in his book.

So, why did he do it, one might ask? If his self-portrait in this scene is at all accurate, Floyd certainly stands as a reluctant food adventurer, an unwilling partaker of the exotic. If he acquires cultural capital by eating a poisonous snake, he certainly also spends a considerable amount of it in his reluctance to do the deed. His is not a typical food adventure story (while it might be a typical food horror story—but these are not usually written by cookbook writers). The most plausible answer to the question "Why?" is "Television." A trip to the local snake restaurant is just the thing to liven up an otherwise dull cooking sequence. But I must admit I remain unsatisfied with this explanation.

For Floyd, the food of the Other remains exotic, its exoticism often standing as evidence not of the fascination of other cultures, but of their inferiority. His stories, while filled with descriptions of the lushness of vegetation, the beauty of the local scenery, and the abundance of fresh fruits and vegetables, always come around to reminding the reader that They (not We) are people who eat snakes and rodents and who cook on dirt floors. Yes, their foods are exotic, but such exoticism simply might not be worth the price. Such a description may be just the thing to entice the zealous food adventurer; what better evidence that a cuisine is still on the cutting edge than a cookbook author who cannot speak of it without a certain amount of disgust? Here is a trend one might be able to ride for several years before it becomes too familiar!

Floyd's cookbook includes many recipes for foods that he assures his readers are delicious. But his revulsion casts a kind of pall over the recipes, leaving the reader unsure whether she really wants to try them at all. It's questionable whether Floyd's approach to preserving authenticity in a cookbook is really successful. Perhaps it is better to leave his book in the category of food adventure writing, even if it does include recipes.

*Chapter 8*

# Aided by My Faithful Old Family Cook

IN HER BOOK *IMPERIAL EYES*, MARY LOUISE PRATT DISCUSSES THE *JOURNAL OF A Residence in Chile during the Year 1822* by Maria Graham Callcott. Describing a section in which Graham tells of learning to make pottery, Pratt writes, "Rather than treating the artisanal pottery works as a deplorable instance of backwardness in need of correction, Graham presents it in this episode almost as a utopia, and a matriarchal one at that. The family-based, non-mechanized production is presided over by a female authority figure. Yet even as she affirms non-industrial and feminocentric values, Graham also affirms European privilege. In relation to her, the potters retain the essential colonized quality of *disponibilité*—they unquestioningly accept Graham's intrusion and spontaneously take up the roles Graham wishes them to."[1] As Pratt suggests here, to treat the ethnic Other as a resource for one's own use can take many forms, even some that involve veneration and admiration. This observation is well worth keeping in mind when one examines ethnic cookbooks; many of them exhibit appreciation for a food tradition, even as they preserve an "essential colonized quality" in the relationship between the cookbook writer and her cook/informant. Sometimes one admires, even loves, the people and things one possesses and uses. (Think of the much-discussed relationships between Black nannies and their white charges, relationships that have often been written about by the whites who experienced this form of child rearing in tones of sentimental nostalgia that tend to minimize or obliterate the degree to which those relationships objectified Black women.) It is little surprise that authors tend to love the cuisines about which they write; what might be harder to believe is that the loving ways they write about those cuisines can perpetuate a hierarchical and marginalizing relationship between themselves and this other culture.

Pratt also describes the stance of the outside (European) observer in all of this; a privileged position that enables her to interrupt the women's work and insert herself in their midst in order to assign them particular poses in her colonial diorama. She has the right to be there, and the power to interpret them—it is their task to live up to that interpretation.

Food adventurers embody the colonizer's tendency to believe that he belongs anywhere, doing anything he wants, whenever he wants. And once we get there, we tend to begin deciding just how the Other should behave, according to our notion of things. (Recall my behavior in a Thai restaurant in Ireland.) Cookbook writers are no exception to these tendencies.

It is easy for me to identify a colonized quality to the relationships between European or Euroamerican cookbook author and non-European cuisine when I look at cookbooks that are several decades old.[2] I read in the introduction to the 1961 book *The Art of South American Cookery* that "South American food is amazingly good—a complete, almost undiscovered cookery style" and I find myself wanting to ask "*Why* is its goodness amazing? And by whom is it undiscovered?"[3] Even though she comes to praise South American cuisine, Myra Waldo, the author of this book, does so in a way that clearly keeps South American cooks firmly in their place over *there*. Frequently in such cookbooks, we are given sketches of the character and personality of an entire ethnic group—and shown that their cuisine is just a natural outgrowth of this supposedly natural character. Caroline Weiss, in *A Collection of Creole Recipes* (from 1941), reports that in Creole cooking, "the Negro cooks had instinctive facility and an inborn genius for combining herbs and seasonings with foods. . . . They took the native French and Spanish dishes and, by the refinement of the trial and error method, made new dishes. . . ."[4] Instinct and inborn genius (with a dash of trial and error), not carefully developed skills, are responsible for African-American contributions to Creole cuisine. Insider cooks sometimes even participate in their own essentializing, as when Freda DeKnight describes herself as "the little brown chef" in her cookbook *A Date with a Dish: A Cook Book of American Negro Recipes,* published in 1948.[5]

These older appeals to ethnic stereotypes strike my ear as incredibly crude, incredibly obvious examples of putting the ethnic cook in their colonized place. Contemporary cookbooks employ rather different, apparently more subtle means. The results, however, are often similar.

In this chapter, I look at two different ways that cookbooks perpetuate the notion that the ethnic other is a resource for my use—recipe theft and recipe development. I also discuss a second worry about authenticity that arises in this context, a companion to the issue I raised in chapter 6: who is entitled to alter a recipe?

## Borrowing or Stealing?

Where do the recipes in cookbooks come from? And when is it proper to say that a recipe was stolen or inadequately credited? When it comes to cookbooks in general, and ethnic cookbooks in particular, the definitions of these terms decidedly favor the interests of authors. A cookbook author is accused of having stolen recipes only if those recipes have previously appeared in published form—a form of communicating that privileges people on the basis of class and education, and often race and sex as well. Thus, in his 1958 cookbook *Tasty Dishes of India*, R. A. P. Hare could write that "before I left India for good in 1947, I had several sessions with my very excellent cook— Khoda Buksh—and noted down the recipes of many dishes he had served up to me over a period of 25 years. The result is this collection to which I have added recipes picked up in my travels and which I taught Khoda Buksh to make."6 One might well ask, Why is Buksh's name not prominently displayed on the cover as a principle author of this cookbook? Well, because all he has done is cook the dishes for twenty-five years; the writing down of the recipes was a second step. And it is that second step that is all important— so important that it apparently eclipses the work of actually perfecting the recipes in the kitchen.

Consider this case: Ann Barr and Paul Levy, in the *Foodie Handbook*, praise Claudia Roden for her careful "anthropological" (their term) work to credit sources of her recipes in her *Book of Middle Eastern Food*.7 But while Roden is meticulously careful to identify the sources of the recipes she reproduces when those sources are cookbooks, she acknowledges *unpublished* sources by name only in the acknowledgements to her book—and then only in a brief list of those to whom she is "particularly indebted."8

Barr and Levy's praise for the integrity of "scholar cooks" like Roden rests upon the unstated assumption that only published sources require crediting—an assumption that is validated by and codified in copyright laws and institutional policies regarding plagiarism.9 This assumption allows them to regard as highly principled Roden's practice of sometimes *describing*, but almost never *naming*, the women from whom she receives unpublished recipes. (They need not be identified definitively, because They cannot be stolen from; They do not own their own creations in any genuine—read: legally binding—sense of the word.) But when coupled with her meticulously careful crediting of previously published recipes, her failure to name these women cooks actually creates cookbooks that reflect and reinforce the colonialist and classist societies into which they are received.

Barr and Levy's comments in praise of Roden come in their discussion of a case of recipe plagiarism. In the Euroamerican tradition of cookbook writing they are examining, the ethics of recipe borrowing seem roughly to follow the rules governing plagiarism. According to these, borrowing only becomes theft if a recipe has already appeared in print and one fails explicitly to acknowledge that fact. Because of the nature of recipes (when is a recipe original?), it will always be much more difficult for a cook successfully to charge theft than for, say, a novelist, but if the charge is ever to stick—or even to make sense—it must be made against someone who reproduces a recipe that has previously appeared in a published work.

If we consider cooking itself—rather than cookbook writing—we may locate another, similar definition of theft. Chefs can be thought of as stealing each other's dishes, particularly signature dishes that they have invented, even if recipes for those dishes have never been published. Famous chefs, who get paid for their work, can most easily make this claim, because they can produce the most evidence for it. Unknown chefs—like unknown songwriters—will have more difficulty proving that they've been robbed of a culinary idea. And people who are not chefs for pay but simply home cooks will have even more difficulty; a recipe must become some kind of a commodity before it can be stolen. The thing to note is that in cooking, as with cookbooks, proving originality is important—but having the power to reinforce a claim to originality is crucial.

Taking up the legal issue, Barr and Levy argue that it is both "mad" and "unenforceable" to suggest that an individual ought to have the right to copyright the directions for an omelet or a traditional French casserole (108); how could any individual own the procedure for making dishes so ubiquitous? In contrast, they favorably report that, in a 1984 case, Richard Olney successfully sued Richard Nelson for copyright infringement, claiming that Nelson had reproduced thirty-nine of Olney's published recipes in one of his own cookbooks. Thus, while they are uncomfortable with the idea of copy-righting some kinds of recipes, Barr and Levy suggest that justice was served in the Olney case, because Olney is an "originator" of recipes—as opposed to an anthologizer (like Nelson) or an "anthropologist" (like Roden) (110).

Olney owned his recipes in a way that no one can own the omelet recipe because he both invented and published them. The latter step apparently is necessary; Barr and Levy have no pity for the author who prints recipes on index cards and distributes them to her friends and then cries "thief." Indeed, the prevalence of recipe card exchanges serves to temper some of their outrage over the Olney-Nelson case; it seems that Richard Nelson got his recipes not out of Richard Olney's book, but from a set of recipes cards he'd received in the mail and had used for years in his cooking class, with no idea of their origins. But in the end, it doesn't matter; just because you receive in the mail an unsigned copy of *On The Road*, written in pencil on paper torn from a wide-ruled spiral notebook, you cannot publish Jack Kerouac's words under your own name.

But what of other cases in which the recipes in question are not origi-nals, but are the ethnic equivalents of the omelet? What are the ownership rights of Barr and Levy's anthropologist cook who publishes the recipes she has collected in the field, only to have someone else republish those recipes in their own book? Is she a victim of theft? Barr and Levy suggest that she is, in their sympathetic consideration of Claudia Roden, whose work has been the site of much borrowing by other cookbook compilers. Barr and Levy re-port that Roden is pleased to see people using the recipes she gathered, but not so pleased to see those recipes reappearing in print. In particular, she is "hurt and angry that Arto der Haroutunian, in his books . . . has a great many of the same recipes as hers (some of which had never been in print be-fore), similarly described and including some of the mistakes. . . . As a writer who gathered her material physically, Mrs. Roden feels 'He has stolen my shadow'" (112). Roden's anger here suggests that it is not only the origi-nator of a recipe whose work can be stolen; one is also a victim of theft if the recipes you "physically" collect and publish are subsequently published by someone else.

That Roden is the victim of a theft of original material seems obvious on one level. In a context defined by copyright law, Haroutunian's acts do con-stitute a form of plagiarism of Roden's original work. But consider the matter again; what he stole were, for the most part, recipes she gathered from other women—along with published texts she excerpted and organized in a particular way. The content of Roden's text was not original to her in any straightforward sense. Apparently publishing, in this context, comes to be its own kind of originality—or comes to *mean* originality.

Furthermore, publishing a thing comes to make it one's own, regardless of who owned it in the first place. Barr and Levy note that Roden does not claim that she created the recipes; indeed, she expressly describes them as belonging to the particular towns, villages, communities, and countries in which she located them (112). Nevertheless, Roden says that *her* shadow has been stolen by Haroutunian. This suggests that these recipes are also hers because she painstakingly brought them to the rest of the world in a book. She would have no grounds to claim injury if she had simply put these recipes on index cards and passed them out at parties (as Madhur Jaffrey did, before deciding to publish her first cookbook).[10] Her claim to ownership rests chiefly on her copyright.

While I agree that some kind of harm has been done to Roden by those who have republished parts of her book, I want to redirect the discussion to the kinds of harm that this explanation obscures—namely, that harm done to the Middle Eastern women at whose stoves she stood, and from whom she learned the recipes she reproduced in her cookbook. This harm does not fall neatly under the category of theft, because they cannot be regarded as the owners of recipes in the sense required. The language of property does not help us to understand such harm for at least two reasons: first, these cooks have not laid any claim to the recipes (say, by publishing them themselves or by cooking them in a restaurant for paying customers), nor will they likely do so because, second, the recipes from which they cook are in many cases as common to them as the omelet is to a French cook, and thus not the sorts of things that they would be inclined to think could be owned. It is not appropriate to describe Claudia Roden as stealing recipes from the women with whom she studied. The harm done to them could not be rectified simply by documenting the originators of her recipes.

John Thorne makes a similar point in the chapter of *Outlaw Cook* titled "My Paula Wolfert Problem." Thorne writes that "What Paula Wolfert has perfected . . . is a method of lifting dishes *out* of the public domain and patenting them as her own. Such a trademark cuisine delights her followers because it provides them with a series of exclusive possessions . . . a Paula Wolfert cassoulet to set next to their Lexus sedan, their Movado watch. But it does this by impoverishing the rest of us, and not least because every dish so patented weakens the very concept of such a commons—a pool of dishes shared by all members of a culture."[11] The fact that an ethical system grounded in property ownership does not help us understand the kind of harm Thorne and I identify, and also cannot repair that harm, only reveals the inadequacy of that system. To try to conceptualize the harm, I turn to Roden's cookbook itself. Roden's method in the book treats the women from whom she learns cookery as resources-for-use. She may exhibit toward them the respect and deference of which Pratt speaks in the passage that opens this chapter, but nevertheless, they also retain Pratt's "essential colonized quality of *disponibilité*."

Roden erases or generalizes the identities of most of the women who give her recipes.[12] She tells colorful stories about some of them in the body of the book, but the reader can match names to stories in only a few cases—and then only with considerable detective work. She does identify various relatives as the sources of recipes, noting, for example, that "My mother discovered [this recipe] in the Sudan, and has made it ever since" (43). But in most recipes, she mentions only the primary region in which a dish is served, and says nothing about the particular woman or women from whom she got the recipe. In contrast to this, she carefully notes the dishes she found in particular published cookbooks. Introducing a chicken dish, she notes "A splendid dish described to me by an aunt in Paris, the origin of which I was thrilled to discover in al-Baghdadi's medieval cooking manual" (184). The effect of this differential treatment is to blur the "ordinary" women who contributed to this cookbook into a mass of interchangeable parts. She renders invisible the work done by members of this mass to create, modify, adapt, and compile recipes; it does not matter which individual was responsible for which modification. Only her own work on these tasks is visible in her text.

A critic can reasonably respond to me, "In fact, these recipes have no originators. You already pointed out that many of them are as ubiquitous in the Middle East as the omelet is in France. Are you advocating that Roden give credit to particular women for their contributions of a particular recipe? Why would that make sense, given their ubiquity?" My first answer, which remains partially within the framework of property ownership, is that it makes as much sense to credit these conduits as it does to credit Roden herself; their participation in making these recipes available is certainly as relevant as hers. The fact of interacting with the machinery of the publishing industry should not alone give her special, superior claims to ownership.

My second answer moves farther away from the property model: I do not really advocate making particular women, or even their communities, the owners of recipes any more than I advocate allowing Roden to make that claim. As I've already said, the model of property is inadequate to these cases, and applying it more stringently would not solve the problem. (It may, however, serve as a powerful defensive strategy in some cases; strategic claims to ownership may function like strategic claims to authenticity, something I will explore in part 4.) I think the problem emerges from the fact that Roden makes traditional recipes into the sorts of things that one can commodify in the first place. She treats the recipes she gathers as resources, raw materials onto which she puts her creative stamp—whether that be in the form of scholarly background information, a personal anecdote, or a relevant quotation from a work of poetry or literature. With this creative transformation, the recipes become property that can be stolen.

Perhaps Roden simply wishes it be noted that she was something like the first collector of these recipes, or that it was in her book that someone else found a recipe. But it could be argued that noting only the last person in the chain of those who used and modified a recipe is to give her or him disproportionate importance. Why should this role be forever enshrined?

Claudia Roden's relationship to the Middle Eastern cooks from whose recipes she has profited resembles certain features of the relationship that has developed between first-world seed companies and third-world farmers. As Jack Kloppenburg and Daniel Lee Kleinman explain the matter in their article "Seed Wars: Common Heritage, Private Property, and Political Strategy," first-world agribusiness interests regard some germplasm to belong to everyone as a "common heritage," free for the taking by any would-be genetic engineer, while other kinds of germplasm can be owned and patented. Common heritage germplasm is that which is found wild—where the term "wild" is actually understood to include plants that have been bred over generations by third-world farmers to manifest particular properties. In contrast, the germplasm bred by first-world seed companies is patentable, and must be bought (sometimes by the very farmers who originally developed the now-patented crop).

A similar two-tier system appears to exist with respect to recipes; some can be gathered and reproduced at will and without credit, while others are the intellectual property of particular persons. As with germplasm, the difference seems to be more a matter of who is doing the engineering/modifying, than of whether or not any modification is being done.

One argument first world seed companies make for distinguishing between two kinds of germplasm is that it only has value after someone has put time and money into it.[13] Similarly, Levy, Barr, and Roden seem to suggest that Roden has some right to these recipes because of the time she spent gathering, compiling, and contextualizing them. Kloppenburg and Kleinman point out, however, that with respect to seeds, this argument assumes that only the time and labor of Northern Hemisphere scientists count. The work Southern Hemisphere farmers have done to develop their genetic resources becomes invisible; the plants they have cultivated, sometimes for centuries, are still defined by northern geneticists as wild, despite this effort. Again, the parallel with Roden is striking. Though recipes are obviously never wild, the concept of common heritage can be made to apply to them; a common heritage recipe would be one whose creators can never be identified, and that is ubiquitous in particular communities (the omelet again). Roden is simply treating these common heritage recipes in the ways that northern geneticists treat common heritage seed. She is thereby free to put in her collecting, cataloging and contextualizing labor, and to name the resultant products hers.

Roden's distinction between what I'm calling "common heritage" recipes and "commodity" recipes benefits those who have access to the means of publication, at the expense of those in the kitchen. Within a context dominated by the notion of property, those who can make some clear claim to ownership (seed companies, cookbook authors) will benefit at the expense of those who cannot (traditional farmers, traditional cooks), and also at the expense of those who regard the concept of property as inappropriate.

Another factor contributing to the complexity of the issue of recipe borrowing versus theft is that everyday recipe creation has traditionally been women's work done in the home, whereas the forms of harm that get identified and codified in law tend to be the kinds of harms that befall the creative work men have traditionally done in more public arenas.

Like other kinds of women's traditional creative work, such as quilting and weaving, recipe creation has tended to be social. By this I mean not only that the physical work may be done in groups, but also that the creative work is frequently the result of many women contributing their own idea to the general plan, often over considerable spans of time. A recipe that passes from one cook to another may undergo slight modifications to accommodate differences in taste or unavailability of an ingredient, to streamline or complicate a process, or for other, unidentifiable reasons.[14] We might say that such a recipe is original to everyone and no one; its beginning is unknown, but the contributions of particular cooks may be read off of it by someone who knows how to decipher such an evolutionary record.[15] (I once heard a food expert analyze the Thanksgiving dinners of several families living in different parts of the United States. On the basis of the foods present in the meal, and the way that those foods were prepared, she was able to identify, with great accuracy, the areas of the country in which that family had lived over the past generations.) Cooks who have contributed to the evolution of a recipe may well be pleased and proud when someone else takes up their modification—whether or not the other cook knows who is responsible for it.

Concepts like originality and plagiarism address problems arising in more individualistic art forms, such as novel writing and painting—forms that have also been regarded as high art and have historically been the purview of a privileged minority of men. These categories do not necessarily translate well to other sorts of art forms, particularly those that are collective and cumulative. However, they often are employed (awkwardly) within these forms, perhaps as an attempt to gain legitimacy for them. Women often have (in reality and in fiction) appealed to claims of originality and ownership, to accuse others of stealing their recipes. The women who have done so are often objects of mockery. (My morning radio station regularly plays a song entitled "Lime Jell-O, Marshmallow, Cottage Cheese Surprise," in which a woman discusses the dishes that have been brought to a "ladies'" potluck luncheon. The singer, who brought the title dish to the potluck, at one point sings, "I did not steal that recipe, it's lies, I tell you, lies!" The line is greeted with guffaws of laughter from the audience.) I would suggest that this mockery reflects both the pervasive sense that an individual's recipes are not original to them and thus cannot be owned by them, and the sense that even if recipes could be stolen, their theft would be no crime, since recipes simply aren't important enough to be the objects of moral concern.

I would contrast this with the respect—bordering on reverence—with which recipes used in restaurants are often treated, the deference with which a customer asks for the recipe for a particular dish, and the gratitude they heap upon the cook/chef willing to pass it along. (My cousin reminded me of this aspect of recipe exchange when she told me a story about visiting a restaurant where she'd had a wonderful chicken dish. She asked for the recipe, and noted that she assumed there was no way she would ever get it. Imagine her surprise when the waitress appeared with a recipe cut out of a magazine, and featuring canned cream of mushroom soup!) In newspaper food sections, this difference between the recipes of home cooks and those of restaurant chefs is sometimes manifested in the presence of two different recipe columns. In one column, readers write in to ask other readers to share a recipe for some particular food ("I'm looking for a good recipe for pumpkin bread. Does anyone have one that uses orange juice?") In the other column, readers write in to ask for specific recipes they have tasted in restaurants—recipes they perhaps were too intimidated to request in person. Almost invariably, these requests are couched in the language of a supplicant: "Do you think you could ever possibly get them to release the recipe for this chicken dish I had?"

### Authenticity Worry #2: Who's Entitled to Change this Recipe?

This discussion of recipe originality raises the second of the two worries about authenticity that I mentioned in chapter 6. When and how may a recipe be modified, and when does a variation leave a recipe no longer an authentic representation of a dish? Who has the right to change a recipe—how is it different when a knowledgeable outsider, rather than an insider, experiments with a traditional dish? And when do variations make a dish into something that is no longer authentic?

In exploring this second authenticity worry, I'll look at how Roden employs the concept of authenticity both in her criticisms of other cookbook writers, and in her advice to readers in her own cookbook. Roden's use of the concept raises a number of additional questions for me: How do her worries about the authenticity of recipe variations differ, depending upon whether she is discussing home cooks or professional cooks/cookbook writers? Does she understand the demands of authenticity to vary, according to whether one is an insider or an outsider to the cuisine?

Roden suggests that, while Middle Eastern cooking is deeply traditional, "after the initial 'trying out' of a new recipe, the reader should trust his taste and allow himself greater freedom in its preparation" (29). In effect, Roden places her trust in the reader of her recipes: if they use their own discretion, knowledge, and good taste, they may experiment with the foods they prepare. After all, she notes, "many . . . variations exist, according to region and even to individual families" (29). Chances are good, in other words, that you're trying something a Middle Eastern cook has already tried for herself.

However, when her readers also become writers of their own cookbooks, Roden is less willing to countenance such liberty. Barr and Levy quote Roden as saying, "It is tragic when food writers add or take away an ingredient to make a lifted recipe 'their own', and pass it off as authentic. They are falsifying tradition. This is how a culture ends up garbled and destroyed in the lap of another." Roden suggests that the practice of lifting recipes "from one book to another each with 'one small change'" leaves us ignorant of "the truth," and possessed of a recipe that has "nothing to do with reality" (112).

What is the difference between these activities, such that in one case, authenticity is at least not harmed, even if it is not perfectly preserved, and in the other, authenticity, reality and truth are destroyed? First of all, publishing one's invented variation, as opposed to simply using it one's home, or sharing it with a friend, will influence far more people than will an individual passing out copies of her recipe at a potluck. But why is this significant? Surely the same holds true of the variations Roden selected for her cookbook; these too will become influential, even to the point of dominating all others and becoming true. (Have you ever caught yourself pronouncing "This isn't the way this is supposed to taste!" purely on the basis of the recipe that you have always followed, and no other evidence whatsoever? Many cooks are like me: we come to see the version of a recipe we first encountered as *the* authoritative one, such that if our Lebanese neighbor suggests a different one, we greet it with intense suspicion.)

But it is more than the power of influence; it is also the fact that the published cookbook writer implicitly claims that the changes they make to recipes have a legitimacy, a faithfulness to tradition that they do not have. Whereas it is perfectly okay for me to add potatoes to my mnazzalleh (eggplant, tomato, and chick pea stew) and serve it to my friends as part of a Middle Eastern (or, better, a "Middle Eastern") meal, I would be overstepping my bounds to print such a variation in a Middle Eastern cookbook—unless, of course, I could trace such a variation to the kitchen(s) of some Middle Eastern cook(s). An outsider to a cuisine cannot vary a recipe, Roden suggests, without stripping it of its "authentic" label.

Another aspect of Roden's worry about recipe variation concerns the domino effect of many people republishing the same recipe, with slight changes. Like the childhood game of Telephone, the opportunistic practices of the cookbook trade, in which authors make minute changes to a recipe in order to legitimate their republishing it under their own name, result in "garbled messages"—recipes that have "nothing to do with reality." As Roden herself points out, small changes are made to recipes all the time; an insider to a tradition makes changes to a recipe in order to give it "the imprint of her own individual taste" (19), and outsider cooks who take her explicit advice do the same thing. It is not only published recipes that go through the telephone—though these run a higher risk of becoming garbled. Insiders to a tradition will have some general understanding of the flexible fabric that is a particular dish. Outsider cooks who read Roden's book will have a little knowledge of the tradition—and can do relatively little harm to it, cooking in their own kitchens. It is outsider cookbook writers with whom she is most concerned; they too may have only a little knowledge, *but* they have the power to spread that little knowledge far. A recipe that runs through a gauntlet of outsider cookbook authors is changed like Neurath's boat; not an ingredient remains "the same" at the end of the process, and the dish is destroyed.[16]

The issue of class also enters into the topic of recipe modification and authenticity in an important way. I would suggest that when chefs create new, wild versions of traditional foods, their work is frequently regarded as legitimate, even sometimes authentic. But when less exalted cooks take such liberties, their efforts often meet with considerable derision. I must admit that I too had a good laugh when some friends shared with me a recipe they had received for "burritos" made with potato lefse (a Scandinavian specialty which is, in fact, quite similar to a soft tortilla) and Dinty Moore beef stew. The recipe came from a booklet sent out by a family-owned potato growing business in Minnesota. Certainly this is an example of the authenticity of a food being pushed to its breaking point (unless we want to say that the word "burrito" refers only to the process of rolling and tucking *some* mixture inside *some* soft flatbread—in which case chocolate crepes are burritos).[17] At the same time, I know that much of the laughter in this particular case stemmed from the use of a "low-class" food like Dinty Moore stew. Would the laughter have been as loud if the lefse had been filled with grilled salmon, topped with a tomatillo salsa?

Roden is an insider to the tradition she is describing. Thus, I believe her worry about preserving authenticity has a different quality than does the worry of outsiders who want to be sure they are getting at the genuine article/ the native version. To put it flatly, Roden wishes to preserve and protect her heritage, particularly from those who seek to make a profit on it. In this, her anger finds company with Joanna Kadi, who, writing about a different cultural production, observes that "Economics impact culture," as illustrated by the present popularity of belly dancing. Kadi notes that "the particular combination of racism and classism that has popularized belly dancing taught by white people has several implications for Arab-American culture. Arab dancers who can't make a living teaching may be eventually forced to give up their serious studies of traditional dance altogether; this is one factor that eventually leads to cultural genocide. . . . For every cultural form happily adopted by the dominant culture's racist and classist system, another falls by the wayside."[18]

No doubt Roden feels similarly outraged that so many Europeans and Americans make money selling cookbooks that exploit the foods of her native region—and that the consequences of their so doing are so high for those within a culture who experience the erosion of their food traditions. In such situations, it is not difficult to understand why Roden and others appeal to authenticity in an effort to retain some kind of ownership of their own traditions.

While I believe Roden's worries are justified, I also remain skeptical about the methods she uses to substantiate those worries. Specifically, I wonder about her suggestion that there is some underlying reality and truth that is being garbled. This way of speaking tends to reify what is in fact a living, changing tradition, to make it a static entity with an essence. No matter how inflexible Middle Eastern cooking traditions are, they do change, regularly. Roden's understanding of the tradition must be able to allow for what even she regards as legitimate variation. I don't think that authenticity, conceived of in terms of truth and reality, makes such allowances. Even if we agree there is a finite number of variations on a dish, might not it be a very large finite number? Might not truth and reality be hopelessly, irreducibly complex?

Furthermore, I would suggest that Roden describes the effects of outsiders' variations in a way that does not leave room for insiders' creative appropriation of their variations. She regards such variations only as problems, unwelcome invasions. But while they might be unwelcome, such invasions can also be put to creative use by insiders to a tradition—as the examples of many colonized cuisines reveal. Consider the elements of French cuisine that Vietnamese cooks appropriated and transformed during the French occupation—the crepe and the omelet, the consommé style soup, and various French cooking terms. Many Americans consider Vietnamese coffee—strong and laced with sweetened condensed milk—to be a mandatory ending to a meal in a Vietnamese restaurant; the coffee is a legacy of the French, while its treatment is obviously a Vietnamese variation. Consider the fact that Hawaiians consume more Spam per capita than residents of any other state—a direct legacy of the presence of the U.S. military during World War II. But whereas in its midwestern home, Minnesota, Spam tends to be cubed and added to canned creamed corn, or sliced, fried, and served on white bread, in Hawaii it will more likely be made into "Spam musubis"—sticky rice balls wrapped in Spam and nori.[19] And consider the fact that some Thai immigrants to the United States sometimes use Jennifer Brennan's *Original Thai Cookbook* to make the foods of their homeland.[20] All these instances exemplify the ways in which colonized people appropriate the colonizers' appropriations.

I find myself much more sympathetic to Roden's strategic use of authenticity, deployed to protect a tradition from destruction at the hands of invaders, than I do with some other forms of authenticity I've discussed so far. (I will revisit strategic authenticity in chapter 11.) Nevertheless, it remains for me a troublesome concept.

## Cookbook Writing as Third-World Development

Cookbook writers, particularly those who are outsiders to the cultures they present, often describe their task as *developing recipes*—where that term comes to mean refining or transforming them into a form usable by other outsiders. What is involved in developing a recipe? How does this process differ from transcribing it, or simply recording it? The language of development, when used by cookbook writers, intentionally or unintentionally emphasizes the view that their work refines the raw materials (recipes) of an indigenous cuisine and makes them more generally usable.

Consider Jennifer Brennan's *Original Thai Cookbook*. Brennan describes herself as developing Thai recipes. Her description of her work as a recipe developer is surprisingly similar to what an enterprising nineteenth-century businessman in the East India Company might have said; like the business-man, Brennan is simply exploiting (in the innocuous sense of that term) a resource for the benefit of Westerners. While her position is certainly not as craven as that of a governor of Indochina, who observed, "It would be puerile to object to the European colonial enterprises in the name of 'an alleged right to possess the land one occupies, and some sort of right to remain in fierce isolation, which would leave unutilized resources to lie forever idle in the hands of incompetents,'"[21] the preface to her book does suggest that Brennan regards herself as performing a valuable service to the English-speaking world by developing a resource the Thais were never going to get around to—their own recipes.

In that preface, Brennan discusses the reasons she decided to write a cookbook. She notes that, as Thai restaurants became popular in the United States, it became possible to purchase the ingredients to make this cuisine, but "there remained a single barrier—a paucity of cookbooks for Thai. . . . For the Thai, like many other races[!], pass their recipes verbally down through generations, seldom committing their accumulated knowledge to paper. Even when pressed for a particular recipe, the Thai have some considerable dif-ficulty translating their knowledge to English; language, procedures and ingredients" (unpaginated preface). Brennan's discussion of the lack of cook-books constructs it as a Thai problem, a function of the fact that they don't write their recipes or speak English. They have simply failed to develop their cuisine in a way that allows English-speaking westerners access to it.

In the next several paragraphs Brennan explains how she arrived at the recipes that appear in the book. She spent hours in markets and in her kitchen, "abetted by a changing parade of patient Thai household cooks, while I discovered and explored the intricacies of this fascinating cuisine." As a result of this work, she came to the United States with a collection of recipes she had developed (her word). Brennan emerges as a latter-day Richard Burton; with the aid of faithful natives, she comes upon new, "un-known" features of the landscape of Thai cuisine.

I am reminded of Mary Louise Pratt's analysis of the art of promontory description: "As a rule the 'discovery' of sites like Lake Tanganyika involved making one's way to the region and asking the local inhabitants if they knew of any big lakes, etc. in the area, then hiring them to take you there, where-upon with their guidance and support, you proceeded to discover what they already knew" (202).[22]

Obviously, Richard Burton's "discovery" and naming of Lake Tanganyika (Lake Victoria to him) is an act the audacity of which is of a far greater magnitude than is Brennan's suggestion that she has discovered various Thai recipes. And a charitable reading of Brennan would understand her use of the term "develop" as scientific, or perhaps purely metaphorical. But even a charitable reading will not erase the cumulative effect of Brennan's descriptions of her work.

Brennan identifies several different kinds of work that she does to develop recipes, work that appeals to a modern westerner's sense that Our culture is more refined than the culture of the Thai. I've mentioned that she emphasizes putting the recipes into writing, moving them out of the oral sphere and giving them not only accessibility, but also a kind of legitimacy in Euroamerican culture that purely oral forms do not have. Furthermore, she notes that she put in "countless hours of rigorous testing and research during, and for, [her] cooking classes"—thus rendering the recipes "scientifically accurate" in the manner we rational Western cooks demand (unpaginated preface).

It is useful to consider this aspect of her work in light of the history of cookery in the United States. Scientific cookery emerged in this country at the turn of the century as part of an attempt to legitimize homemaking activities as a field of study, by rendering them exact sciences.[23] The language of science came to permeate much cookery writing, with ethnic cookbooks being no exception. In cookery writing, scientization meant modernization, and modernization meant development. So, for example, Erna Fergusson could write in her 1934 *Mexican Cookbook,*

> All old and excellent cooks maintain that the full flavor of Mexican cookery depends upon doing everything as in the old days, when women worked slowly with their hands and with only the simplest equipment.
>    To an extent this is true, but Miss Estelle Weisenbach, a domestic science teacher who has tested all these recipes, finds them thoroughly practical for a modern cook in a modern kitchen.[24]

Modernization, Fergusson tells us, needn't come at the price of authenticity.[25] Nearly fifty years later, Brennan offers a similar observation about her renditions of Thai cookery.

Brennan may understand herself as a developer in another sense—the sense in which she figures her manipulation of traditional Thai recipes as a kind of refinement of them. Recall my discussion in chapter 5 of Jean-François Revel's distinction between regional cuisines and international cuisine; the latter, he asserts, is a "genuine art," as opposed to the "mixture of biology and ethnology" that constitutes the former. He notes that "gastronomical art is able, when necessary and possible, to find the equivalents of certain products or of certain ingredients and use them to replace other products and other ingredients that cannot be obtained in certain places."[26] Brennan's attempts to systematize and standardize Thai recipes, and to establish equivalent ingredients for those not available here may also be an effort to transform "primitive" Thai food into an international cuisine, a genuine art.

But how else might we describe what Brennan did in her kitchen with her cook, if we do not want to subscribe to this model? It is possible to explain the work she did compiling a cookbook in ways that do not valorize her activity as development. Such descriptions, while less glamorous than the one she chooses, are nevertheless accurate to the work she did. Here are some possibilities: 1) She formulated a way to write down *existing* Thai recipes for Westerners, who are limited by their linguistic ignorance and their ignorance of Thai food and cookery.[27] To describe her cookbook this way highlights Brennan's work to turn an oral form into a written form usable by another culture, and the work she did to translate Thai ingredients into American ones. (It also highlights Americans' ignorance—of food—whereas her account highlights Thai ignorance of English.) As such, we might think of her as a translator. 2) She learned how to cook. This description acknowledges the role played by the many cooks with whom she worked, and emphasizes the fact that Brennan moved from a position of relative ignorance to one of knowledge. It also casts doubt upon her understanding of herself as a kind of scientist, developing raw materials into tested recipes. Rather than the knower, she becomes a learner—albeit a learner who makes important contributions to the practice she is learning.

I don't want to suggest that Brennan made *no* contribution to Thai food at all and merely acted as a scribe. Rather, I want to challenge the U.S.-centered way in which she describes her activity, an orientation that makes her own work unreasonably important. I want to put her contribution on the same plane of activity as the contributions of Thai cooks who modify, change, and pass on recipes within their own community.

At the beginning of part 3 of this volume, Jennifer Brennan asked us to imagine ourselves in a chauffeur-driven Mercedes, arriving at an elegant Thai house where an elegant Thai woman serves us "a parade of unfamiliar and exotic dishes"—dishes that Brennan promised to teach us to cook. In these chapters, I've tried to dispel the argument that cooking is a magic bullet, an easy way for Euroamericans to decolonize our ethnic food consumption. While we might be tempted to believe that the colonialist elements of ethnic dining are dissipated automatically, once we are inspired to cook these ethnic foods for ourselves, in fact those elements simply take on different forms in the cookbooks that teach us how to cook ethnic.

So does that mean that the problem lies with the very fact of Euroamericans eating ethnic food at all? Shouldn't we all just stay home, as it were, and eat only the foods our great-grandparents would have eaten? I will briefly consider this option in chapter 9, before turning to more fruitful strategies for cultural food anticolonialism in the last two chapters.

PART FOUR

# Toward Anticolonialist Eating

WARD CHURCHILL, IN HIS BOOK, *INDIANS ARE US? CULTURE AND GENOCIDE IN NATIVE North America*, argues that it is impossible for cultural exchange to take place between Indians and Euroamericans in ways that do not exploit Indian peoples. The only two choices available to Indian peoples are to resist all incursions into their cultures, or to sell out and become a "hang-around-the-fort Indian." Historically, "when confronted with white imperial pretensions, each nation quickly came to manifest at least two mutually exclusive histories and traditions. On the one hand is the reality of native patriotism signified by those who fought back against overwhelming odds to defend their people's rights and ways of life. On the other is an equally important, if much less discussed, history of those who weren't up to the task, who obediently, and often for petty reasons of perceived self-interest, joined hands with the invaders to destroy their people's ability to resist colonization."[1] Reading Churchill in the context of examining culinary forms of colonization, the dichotomy becomes a choice between marginalized and colonized cultures keeping their food traditions to themselves, fighting off any attempts to borrow them, and resigning themselves to the colonization of those traditions, perhaps by welcoming the cookbook writers and restaurant franchisers into their kitchens. There is, in his view, no third option. Exploitation is inevitable whenever a more powerful culture comes in contact with a less powerful one, and the only way to *minimize* that exploitation is for members of the less powerful culture to refuse to participate, whenever and wherever possible, in their own exploitation.

Would Churchill throw up his hands in dismay, then, at the Hopi nation's decision to build a restaurant on their reservation, a restaurant serving piki bread (the traditional paper-thin, crisp, rolled bread made from blue corn) and Hopi tacos to the tourists who roll through hoping for a glimpse into the ancient civilization? Probably. How could such an attempt to appeal (or would Churchill say "pander"?) to tourists' interests have any positive consequences for the life of the Hopi people? And indeed, should anyone be surprised that the deeply symbolic Hopi blue corn is now found in every upscale grocery store in the country, in the form of pancake mix, tortilla chips, and facial cleansers? If the Hopi people are interested in protecting their rich culture—including their food heritage—they would be much better off throwing their efforts into fending off tourists by any means necessary—not inviting them to stick around the reservation for dinner.

Churchill's stark position makes a lot of sense to me. I find myself compelled by arguments for cultural separatism advanced by marginalized peoples—and I want to stay home as a way of honoring those efforts at separation.

Nevertheless, food adventurer that I am, I went to the Hopi Cultural Center Restaurant, on the strength of a recommendation from foodwriters Jane and Michael Stern, who lured me in with their description of the bread: "The blue piki bread . . . is still made in the centuries-old way, on smooth piki stones, heirlooms passed down from mother to daughter. The stones are heated and greased with sheep's brains until they are slick; then the finely ground blue cornmeal is laid on."[2]

I went to the restaurant for dinner, after visiting the cultural center's exhibits detailing various aspects of traditional Hopi culture, and before spending the night in the adjacent parking lot/campground. In the museum, I found myself most engrossed in the exhibits that show how Hopi cultural creations and the Hopi worldview have been assaulted by outsiders to their nation—in comic books in which Kachinas, sacred figures in the Hopi worldview, are depicted doing evil acts; in the practice of locking away in Euroamerican museums the masks and figures used in Hopi sacred rituals; in the fact that Hopi ceremonies have become flooded with outsider spectators who crowd out the Hopi participants and take pictures of everything in sight. I learned a great deal about the ways a small, struggling culture can be harmed, even by well-intentioned, respectful interests of outsiders—especially when those outsiders come trailing television cameras and movie deals. (Note that it is the fact of the size and relative powerlessness of the Hopi nation that makes some of these acts objectionable. I do not mean to say that it is never acceptable to alter other cultures' traditions in ways that may be unacceptable to members of that culture. But when a culture is so small as to be invisible to the rest of the world *except* through these outsiders' altered images of it, then it is unacceptable.)

Then I went to dinner. There were very few people in the restaurant that evening, but, like the Sterns, I found myself eating alongside tourists like myself and Hopi community members (the restaurant is really the only restaurant on the reservation for *non*tourists also—an interesting thing for me to contemplate). We all chose from a menu that featured both piki bread and bacon, lettuce, and tomato sandwiches (the Sterns were disconcerted by that mixed cultural message). The menu itself illustrates the precarious balance in which Hopi culture lives alongside Euroamerican culture—especially precarious because the Hopi population is tiny, but things Hopi attract hordes of people, from scholars to seekers to gawkers. Many Euroamericans collect Hopi Kachinas as art or craft objects—Barry Goldwater had a famous collection—and I've even seen drawings of Kachinas on bottles of something called Goldwater's salad dressing. The population of the Hopi villages—only a thousand or so people in the largest one—is dwarfed by the number of visitors who tour them each year. A standing joke claims that a Hopi family consists of grandparents, parents, aunties, uncles, sons, daughters—and an anthropologist.

In self protection, members of the Hopi nation have declared many parts of their culture off limits to outsiders; many festivals and ceremonies are now closed to any but Hopi villagers and their guests, photography is forbidden in several of the villages, and many kinds of artifacts are no longer for sale anywhere in the Hopi Nation. But the Nation also opened a cultural center and restaurant.

Can the center serve as a means of introducing intensely curious Euroamericans to Hopi culture and Hopi food in a way that will not simply lead to more exploitation? Can it at least keep us outsiders from knocking on the doors of their private homes and taking pictures of them tending their corn? If Churchill, in his most pessimistic moments, is right, it cannot; attempting to protect your culture by offering even a highly controlled slice of it to outsiders simply amounts to destroying the village—and the villagers—in order to save them.

Churchill directs much of his attention (and thus his anger) toward insiders— and specifically those insiders who, on his analysis, facilitate the destruction of Indian cultures by offering them up for sale to white people. But obviously there is a message here for food-adventuring outsiders like me as well: If I'm serious about trying to be a food anticolonizer, I ought to put down my napkin and go home.

As someone committed to challenging colonialist attitudes in my own life, I realized early in this project that I had to find a viable alternative to my adventuring— a relationship to food that did not rest on the triple foundations of the quest for exoticism, the desire for authenticity, and the view that the Other is a resource for my own enrichment. Does staying home to eat constitute such an alternative for the food adventurer? If eating the food of the Other is what gets me implicated in colonialism in the first place, then isn't the solution simply to eat only my own foods— the foods of my own tradition(s)?

In short, no. This section is not an extended exploration of how to wean yourself from your food-colonizing ways by eating only the foods your great-great-grandmother cooked. Instead, here I'll examine ways to resist the colonizing aspects of food adventuring that do not entail giving up the exploration of cuisines outside your own heritage. I hope to show that one can be an *anticolonialist* food adventurer—that food adventuring is in fact an activity through which one can develop a way of being in the world that resists the tendencies to appropriation and exploitation that I have cataloged thus far.

In this work, I've grounded my discussion of food adventuring in three elements of a cultural colonizer's attitude. Turning to the project of anticolonialist adventuring, I identify two elements of a food-anticolonialist attitude, to which I attach the short-hand labels "self-questioning" and "contextualism." Each of them responds to, and engages with, one or more elements of the food colonizing attitude. Self-questioning, the element I explore in chapter 10, most directly addresses the tendency to regard the Other as a resource for my use. Contextualism, the subject of chapter 11, addresses both the obsession with authenticity and the quest for exoticism.

But first, in chapter 9, I consider staying home in order to give my dismissal of this solution some credibility. After all, it does seem like such a good way to resist cultural food colonialism. *Why* does it seem that way—and why *isn't* it?

*Chapter 9*

# Okay, Let's Stay Home

EATING AT HOME—THAT IS, EATING THE CUISINES OF ONE'S HERITAGE—RESPONDS
to *cultural* colonialism in a way that mirrors a familiar and well-articulated
response to *material* colonizing. Eating locally, a practice advocated by bio-
regionalists and advocates of organic agriculture, has clear environmental
and economic benefits. For instance, by eating foods from my own garden
or purchased from local growers and processors I reduce my participation in
and support for the world food system, a system that provides me with
cheap foods at others' expense, including farmers, food industry workers,
and nonhuman animals. Eating locally produced food is more environmentally sustainable, because, among other things, it reduces the need for non-
renewable fossil fuel to haul, ship, and tote food all over the world. It reduces
the "need" to engineer foods that hold up well under the rigors of such
cross-country travel—irrespective of whether such engineering improves
the flavor or nutritional value of foods. (The plastic tomato stands as a familiar emblem of this sort of engineering.) It enables me to support employ-
ers whose progressive labor practices I can witness firsthand. Is it possible to
identify similar virtues for choosing to eat only my home culture's foods—
the cultural version of "eating locally?"

Certainly there is potential here. In this chapter I explore the potential,
using my own context as a kind of case study. Ultimately, I'll argue that staying home is not an all-purpose strategy for resisting colonialism, although
used situationally, it can be a very powerful tool.

By eating only the foods of my own heritage (bracketing, just for the moment, the vexed question of what my heritage includes), I necessarily reject
the novelty and exoticism on which food adventurers thrive, but which can
so quickly enmesh us in the fabric of colonialism. And by choosing not to
eat the food of Others, I must eliminate the very possibility of treating those
Others as resources. Haven't we seen enough of the problems that arise from

adventuring, to make us realize that choosing to reject it has to be a step in the right direction?

## Less *Is* More

In addition to avoiding the vicious cycle into which our adventure eating leads us, are there not also virtues in choosing *to* eat one's home foods? By eating only the foods of my own ethnic background, I promote a welcome simplicity in my diet, a respite from the flood of choices that confront me every time I walk into the supermarket. I minimize the importance of variety—or, better, I cultivate variety in different ways—when I confine my eating to those foods that have long been a part of my heritage. Instead of developing an ever-expanding repertoire of dishes, I develop my ability to make—and to *taste* knowledgeably—a small but ever more deeply familiar set of them. This way of cooking and eating allows a certain kind of creativity to develop in me—a kind that cannot develop when I have all the choices in the world. I see an analogy to sixteenth-century composers—contrapuntalists whose musical compositions were hemmed in on all sides by stern, unbreakable rules. Within the austere confines of those rules, composers created music of tremendous beauty and complexity. When I attempted to write music employing these rules, it became clear to me that their compositions were beautiful not in spite of the limitations, but in part because of them. The same thing can be true of food; fewer culinary choices need not spell the impoverishment of one's eating pleasure.

Examples of the richness of this simpler approach to food can be found in current foodwriting. John Thorne, for example, describes his decision to learn to bake bread with only three ingredients—flour, water, and salt—and to concentrate his bread making skills on such basic French-style breads, rather than getting caught up in a whirl of special ingredients, special pans, special procedures.[1] Reading him, I am compelled to try to do the same thing myself, to understand these three basic ingredients deeply and well. I know for a fact that the breads one can produce with these ingredients are repeatedly satisfying, in a way that sun-dried tomato this and sunflower seed that often aren't.

I feel a similar attraction to Claudia Roden's descriptions of the traditional world of Middle Eastern cookery—the attraction of an outsider, to be sure, and therefore no doubt touched with an unrealistic romanticism. But cutting through the romanticism, I wonder if perhaps I could develop a similar relationship. Not "Could I cook all and only Middle Eastern cuisine?" (something the food adventurer in me has occasionally contemplated, in my search for the Real source of authenticity), but "Could I cook and eat all and only the foods of my own Midwestern, Northern-European American heritage?" And (important), "Could I do it in the midst of the cacophony that is the American food scene?" Is it even possible for a dyed-in-the-wool adventurer like me to be a traditionalist in a nation of megafood warehouses, stuffed to the brim with every imaginable variety of food, exclusive food boutiques offering delights from all over the world, and restaurants featuring uncountably many cuisines? Perhaps it is possible—and perhaps, given the power of Churchill's critique, I should.

## Everyone's a Critic

Staying home to eat also situates me more firmly within my own tradition. By eating foods I grew up eating, I connect myself to a past and place myself in a tradition. When I prepare or even just eat the foods cooked by my great-grandmother, my grandmother, my mother, I connect my life to theirs. I acknowledge their lessons to me, my debts to them. I treat my ethnic heritage as a living, changing tradition, of which I am an active part.

Unlike the kind of aimlessness that is often engendered by food adventuring, staying at home fixes me in a context that is in some important sense my own, one I have not arbitrarily selected for its exotic allure. Perhaps I can develop an *authentic* relationship to my home food, rather than seeking authenticity in the culinary riches of other cultures—cultures in which I may be nothing more than a trespasser or an unwelcome collector. Perhaps a desire for *this* kind of authenticity would be more sustainable, less problematic than the desire that makes me see authenticity in every new dish I encounter.

*Cook's Illustrated* editor Christopher Kimball writes in hopes of such a relationship to food in an editorial for that magazine. Kimball assesses the current state of culinary affairs somewhat as I might: "In reaction to both our homogenized culture and our declining cuisine, Americans have embarked on a commendable search for improvement. But in this search for satisfying culture and cuisine, many of us have opted for an archaeological pursuit of cuisines from around the world. We want to discover the true culinary heritage of Tuscany or the real method for making couscous from scratch. . . . These culinary expeditions set out with romantic notions about other cultures, past or present, and often disregard the realities of modern American life."[2] But what is the alternative? For Kimball, it is staying home: "As we race to reinvent our culinary present, let's remind ourselves of our own history of practicality and economy. Just as the Puritans had to work around the realities of daily life, we should do the same. Instead of importing ingredients, let's use what is grown locally. Let's once again eat with the seasons, when the produce is both cheapest and at its best" (agricultural motivations). And (introducing the cultural dimension), "Let's stop running helter-skelter down the road to diversity, a path that leads to culinary anarchy" (3). For Kimball, the choice is clear: hold to the food traditions on which this country was founded (his examples represent the traditions of white New Englanders and Southerners), or dissolve into culinary anarchy: "As a culture, we gain much from a shared cuisine. It helps to bind us together in a time when we are constantly being urged to pull apart by expressing our individuality" (3).

It is telling that Kimball does not include the traditions of African Americans, Asian Americans, Latina/os, or other Americans of color in his list of the culinary traditions on which this country was founded. Some of those traditions have been a part of American foodways as long as the Puritan tradition he lauds (and even longer, in the case of Native Americans). And certainly some of those traditions have had deep, significant effects on the way white, mainstream culture eats. (For that matter, Native Americans made monumental contributions to the way the Puritans ate, contributions that spelled the difference between literal starvation and survival.) Kimball's exclusion of these cooking traditions is at best a remarkable and irresponsible oversight; at worst the manifestation of a troubling ethnocentrism. I'll return to this issue shortly.

That serious criticism notwithstanding, I do understand Kimball's desire for a cuisine in which he and those around him feel deeply invested. In *The Tuscan Year,* the British food writer Elizabeth Romer ponders what it is like to cook for a table full of food critics every meal of every day. Such is the situation confronting her neighbor in Tuscany, a farm woman whose household chores include preparing a daily feast at noon for the workers on her farm, made from the foods they grow and process. Every one of those workers is an expert in Tuscan cookery—every one of them has a deep, studied, well-grounded opinion about how that food should taste, because they've been eating it and talking about it daily since they could talk. Clearly, cooking and eating in such a context would be anything but boring or mundane. I'm intrigued: if I could situate myself in a community like this, then perhaps I could resign my food-adventuring ways—and by that route give up cultural food colonization.

But staying home in this cultural sense won't work for someone like me—for reasons both practical and theoretical.

## Who Are My People Again?

The practical impossibility of eating at home stems from the fact that it's not entirely clear just where home would be for me, culinarily. Would it be based on my ethnicity? Like many Euroamericans, mine is a hodgepodge; how would I decide *which* of my ethnicities to stay home in? (Majority rule? Most recent immigration to this country? The one whose foods I like the most?) Or should I think in terms of the cuisines of my geographic home, irrespective of my own ethnic heritage? Is my culinary home the Midwest—or even Wisconsin, specifically? Northern Wisconsin? Barron County, with its majority German immigrants, yes, but also its Bohemian, Italian, Scandinavian, and Jewish immigrants, and its original Native American inhabitants? No matter how small I slice it, the piece of my heritage that remains is always still a hodgepodge.

And when you get right down to it, the foods of my various homes already bear the stamp of earlier colonization. Like other aspects of my heritage, the food practices I've inherited are a patchwork of recipes, cooking techniques, and specific foods that have been collected by the various branches of my European ancestry during their colonizing incursions into Africa, Asia, and the Americas themselves. For example, potatoes, tomatoes, peppers, squash, and corn are foods Europeans were taught to cultivate and eat by the Native American peoples whom they subsequently forced off their own lands. Black pepper, cinnamon, and other spices I use regularly were collected by earlier European explorers during numerous raids on China,

India, and Southeast Asia. My grocery list alone is a virtual gazetteer of earlier European and subsequent American imperialist and colonialist activity.
If I'm trying to avoid colonization, it won't happen by staying home—at best,
it will push the problems back a century or two.

It's not at all clear how I would go about deciding what foods I would
even include on my list of home foods. And even if I could make the decision, it is not clear where I would locate the requisite community with whom
to share the cooking and eating of these foods; I now live in an academic
community in which people from all over the United States and many other
nations eat and cook for each other. I never cook for a tableful of experts;
usually I end up making dishes that one person at the table has never even
heard of before, but that were the comfort food of another person's childhood. With such a polyglot community, it's not clear how I could reap the
various benefits of eating at home that Elizabeth Romer describes.

Christopher Kimball's celebration of "our own history" manifests the practical problems of staying home to eat, but in a slightly different way. Calling
for us to celebrate the roots of our cuisine, and then describing those roots
as Puritan and white Southern, Kimball simply erases the contributions of all
sorts of Americans whose roots go back not to Britain but to other parts of
Europe, or to Africa, Asia, and the Americas themselves. "We," the readers of
Cook's Illustrated, are all of these people. It will not do to try to solve the
shallowness and rootlessness of American eating habits by simply defining
as un-American the vast numbers of cuisines that have been historically
cooked and eaten by Americans. When Kimball dismisses attempts to learn
to make couscous from scratch (evidence, to him, of our rootlessness), he
fails to notice that at least some of the Americans who are making that attempt are themselves of Middle Eastern descent. For them, this is not a "helter-
skelter" run toward diversity, but a reconnection with their own heritage, or
the heritage of a family member. (I was heartened, following the September
11, 2001, tragedies, to see significant numbers of non–Arab Americans
choosing to eat in Middle Eastern and Afghani restaurants; some restaurants
even reported a small upturn in business. Some of those patrons specifically
asserted that eating in these restaurants was one way of symbolically acknowledging that persons of Arab and Afghan descent are also part of the
American "we.")

Kimball's description of the dichotomy—either stay home or chase
around the globe—will not hold up. (His dichotomy is also strikingly simi-

lar to Churchill's.) At least in the United States, the two alternatives begin to collapse into each other, such that staying home ends up looking a lot like last century's food colonialism; we're simply eating the booty from earlier generations' globe-chasings.

## Not Colonialist, But Imperialist

Becoming a kind of food isolationist is not only impossible practically, but also unsound theoretically. In attempting to prevent the harm I cause myself and others by my colonialist borrowings, I instead cause harm by my refusal to enter into any relations. I become inflexible, rigid, unbending, closed. If I eat all and only what I've grown up eating (or whatever I've defined as constituting my heritage), I run the risk of becoming a person closed off from new experiences, who cannot learn even if those experiences present themselves. I make the mistake of assuming that we adventurers are wrong not simply because of the exploitive ways we eat ethnic foods, but because we eat ethnic foods at all.

Such an attitude ends up manifesting a kind of cultural imperialism, for it assumes something only a member of a dominant culture can assume with any degree of assurance—that the influence of other cultures is dispensable and avoidable, that I can choose not to be influenced by others, and that it is in my power to restrict other cultures' access to me. Imperialism includes not only the power to impose one's systems on another culture, but also the power to close oneself off from the influences of other cultures. Consider the ways in which members of some colonial powers brought their entire culture with them when they came to govern a colony. Life was to continue exactly as it would at home—right down to the kind of tea one drank at breakfast and the cut of meat one ate for dinner. This dietary rigidity carried with it a strong ideological message: these people are our inferiors. They eat things that are not even food.[3]

Similarly, for me to decide to eat only foods of my own ethnicity is to close my doors, not to allow any foreign influence in. It is also a decision to impoverish my life by remaining ignorant of other cultures.

Culturally colonized and marginalized people generally do not get the opportunity to hold the imperialist assumption; they recognize that, welcome or no, interaction with, and transformation at the hands of, other cultures will come—indeed, it will be imposed upon them. That's part of what it is to

be colonized. That is why, following Churchill, we may want to say that refusing to eat the foods of the dominant culture, and refusing the dominant
culture access to one's food traditions, can constitute forms of resistance for
members of marginalized cultures.

One vivid example of this strategy (though one in which the relations of
domination are obviously highly complex and multi-vectored) can be found
in Palestine, around the time of Israel's establishment. As food theorist Yael
Raviv notes in her "The Hebrew Banana," beginning in the 1920s, the Department of Commerce and Industry of the Zionist Administration instituted
a policy mandating that shops and restaurants sell only *tozeret haaretz*—
local crops grown by Jews. The practice of "buying Hebrew" was motivated
by a variety of aims, including the concrete economic goal of creating a market for local crops (crops often unfamiliar to European immigrants to the region), but also "preferring Hebrew products over Arab ones. . . ." "Buying
Hebrew" thus had two effects: it "helped in playing down the Arab presence
in Palestine both during the past 2000 years and at the present moment,
leaving it 'empty' for Jewish settlers to inhabit and revive" (an important
propaganda tool for a nation creating itself on top of, and over the vocifer-
ous protests of, an existing society) and, interestingly, it helped in "severing
ties with the Diaspora" (in order to prove the self-sufficiency of the emerging
nation).[4] Buying and eating only "Hebrew bananas"—as well as Hebrew watermelons, eggs, eggplants, and zucchini even when those crops were more
expensive or inferior to imported products, literally helped to create Israel
by creating a diet closed to outside vegetable influences—both those of the
Arabs whom they were actively displacing and those of Jews who had not
chosen to resettle in the new Israel.

Food theorist Krishnendu Ray identifies another instance of the use of
this strategy of refusal—one that more directly addresses cuisine as opposed
to crops. In the context of an analysis of the food practices of recent Bengali
immigrants to the United States, Ray notes, "I do not believe that marginalized communities, even at the height of the food fights, were completely
colonized. They often met [mainstream] disdain with disdain."[5] So, for instance, the immigrants Ray studies describe American food as "normless,
easy, and 'uncultured',"[6] and refuse to have anything to do with it. He notes
that such "Insider caricatures of dominant outsiders are an important resource
in the fight for survival. It [sic] is a classic 'weapon of the weak'" (2000b).

Concurring with Ray, food theorist Arlene Voski Avakian notes that "As an [sic] first generation Armenian I grew up with my family's disdain—that IS the word—for American food. An Armenian expression I heard often was that Americans didn't know the taste of their own mouths. On the rare occasions that my family shared food with Americans they went on and on about how the Americans loved the food, and the implication was clearly that they had now tasted real food and could, with the help of Armenians, learn the taste of their own mouths."[7] Closing the borders may be a powerful way for culturally marginalized groups to strike a blow against their marginalization.

But, while marginalized communities are never completely colonized, just as surely dominant cultures never have complete control over the cultural influences on them. While outside influences upon my food practices may not be forced on me directly, other cultures dramatically influence what I eat in all sorts of more indirect ways; I might be Avakian's neighbor, for example. Or her child might attend the same school as my child. She may run the best, most affordable restaurant in the neighborhood. Recall (on a larger scale) that the British diet *did* change in important ways as a result of Britain's occupation of India; curry now appears on pub menus across Britain. (Whether or not Indians want to claim those influences on Britain, the fact remains that Indian cooking changed British cooking forever.) The American guests in Arlene Avakian's home *did* learn the taste of their own mouths. And while my Aunt Loretta may never have reconciled herself to pizza, the rest of the country surely has—and tabouli and pad thai are not all that far behind. Influence is the rule, not the exception in cuisine—and influence runs in all directions, not only from the powerful to the powerless. All measures to prevent it—for reasons noble or nefarious—end up being partial at most.

Furthermore, given the ubiquity and multidirectionality of influences, we might question Churchill's conviction that the only two choices available to those *inside* a culture threatened by colonialism and imperialism are to resist all forms of interaction or to become a hang-around-the-fort Indian. Churchill's is a stark, dichotomous view of the possible ways cultures can interact. Many, if not most, cultural interactions are much more ambiguous than this dichotomy suggests, the possibilities for action more diverse.[8]

The hang-around-the-fort Indians, for instance, have sometimes had profound effects on white America—effects that, while hardly unambiguously

positive for Native peoples, are nonetheless serious, substantive, even transformative of Euroamerican cultures and their understanding of Native peoples. This, too, is a kind of resistance—albeit one that comes at a cost.[9] And
even in cases in which Native cultures have been forcibly transformed by
the cultures around them, resistance still lives. I think, for just one example,
of the way in which Dakota women at the time of contact used the institu-
tion of the Christian church to do community organizing. Whites did not
allow Dakota men to gather in groups—a means of preventing uprisings.
However, women were encouraged to do so—at church services and at hand-
icraft sessions, during which they might make things like beaded Bible covers. Dakota women took advantage of these sanctioned gatherings, rooted in
Euroamerican traditions, to do political work, undetected by white people.

Cuisines are full of examples of these kinds of creative appropriations of
the colonizers' foods—of using foodstuffs forced upon one's culture in utterly new and unexpected ways, or of preparing the colonizer's most familiar
dishes in ways they'd never before experienced them, ways that bear the un-
mistakable flavor of the colonized. What Hawaiians do with Spam bears no
resemblance to the concoctions dished out by American mess hall cooks
during World War II, or to the Spam dishes featured on the northern Wisconsin dinner tables of my youth. While it may seem a bit florid to describe
the Spam musubi—that rectangle of Spam, sticky rice, and nori—as "resistant," that is exactly what I am suggesting.

Would-be food anticolonialists ought never forget the position Churchill
espouses here—that, if we recognize (as I believe we must) that relations between members of cultures with disproportionate power between them *will*
be exploitive, then we must recognize that there is a good case to be made
for Them to refuse to voluntarily engage with Us. And we ought to regard
Churchill's position with more than academic curiosity. In particular situations, I believe it ought to guide our actions; sometimes the best way for me
to resist the forces of colonization is to choose not to try to gain access to
some aspect of another culture. This can be one important way for outsiders
to a culture to act in solidarity with insiders who are trying to resist the ex-
propriation of their culture.

But, as I have argued here, staying home is neither the only nor the most
useful way for adventurers to avoid cultural food colonialism (or for the culturally colonized to resist). For persons from dominant cultures, it is also

extremely important to develop cultural flexibility and experimentality. As Madhur Jaffrey puts it, "Childhood taste habits never completely die out. They seem to leave their mark on us and often dictate the areas that we are willing to explore or not explore as adults. That is why I feel, rather strongly, that children should be exposed to not only the best foods but also foods of as many different countries as possible. Culinary insularity is really nothing more than a set of stubborn taste habits."[10]

Aimé Césaire, in his *Discourse on Colonialism*, writes, "I admit that it is a good thing to place different civilizations in contact with each other; that it is an excellent thing to blend different worlds; that whatever its own partic-ular genius may be, a civilization that withdraws into itself atrophies; that for civilizations, exchange is oxygen . . ." He goes on, however, to say: "But then I ask the following question; has colonization really *placed civilizations in contact?* Or, if you prefer, of all the ways of *establishing contact,* was it the best? I answer *no.*"[11] Césaire, writing from the position of the colonized, re-jects not only cultural food colonialism but *also* staying at home, for neither of these options places cultures in contact with each other in ways he be-lieves are desirable.

bell hooks, like Césaire, argues that even the interests of oppressed and marginalized people are not best served by isolationism—even their own isolationism. She writes, "[Nationalist Black voices] are misguided when they suggest that white cultural imperialism is best critiqued and resisted by black separatism, or when they evoke outmoded notions of ethnic purity that deny the way in which black people exist in the west, are western, and are at times positively influenced by aspects of white culture."[12] Given the history of, and the ongoing reality of, cultural contact, it does not even ben-efit colonized peoples to erect barriers to that contact.

But by the same token, "Whether or not desire for contact with the Other, for connection rooted in the longing for pleasure, can act as a critical intervention challenging and subverting racist domination, inviting and en-abling critical resistance, is an unrealized political possibility" (22). For hooks, it is an open question whether or not the pleasure of food adventur-ing can be turned from supporting and maintaining systems of hierarchy, to an activity that actually challenges and resists such systems. I believe that it can; that culinary exchanges might actually contribute to the dissolution of relations and attitudes of colonialist domination. If they are to do so, however, our eating must take place within a different kind of framework, one that recognizes always the pervasiveness, durability, and flexibility of such relations.

The challenge of food anticolonialism is to develop ways of approaching food that foster a respect for one's own traditions without advocating isolationism, and that cultivate an openness to other traditions without objectifying them or treating them as resources from which to support one's own lifestyle. This challenge is both deeply theoretical and deeply practical, calling upon food adventurers both to challenge and transform the unspoken assumptions upon which our lives are constructed, and to do so through the everyday acts of cooking and eating. We need to find useful, anticolonialist ways to decide what to have for dinner.

*Chapter 10*

# The Skeptical Palate

IN CHAPTER 1, I SUGGESTED THAT ATTITUDES MAY PLAY AN IMPORTANT ROLE IN bringing about concrete social change. There, I identified a relationship between the attitudes held by individuals and the ideologies that permeate a culture; I suggested that attempts to transform individual attitudes can help produce cumulative, culture-wide effects. However, the intimate relationship between individual attitudes and cultural ideologies creates a kind of paradox with respect to the possibility of making change. Because individual attitudes are instantiations of collective ideologies, others always interpret our practices through the lenses of those ideologies. Therefore, it is impossible for individuals, acting as individuals, completely to transform even their own attitudes, let alone the ideologies of a society; no matter how differently we believe we are acting, others will still interpret our actions with their old frame of reference. Much as we wish we could, we simply *cannot* change the world one meal at a time.

But at the same time, collective ideologies are constituted out of the attitudes of individuals. Therefore, changing the former seems to require changing the latter. The result, it would seem, is that neither activity can be done without the other's being done beforehand; ideologies can't change unless attitudes do, and attitudes won't change until ideologies do. In a culture of colonialism, this would seem to mean that individuals can never really *be* anticolonialist; our actions will always already be reinterpreted through those colonialist lenses, no matter our intended meanings. Likewise, societal ideologies can never really be transformed, because the constitutive individual attitudes cannot ever really change.

Real life is never as neat as are the models philosophers make of it when we create logical puzzles for ourselves—a fact that is fortunate in this particular case. For, while it is true in a general sense that attitudes are the instantiations of ideologies, and ideologies are the composites of attitudes, the system is not so hermetically sealed as all that. Cracks, fissures, and wrinkles of all sorts make available the space in which we may effect change. Social philosopher Peg O'Connor makes this point, in her Wittgensteinian analysis of the nature of oppression and responsibility. Employing Ludwig Wittgenstein's notion of the "background" as that set of beliefs and practices that ground and make sense of our "foreground" activities, O'Connor notes that "backgrounds are not monolitic entities, and the agreement underlying them is not absolute. Practices with their underlying rules are not immutable entities that are simply given."[1] The background (or ideology, though the words are not interchangeable for Wittgenstein) against which we act out our colonialist dramas is actually a set of not-fully-consistent beliefs and not-fully-coherent-practices, understood less than completely by the people who depend upon them.

The strength of this chicken-or-egg paradox—how can we change *either* attitudes *or* ideologies, given their interdependence?—is thus a linguistic strength only. In actuality, transformative action takes place every day, in the wrinkles and gaps of the background. There, where the links between individual attitudes and collective ideologies are the murkiest or most tenuous, individuals and small groups of people have the most power to effect transformation. When the existing fabric of beliefs fails to capture—or inconsistently captures—individuals' experience, they begin to create new analyses of that experience, and to try out their analyses on others who seem similarly disaffected.

O'Connor cites the development of the concept of "coming out," and survivors of sexual abuse learning to "break silence" as examples of the ways persons acting in small groups can use gaps the background to create new forms of resistance to oppressive practices.[2] These actions did not exist until members of those groups took advantage of the messiness of existing beliefs about gay and lesbian, bisexual, and transgender identity and about sexual abuse survivors in order to create new concepts that better spoke to their experience. We who would create a network of cultural food anticolonialists can engage in similar work.

Such transformative work is not easy. For all their messiness and inconsistency, the ideologies of colonialism are also pervasive, resilient, and flexible. They have the capacity to absorb strategies aimed at resisting colonialism and transform them into acts that support the colonialist project. The would-be cultural food anticolonialist must develop an attitude that can compete with such resilience and creative flexibility.

One of the most useful tools an anticolonialist food adventurer can learn to manipulate is a healthy and persistent skepticism about one's own motivations—in this case, motivations for eating ethnic cuisines. I term this tool (or component of an anticolonialist attitude) "self-questioning." Used persistently, self-questioning can work to challenge the hierarchical dichotomy that separates knowing, powerful subject from known, subordinate object, and that serves as one of the defining elements of the colonizer's attitude.

What do I mean by self-questioning? As we work to cultivate anticolonialist ways of eating, adventurers should continually ask ourselves, Why am I interested in becoming a food anticolonialist? Many of the reasons that motivate us should give us pause, for they are themselves born of our imperialist and colonialist heritage and continue to reflect and support it.[3] Am I trying for a clean conscience and clean hands? Given the many other forms of colonialism in which I still participate, and from which I benefit, this is an unreasonable motive; furthermore, it smacks of a belief in the possibility of moral purity—an illusion that only overprivileged persons tend to cultivate. Is my aim to "help" oppressed, colonized peoples? It is not clear that resisting cultural food colonialism will, in and of itself, have any impact on the real lives of colonized people, and even if it did, such a motivation runs the risk of dissolving into a missionary attitude. Am I doing it to score Good White Person points with people of another ethnicity? This motive again smacks of the benevolent colonizer. Do I simply want to acquire more cultural capital, to become more of a food snob by knowing something about a culture as well as something about its food? If so, I betray the aims of anticolonialism.

We who are systematically privileged—whether by virtue of race, class, education, or gender—cannot escape the fact that, in every choice we make, every action we take, we exercise that privilege. The question we must ask is not "How can we avoid privilege?" but "How can we work to undermine the structures that give me privilege in the first place?" The first question speaks of a longing for individual moral purity, for blamelessness in an evil world; the second reflects a desire to transform the conditions that create injustice in the first place. The difficulty for would-be anticolonialists lies in manifesting that desire both sincerely and effectively.

In calling for would-be anticolonialists to be *both* sincere and effective, I mean for them to recognize and embody the relationship between attitudes and actions that I identified in part 1. There I suggested, following John Dewey, that attitudes and actions are two faces, two phases of our moral life; in Dewey's words, they are "morally one and the same, first taken as effect [action or conduct] and then as causal and productive factor [attitude or character]."[4] If Dewey and I are correct about the mutually constitutive relation between attitudes and actions, it would be impossible for someone to cultivate, over time, a genuinely sincere anticolonialist attitude that was not also manifested as a set of generally effective anticolonialist actions. One's actions as an anticolonialist arise from one's attitude—and one's attitude accretes out of one's actions. (This is of course not to say that each of one's actions will be effective, or that each thought one has will be sincere; we are interested here in the aggregate of one's thoughts and activities.) Immanuel Kant's protests about the centrality of intentions notwithstanding, a transformation in attitude that does not result in a transformation in action is not effective; nor, ultimately, can it be sincere. One cannot be an anticolonialist adventurer entirely in one's head. Not all attitudes are immediately visible in particular actions, but over time, changes in attitudes will—*must*—be manifested in changes in actions.

Some readers might acknowledge the need to question one's motives but ask, Why the need for *continual* self-questioning? Isn't it overly pessimistic (and perhaps just a touch hair-shirtish) to require us to interrogate our motives perpetually? Can't we just do all our questioning of aims and motives at once and be done with it? No, we can't, just as we cannot eat just once and be done with it. The meanings of our actions do not remain constant, but shift and change with the changes in their context. We can never "finish" questioning ourselves, because our attitudes are never fixed, firm, final; this fact follows of necessity from the recognition that attitude and action, character and conduct stand in mutually constitutive relation to each other. The old background shifts to accommodate, absorb, and redefine these new acts. Yesterday's resistance becomes tomorrow's mass-produced good. We would be wise to resist feeling either angry or depressed about this fundamental feature of the way in which we and the world are enmeshed.

So, how might we undertake to question our motives? From what vantage point might we try to do so? How can we position ourselves so as to see how our supposedly resistant beliefs in fact cohere to the mainstream ideology? How can we situate ourselves in order to reveal the cracks and fissures in which alternate attitudes and action can form? Feminist philosopher Sandra Harding has developed a concept that is useful for just this purpose. "Traitorous identities" are identities privileged persons can develop that will work to betray or undermine the very systems that give us our unjust privilege (she calls it "overprivilege"). When I refuse to accept, unquestioningly, the way that the world appears from my position as a working-class/middle-class white woman in the United States, when I refuse to accept without question the beliefs that go along with this privileged position, and when I seek to understand how those beliefs in fact work to shore up my privilege, I begin to develop a traitorous identity. Traitorous identities are platforms from which food adventurers can engage in critical self-questioning about their actions.

The process of developing a traitorous identity is inextricably bound up with the process of trying to understand ourselves through critical reflections developed by marginalized people. Harding gives the example of Minnie Bruce Pratt, a white woman, who "reenvisions the southern town in which she grew up, contrasting the partial and distorted view that her father . . . tried to give her with what she knows of it after relearning history from the perspective of black lives."[5] Those perspectives were made invisible to her in her white-centered education. Pratt becomes a traitorous white person because her identity and her actions challenge a system of white racism that privileges her at the expense of Blacks and other persons of color.[6]

Anticolonialist food adventurers who wish to develop their capacity for self-questioning ought to look for analyses and critiques of cultural exchange that interrogate our motivations for food adventuring. We can and should cultivate—and continually refresh—our skepticism about our own anticolonialist motivations by thinking with the aid of theorists writing from the margins.

In the remainder of this chapter, I present some examples of the ways in which food adventurers might question their motives when they set out from positions that have been shaped by the challenges of theorists writing from colonized and racially marginalized perspectives. There is no unanimity to the three kinds of theoretical challenges I explore. In fact, they differ quite sharply with respect to the question "How ought we marginalized persons respond to our objectification at the hands of those who stand in positions of privilege in relation to us?" Part of the value of considering the three positions together is precisely their lack of unanimity on this question; they deny me the opportunity to decide, simplistically, that "this is the right way for me to act," because "this is What (All) Marginalized People Want." Self-questioning eschews such global solutions.

Ward Churchill's separatist prescription, with which I began part 4, can stand as the first challenge to my eating practices; if the dishes on the wall are written in Chinese, and if the waiter tells me I won't like them, sometimes my response must be to respect the boundary.

But unthinkingly subscribing to Churchill's argument will not make me an anticolonialist food adventurer either. As Harding emphasizes, I need to reflect *for myself* on the meaning, validity and applicability of Churchill's argument. Otherwise, I simply create a new kind of division between Us and Them; We are the ones whose arguments are to be taken seriously, subjected to scrutiny, while They are the ones whose claims should just be taken at face value.[7] I might, for example, reflect on whether I must *always* retreat from contact with insiders to a culture whenever I meet with the disdain that Krishendu Ray and Arlene Avakian describe (see chapter 9). Might there not be times when it is more appropriate for me to politely but persistently ask if this is the place that's giving lessons in the taste of one's own mouth?

Trinh Minh-ha presents the second perspective from which one might cultivate a traitorous identity with which to question food adventuring practices.

## Exclusion with a Human Face

Anthropologist Clifford Geertz suggests that "the essential vocation of interpretive anthropology is . . . to make available to us answers that others . . . have given, and thus to include them in the consultable record of what man has said."[8] Challenging Geertz's suggestion, Trinh writes, "The question remains whether this inclusion is disinterested or not. If it is not, as in this case—what is apparently aimed at is 'to make available to us' who need it a 'consultable record of what man has said'—the result will simply be the opposite or a by-product of 'exclusion,' and a stirring about within the same pattern of logic. The 'conversation of man with man' is, therefore, mainly a conversation of 'us' with 'us' about 'them'. . . ." (65). Trinh challenges the notion that interest and inclusion—mere *appreciation* of the creations of the Other—are inherently nondominant, liberatory activities. In Geertz, Trinh argues that such interest simply replicates an us/them dichotomy. Inclusion, when it takes place entirely according to the terms of the colonizer, is simply a companion to exclusion, not a rejection or transformation of it.

Trinh's analysis of Geertz puts me in mind of television chef Jeff Smith, writing in *The Frugal Gourmet Cooks Three Ancient Cuisines*. While there is much for the anticolonizing adventurer to admire in Smith's book—his assertion that one ought to know the history of cuisines, the origin of particular dishes and cooking techniques, for example—his approach to this information retains the familiar us/them dichotomy, replacing the exclusion of the Other with an inclusion that is its first cousin.

I find this exclusionary inclusion most markedly present in his treatment of the cuisines of China. I am struck by the sharp contrasts between his discussion of Chinese cuisine and the cuisines of Rome and Greece (the other two ancient cuisines in his book). In brief introductory discussions of the three cultures, for example, we find sections entitled "Modern Greece" and "Rome at Present." There is no companion "China Today." Is this because China is locked into a permanent, immutable past? Regarding Chinese food-buying practices, Smith tells us that "we find this system strange, but please consider that we are terribly inefficient. . . . The Chinese just do not think that way."[9] (Are "we" inefficient even if "we" are of Chinese descent? Do *no* Chinese think that way?) With respect to table habits, he reminds readers that "the Chinese enjoy food unabashedly and without hesitation. Therefore they do not pretend that they are *not* eating when they are. That is our game in the West" (59). Smith is writing to a readership that apparently does not include the Chinese or Chinese Americans—and in which all their traditions may be summed up in simple, declarative statements. Here is the "consultable record" of which Trinh speaks—one of Us writing to Us about Them.

Trinh, for her part, tries to imagine how we can move beyond the practice of white women inviting women of color to be consultants to projects they have organized. How can women of color get to set the terms of such projects and then have white women participate in them? Likewise, I want to ask: What would Smith's cookbook be like if he really attempted to challenge this Us-on-Them script? How could Smith create—or help to create—a cookbook called *Three Ancient Cuisines* that did not turn the Chinese into outside consultants (at best)? An advisory panel won't do it; every halfway decent cookbook lists a panel of experts its author consults. Would joint authorship with insider chefs from each of the cuisines suffice? It would begin to do so, although not if outsider chefs continue to set the terms of the collaboration.

I find expressions of a desire for such deep collaboration in various cookbooks, but not much that is more substantial than hope. For example, in various cookbooks from the fifties through the seventies written by insiders, I find introductions filled with the authors' fervent hopes that their cookbooks will further the conversation between the people of their nation and those of the United States. Dolores Botafogo writes, "To make the friendship between our two countries stronger, I offer you dishes which will remind you of Brazil, its customs and its cordial and kindly people. Some may seem strange to you, but their preparation will be like a cooking adventure in a foreign country and perhaps they may become family favorites and thus be incorporated into North American cookery."[10] But such expressions of hope from a Brazilian author are only the barest beginning of the kind of dialogue that Trinh envisions, and they run the risk of becoming empty platitudes in a world filled with diversity patter. A more deeply dialogic effort (again an effort made by an insider) is Malulee Pinsuvana's *Cooking Thai Food in American Kitchens*, a book I discussed in part 2. The author writes out of her experience of trying to cook Thai food herself in the United States, and also out of talking with others—U.S. and Thai—about how to do it. The project is Pinsuvana's, the audience one that she has identified.

But most of us don't write cookbooks, so to interpret Trinh's implicit challenge only in terms of them won't suffice. Surely as eaters we can also cultivate our traitorousness by thinking critically with that challenge. How can an adventure eater disrupt the us-talking-with-us-about-them dynamic that so often flavors our meals in an ethnic restaurant and scents the prose of an ethnic restaurant review? Or, more to the point, how can outsiders honor the attempts of ethnic insiders to disrupt that dynamic? Sincere questions asked of the wait staff do not, on their own, suffice. It is possible to be "sincerely interested in the natives" without disrupting the Us/Them dynamic one iota—in fact, it can reinforce it still more, by making the staff responsible for yet one more aspect of your pleasure.

The fact that this is a consumer relationship—that food here has become a commodity—makes the task of disrupting it even more difficult. Perhaps in the restaurant, adventure eaters ought to focus our attention on *not* attempting to establish genuine contact with the cultural insiders hired to prepare and serve us food. Why should they want to establish some genuine contact with me, when, for all its "genuineness," such contact is still nevertheless confined within the four walls of a restaurant and the parameters of a commodity relation? In what sense have they been able to set the terms of the exchange, if I persist in seeking some sort of deeper, more sincere contact, in a setting in which they aren't free to say no? (The customer is always right, after all!)

Is there no way to change this dynamic, then? Certainly there is; but it is more likely to arise as a result of long, sustained interaction that takes place in more than one venue than over dinner in your favorite ethnic café.[11] (And why would we expect otherwise? Do we think we should be able to develop deep, genuine rapport with others who provide services for us? Do we imagine genuine connections with the plumber who comes to unclog the sink? No? Why, then, would we think it possible or appropriate to expect such rapport in an ethnic restaurant? "Because we want it to be possible" is perhaps the most honest answer the food adventurer can give.) Food may be a wonderful way to begin creating a connection between Us and Them—but no such connection is instantaneous, and even the flexible, interactive, welcoming medium of food cannot make it so.

Am I not just handing out the old familiar advice to avoid being an ugly American when you travel into another culture? Not really. One can avoid being an ugly American—rude, outwardly presumptuous, loud—without really disrupting the structures and presumptions on which such rudeness rests. I'm digging in, a layer deeper, to suggest that we think and act from a consciousness of our privilege—from an acknowledgment that, among other things, we *are* always ugly Americans by default. Trinh describes the possible/impossible nature of such cross-cultural exchanges when she writes, "Can knowledge circulate without a position of mastery? No, because there is no end to understanding power relations which are rooted deep in the social nexus. . . . Yes, however, because in-between grounds always exist, and cracks and interstices are like gaps of fresh air . . ." (41).

Trinh's challenge to move beyond mere appreciation of other cultures prompts a related question for me: How might restaurateurs from various marginalized cultures run their restaurants in the United States, if they were able to follow motivations other than surviving in a cutthroat restaurant

market in which Euroamerican consumers predominate? The question is
not, What would such restaurants be like in the absence of whites altogether? The issue is not cultural purity. I'm asking what it would be like if
restaurants emerged in contexts of cultural interaction not fundamentally
shaped by colonizing—hooks's and Cesaire's question. This is a significant
thing for self-questioning food adventurers to ask, not because many of us
will ever *be* third-world restaurateurs, or because any of us will live in a
world free of the dynamics of colonialism, but because it can give eaters
ideas and inspiration about how to *be* in ethnic restaurants.[12] If we imagine
what such a restaurant might be like (Would it serve this much meat?
Would these special-occasion dishes appear as a matter of course? Would I
assume the wait staff was responsible for providing me with a "complete
cultural experience?"), we can try to move ourselves from the actual present
to that imagined possibility. We can try to be the patrons of such a restaurant.

In sum, what I take from Trinh is the realization that a food anticolonialist attitude cannot rest upon the easy assumption that reducing one's ignorance
about another culture is always a positive activity; acquiring knowledge
about another culture can, in fact, be just another effort to shore up the relationship of inquiring subject and inquired-into object. ("Some of my best
recipes are Szechuan.") Trinh demands that we move beyond this simplistic
version of exclusion-by-inclusion, in which control of the exchange remains
firmly in the hands of Us. The food adventurer must continually ask herself
how she might work to bring this about, and whether her current attitudes
and actions are working to do so.

## Forced Intimacy

bell hooks, writing about whites' fascination with Blackness as expressed in
popular culture, argues that "subject to subject contact between white and
black which signals the absence of domination . . . must emerge through mutual choice and negotiation. . . . [S]imply by expressing their desire for 'intimate' contact with black people, white people do not eradicate the politics of
racial domination. . . ."[13] Cookbook author Jennifer Brennan does not magi-
cally neutralize the colonialist dynamic between herself and her private cook
simply by making herself at home in the kitchen and cozying up to the cook to
ask sincere questions about whether the Thai really use ketchup in their pad

thai. Such presumed intimacy can reinforce the dynamic, because it highlights the fact that Brennan has kinds of access to her cook that her cook does not have to her. (Brennan's cook can't just barge into Brennan's cooking classroom, for example, and start asking her questions about her teaching methods.)

What would "mutual choice and negotiation" require in such an interaction? What would need to happen in order to change this relationship into something other than a subject-object exchange? At the very least, Brennan and her "changing parade of household cooks" would have to discuss the terms under which it would be justifiable for Brennan to publish their work, their skills and recipes. It would require that the cooks be able to make an informed choice about whether or not to participate in this cookbook-making enterprise in the first place—that they understand the larger, long-term consequences of participating in it. Would they still want to participate if they knew of Claudia Roden's anger over the misappropriation of Middle Eastern cuisine by Euroamerican authors? They may; my point is that mutual choice would require that both parties making the choices have sufficient information on which to base their choices. Given that Brennan has the power to publish—and also the most access to information about how these recipes will be used—she has a particular obligation to exchange that information with the cooks from whom she is learning.

hooks goes on to say that "Mutual recognition of racism, its impact both on those who are dominated and [on] those who dominate, is the only standpoint that makes possible an encounter between races that is not based on denial and fantasy" (28).[14] Such a requirement would transform the way in which European and Euroamerican cookbook writers like Brennan collect their materials for ethnic cookbooks; it would also result in cookbooks with substantially different kinds of approach to their subject matter. Perhaps ethnic cookbooks or dining guides written by outsiders to a cuisine could be constructed in ways that actually acknowledge and grapple with the fact of continued colonialist domination by Western cultures. How have the boom in export agriculture and the presence of multinational food corporations changed cooking practices in country, for example? (How have parents grappled with their children's fascination with all things McDonald?) What are some of the ways that the colonized culture changed the food practices of the colonizer—and vice versa? How have voluntary and forced migration to the United States affected the country's cuisine?

This is a tall order. As we've seen, cookbooks, and in fact most popular foodwriting, tend to be extremely apolitical, avoiding any but the most superficial discussions of war, famine, colonization, and other "unpleasantnesses"—and placing most such unpleasantness safely in the past. In cookbooks and restaurant reviews, the world tends to be a delightful place indeed; I once read a glowing review of a new Ethiopian restaurant in Manhattan that surreally describes it as enabling you to "fantasize you're sitting in a hip restaurant in the trendiest neighborhood in Addis Ababa"[15]—a description that conveniently portrayed Ethiopia as a chic site of culinary innovation and bracketed the fact that the country was enduring an agonizing famine.

Not surprisingly in this apolitical climate, I can't point to examples of cookbooks (or any writing other than the occasional restaurant review) that address the reality of colonization head on. The closest I can come are cookbooks written about soul food and other African American cooking styles written by insider African Americans, not white outsiders. Several of these cookbooks discuss the ways in which racism has made it difficult for African American cuisines even to be recognized *as* cuisine—to say nothing of the challenge of getting books on these subjects published. Helen Mendes writes of the origins of soul food in the slave cooking in early America, and notes that stereotypes keep non–African American people from even trying it, but not from being disdainful of it.[16] Howard Paige tells the story of having an article on soul food rejected by a dozen food magazines because there was "no interest" in the subject.[17] And Vertamae Smart-Grosvenor notes, in the introduction to the second edition of her book *Vibration Cooking*, that "When *Vibration Cooking* came out in 1970, there were fewer than ten published cookbooks by Afro-Americans. There are not many more than that today. That's a scandal. . . ."[18]

In contrast, two Creole cookbooks written by whites—one in 1903 and one in 1941—write about the end of slavery with, unbelievably enough, a genuine sense of loss: "A friend of mine, in the South, once said to me that the surrender at Appomatox had brought about two serious calamities—an end to duelling and the disappearance of the colored cook."[19] And, forty years later, "The Negro cooks had instinctive faculty and an inborn genius for combining herbs and seasonings with food. . . ."[20] Nostalgia for slavery: a particular form of nostalgia for imperialism.

What will it take for outsider cookbook writers, writing about the food of marginalized and colonized cultures, to address such racism and ethnocentrism head on? I'm not sure. So far, we seem to have reached the stage in which some authors insist upon the greatness of a particular cuisine from Asia or South America—arguing that it, too, ranks right up there with French and Italian food in sophistication and gastronomic merit. This may be their (very subtle!) way of saying, "Racism and colonialism have assigned this cuisine the role of second fiddle for too long; I want to change that by showing the true value of this food." But such subtle boosterism does not yet count as a genuine acknowledgment of or wrestling with the legacy of colonialism. It is akin to the early efforts at recovering women's history, in which a few great women were selected for attention. Such efforts involved no reconceptualization of the notion of greatness, no acknowledgment of the ways in which sexism kept women from performing other roles, and devalued the roles that they did play. The same is true for these cookbooks.

As for attempts at genuine collaboration with insider cooks, the best example I have found in an outsider cookbook is *Rick Bayless's Mexican Kitchen*, which Bayless wrote with Deann Bayless and JeanMarie Bronson. What I find unique about this cookbook (which is, after all, just one of many such "star" volumes written by a Euroamerican owner of a well-known restaurant) is not simply that Rick Bayless opens the book by thanking—by name—the specific Mexican cooks with whom he studied, but that he describes his own role in the creation of this cookbook in terms that do not position him as the all-powerful subject, the one setting the agenda. Bayless, born to a restaurant family in Oklahoma and almost-possessor of a Ph.D. in Latin American cultural studies, addresses head-on the legitimacy of his efforts to write a Mexican cookbook: "Can a gringo guy with popular Stateside restaurants flesh out the nuances of Mexico's real cooking?" Yes, he can, but in doing so, he acts not as a developer (the kind of role that maintains the sharp hierarchical division between Us and Them), but as *translator*, working to make the complex cuisines of Mexico understandable for someone unfamiliar with them, someone also hobbled by working in an American kitchen: "Frequently, the translation is easy: Ingredients, techniques and ways of serving are equivalent here and in Mexico. Other times I have to translate the delicious integrity of authentic Mexican cooking into a vernacular my compatriots can understand."[21] A bit later, he describes this cookbook as a "first pass" at presenting recipes for certain building blocks of Mexican cookery—not the definitive volume on the cuisine, but an attempt that he hopes will be built upon by others. Bayless is not simply putting on a humble act; he seems to be trying to represent himself as standing in a subject-to-subject relation with the many Mexican chefs and cooks from whom he has learned. He acknowledges that he has an important role in this process, but recognizes that it is nonetheless a limited role. He is not "clarifying" Mexican cookery for the Mexicans (as Revel might have it), or developing it in order to render it sophisticated enough for Americans (as Brennan might describe it). He's just figuring out a way to make it understandable to those of us born outside the traditions of Mexican cookery, and thereby both ignorant of them and lacking some of the culinary and linguistic tools necessary to be able to learn about them.

Mutual recognition of colonialism and racism would also certainly transform the actions of eaters. hooks's message, translated into the language of food adventuring, is that our only hope for becoming anticolonialists lies in placing the colonizing relationship squarely in the center of the dining table; only by addressing colonialism directly through our cooking and eating can we possibly transform them into activities that resist exploitation. If eating ethnic cannot remain pleasurable once we acknowledge the ways that domination shapes our exchanges with the Other, then we must acknowledge that it is a pleasure well lost.

Do I mean to suggest that our actual aesthetic pleasure in food could and should be affected by our acknowledgment of the colonizing relationships that prevail between first-world restaurantgoers and their third-world servers? Indeed I do. The sharp division usually assumed to exist between aesthetic appreciation and moral sensibility discourages us from attending to the ways in which the pleasure we take in our food can be enhanced or diminished by coming to understand more about its context.[22]

The claim that ethics and aesthetics ought to be more closely linked is hardly without precedent in discussions of food. Arguments for vegetarianism, arguments in support of migrant workers' rights, and arguments against genetically engineered foods and pesticides often appeal to aesthetic dimensions of food. Wendell Berry eloquently delivers one such argument, in a brief essay titled "The Pleasures of Eating." He writes that the pleasure of eating should be an "extensive pleasure," one that comes from knowing that the foods you are eating have grown in an environment you can think about without wincing. He explains his choice to eat seafood when he travels: "Though I am by no means a vegetarian, I dislike the thought that some animal has been made miserable in order to feed me."[23] We could expand

Berry's prescriptions for eating by trying to avoid any foods that have been grown in ways that make the soil and water "miserable" as well; Wes Jackson, for example, suggests that we ought to try to "meet the expectations of the land"—to produce our foods in such a way that the needs of the very soil are recognized and met. Such eating could engender what Corrinne Bedecarré has called, in conversation, "radical joy"—a deep aesthetic pleasure that does not require one to divert one's attention from ethical and environmental questions about the origins of one's food.

"Eating with the fullest pleasure—pleasure, that is, that does not depend on ignorance—is perhaps the profoundest enactment of our connection with the world," notes Berry (378). And for me, that world is not only a physical environment, but also a social one—one in which others have not only grown, gathered, and prepared foods for me to eat, but have also created and endlessly refined the ways in which those foods have been prepared for me. I do not know for sure what it would be like to know that those cooking traditions are being treated respectfully by all those who use them—I know far less about what this would mean than about what it would mean to say that an animal was being raised respectfully, or that farm workers were working under conditions that respected their full humanity. But I am convinced that, if I am to eat without flinching, I must keep finding out what it means.

For an example of such radical joy—though one that still addresses ecological, rather than cultural, respect—I turn to a memoir by Alix Kates Shulman describing several summers she spent alone on an island in Penobscot Bay, Maine. After her first (long, tedious, and ultimately disappointing) trip to the island grocery store, Shulman decides to make use of the copy of a Euell Gibbons guide that she finds on her cabin shelf and teach herself how to eat the things living around her. What began as a means of saving time and avoiding expensive, limp produce eventually becomes a passionate commitment to eating with the intimate understanding that her life and health are directly intertwined with the life and health of every living thing she encounters. The list of foods she eventually harvests (all in a ten-minute walk from her door) spans a full page. And she doesn't stop at Maine; she learns to eat what's growing in the mountains of Colorado, between the cracks of a Cleveland sidewalk, and in the backyards of Santa Fe.

Her descriptions of eating captivate me because although she is deeply motivated by a set of ethical, environmental, and political concerns, hers are so clearly not the descriptions of food eaten by someone operating out of some Kantian moral imperative—eating devoid of pleasure, so one can be sure one is really motivated by duty. Quite the reverse: her meals are luscious, extravagant feasts, filled with unbelievable delicacies, cooked into dishes she creates through a wonderful process that employs equal parts daring, experimentation, and creativity.

Her city friends, meanwhile, worry about her; isn't she starving to death? How can she possibly be getting by without anything to eat? A French friend writes to ask if she isn't "longing by now for a boeuf en daube or a galantine de volaille?" She and her visiting friend laugh, she writes, "as we stuff ourselves with bouillabaisse."[24]

Shulman's eating is not the subsistence of an environmental martyr; it is the repast of a gourmet, an *extensive* gourmet experiencing radical joy in the foods that surround her. For the self-questioning food adventurer the question is, How might we cultivate radical joy in our adventuring—joy that is grounded in hooks's mutual recognition of systems of domination and subordination?

## Dropping the Subject

Yvonne Dion-Buffalo and John Mohawk challenge the Us/Them dichotomy in still another way, one that presents the greatest challenge to anticolonialist food adventurers, even as it also holds the greatest promise for cultivating an attitude of continual self-questioning. They identify three choices that colonized people may take in response to their colonization: "become 'good subjects,' accepting the premises of the modern West without much question, become 'bad subjects,' always revolting within the parameters of the colonizing world, or become 'nonsubjects,' acting and thinking in ways far removed from those of the modern West."[25] Dion-Buffalo and Mohawk advocate the last for all colonized people. This choice empowers members of a culture by acknowledging that engagement with other cultures, even colonizing ones, is inevitable (and can be both beneficial and harmful), and by calling for colonized cultures to set their own terms for that engagement—stepping out of the subject/object frame of colonialism in order to do so.[26] (Note: when Dion-Buffalo and Mohawk use the word "subjects," they mean "the subjected ones"—the ones I would refer to as "objects." Nevertheless, I shall stick with their term "subject," though it creates some confusion later on, when I come to talk about subjects in my sense—subjects as the ones in control.)

By refusing the Us/Them framework of the colonizing relationship, members of marginalized cultures also tacitly challenge those of us adventurers who would be anticolonizers to redefine our own role within this alternate paradigm. What would it mean for food adventurers to act in solidarity with these "nonsubjects?"

Frederique Apffel-Marglin, in an essay called "Development or Decolonization in the Andes?" uses Dion-Buffalo and Mohawk's notion of nonsubjecthood as a way to characterize the work of the Proyecto Andino de Tecnologias Campesinas (PRATEC), a Peruvian group devoted to "writing about Andean technologies, knowledge and world view."[27] We might therefore read Apffel-Marglin herself as a traitor in Harding's sense; she stands behind the PRATEC writers, and considers the Western world from that location. From it, she can see things about the structure of Western colonial relations that are all but impossible to see when one uncritically occupies a Western viewpoint. PRATEC creates and maintains its nonsubject stance through dialogue with many other cultures—including those that have colonized the Andean region and have been responsible for much harm. The nonsubject does not refuse engagement with other cultures on the basis of this harm. Avoiding all things Western at all costs—because they are bad and evil, because they are the products of a colonizing culture—leaves the colonized still within the colonizing relationship, fighting it on its own terms (terms on which the colonized are bound to fail), but also depriving themselves of whatever benefits they could glean from Western culture (Apffel-Marglin refers to that view as "cultural fundamentalism" [4]). Instead, members of PRATEC develop ways to engage in dialogue with these others, ways that slip the confines of the colonizing framework.

Apffel-Marglin notes that Eduardo Grillo Fernandez of PRATEC describes this dialogue as "digesting" the influences of European colonization, "incorporating what they can use and excreting what they do not need or want"—an intentionally bodily description of a process that transforms both colonizing and colonized cultures (7). But on the nonsubject model the colonized culture is transformed on terms of its own making—not those of the colonizer—nor those of the colonized in reaction to colonization. When an Andean culture takes up elements of European culture, it is not a sign of Westernization but an indication that the indigenous culture has decided this is an element worth using—be it the Spanish language or European cattle. The "digestive power" of the Andean people, notes Apffel-Marglin "is their capacity to creatively incorporate alien features into their own world view, without creating a radical discontinuity"—and without surrendering to the terms of Western colonialism in order to do so (10).[28]

It is quite easy to extend this notion of nonsubjecthood and dialogue to the domain of food. I've remarked frequently that cuisines are always a patchwork of borrowings and lendings, undertaken under various conditions of liberty and bondage. The notion of nonsubjecthood gives me a way to describe these borrowings that is not rooted in a subject/object relationship. Considering the possibility that members of a culture may be responding to colonization as nonsubjects who are deciding for themselves whether and how they will incorporate the strange foods that are making their way into the community helps me to recognize their autonomy, creativity, and capacity for self-definition. Think how we might regard the presence of condensed milk and ketchup in Thai food, or Spam in Hawaiian cuisine, if we were to see the presence of these ingredients as the result of Thai and Hawaiian dialogues with the cultures that introduced them, dialogues that resulted in the decision that these ingredients could work well within the existing cuisine. What if we understood satay as a brilliant "digestion" of American steak, rather than a dish that has been "garbled in translation?" How would we eat the chocolate cake that is apparently ubiquitous in the cafes of Kathmandu (courtesy of a recipe left by a former Peace Corps worker)?[29]

How different this approach is from regarding such interactions as capitulations to power or erosions of the authentic culture! In Apffel-Marglin's words, these cuisines "creatively regenerate themselves without radically breaking with their history" (12). Understanding one's culture in this way would directly challenge any definition of authenticity that rests on static timelessness and false notions of purity—and it similarly challenges outsiders who believe they are protecting cultures when they demand such authenticity in a cuisine.

I had what might be described as a "nonsubject revelation"—though not a food-related one—when I went to a performance of the American Indian Dance Theater, a company that performs traditional dances from Native nations all across the United States. I was taken aback to see that the dancers' traditional costumes included laces and other accents in bright Day-Glo colors. "How dare they perform the Grass Dance in Day-Glo pink?" I thought to myself. Then I thought about the fact that the jingles on jingle dancers' dresses were once made with deer hooves—but then they came to be made with metal chewing tobacco can lids; by the time I saw the jingle dance for the first time, there wasn't a deer hoof in sight. Fernandez might say that both the Day-Glo and the tobacco lids are wonderful examples of Native Americans digesting Euroamerican culture and incorporating the useful elements into a tradition that remains undeniably their own.

Not every incorporation can be understood this way; I'm not suggesting that we rewrite the history of colonization in a way that redescribes force as choice.[30] But I am deeply challenged to think about alternative ways to interpret the exchanges between colonizer and colonized. Perhaps, in any particular situation, *We* are playing the colonization game, but perhaps *They* are playing quite another game altogether. So why would our interpretation be the only relevant one? And what if some of us try to play along with them? (We'll do so not as their kind of nonsubject, but as our own.)

Obviously, for those of us used to being knowing, controlling subjects, the path to nonsubjecthood looks quite different from the way it looks to those who usually occupy the role of objects (or subjects, in Dion-Buffalo and Mohawk's sense). *We* cannot resist colonialism by ingesting more cultures and excreting the parts of them that do not work. This is in fact one way to describe just what colonizing cultures have tended to do right along. Setting ourselves blanket prescriptions—"Don't just take up bits and pieces of one culture after another, but don't attempt to close yourself off from all borrowing either"—won't work either; it's impossible to come up with a general protocol, applicable in all contexts. Nor does such an approach cut deep enough.

What we need are alternatives to *subjecthood* (in both senses)—alternative ways to understand our role in cross-cultural dialogues that do not grow out of an Us/Them, studier/studied, dichotomy. We ought to try to cultivate those alternatives within the very sorts of cross-cultural dialogue that PRATEC members seek to create.

What should we look for in alternatives? For starters, a loss of authority, of centrality, of the power to define the context for everyone in it. Acting in solidarity with nonsubjects means creating more possibilities for nonsubjecthood to flourish—which means chipping away at the ubiquity of Us. For me, that means trying to create some kind of dynamic in which I am not at the center—either as the learned authority *or* as the grasping, demanding learner. It means being ignorant, out of one's element and not regarding the elimination of one's ignorance and the restoration of one's comfort as the central projects to be undertaken. It means realizing not only that one is not the center of the wheel (recall my revelation in the Irish Thai restaurant), but that thinking about the world as a wheel with a center is a highly subject-centered way to proceed in the first place.

Melissa Burchard has suggested, in conversation, that one way adventurers may explore non-subjecthood is by cultivating a playful attitude—a suggestion that has much to recommend itself.[31] For one thing, playfulness allows food adventurers to question the us/them dynamic in contexts that do not threaten us, in ways that will send us running in the opposite direction, clutching our subject privilege firmly to our chests. For another, taking ourselves less seriously relieves us of the responsibility to be the expert—or to be in the process of acquiring the knowledge that will enable us to be the expert. Finally, cultivating playfulness is, in and of itself, a useful thing to try to cultivate, because playfulness is an intrinsically useful way of being in the world, particularly for people accustomed to carrying their white man's burden with deadly seriousness.

And perhaps this is precisely why I find this project so difficult to take up—because I take myself so very seriously. My seriousness has the (unintended, perhaps, but real) effect of keeping me smack at the center of things even as I seek to decenter myself, to shrug off power. Thus I find it relatively easy to grant (in the spirit of Ward Churchill) that every interaction between me and a Vietnamese grocery store owner turns that grocer into just a little bit more of the Vietnamese equivalent of a hang-around-the-fort Indian; that every interaction I have with a Thai waitress in a restaurant erodes her relationship to her culture just a bit more; that my only recourse (which is, conveniently enough, impossible) is to stay home and never eat Their food. I find it familiar and comfortable to seriously—agonizingly—understand myself as either part of the problem or part of the solution (never both, and *never* neither).

It is exceedingly *un*comfortable for me to be a bit player, to be a bit of a fool, to be inept (but amiable), to be someone whose questions are *not* the ones that must be answered. I'm the sort of person who *does* consult the dining guide before she goes out to dinner; who memorizes anything she has ever heard anyone say about any cuisine she might ever be in a position to try; who watches the "natives" in the restaurant, to make sure she at least *looks* like she has a clue (a tendency that led me, my first day in India, to fold my paper napkin into various shapes for a good ten minutes before I finally realized that the Indian with whom I was dining and whose actions I was copying was simply a fidgeter). But I think this is just the sort of thing I need to be willing to do/be if I want to participate in this nonsubject-making process. I must give up—playfully, awkwardly, ignorantly—my belief that I, and folks like me, define the agenda, whether by our actions or by our inactions, our knowledge or our ignorance.

Churchill's analysis gives me a clear understanding of the two positions I can occupy; either I'm engaging with the Other and am thereby perpetuating the harms of colonialism, or I can seek to disengage and stop those harms. That's why I like it so well. Mohawk and Dion-Buffalo refuse that dichotomy, and in so doing, deny me a tidy, identifiable position. They challenge me to be willing to be not wrong, but *silly*, not even powerful enough to be harmful, but extraneous or beside the point.[32] Or maybe sometimes interesting and useful, but not when I expect to be. I think about how differently I would have behaved and felt if, in that Thai restaurant in Dublin, I had been attempting to act as a *non*subject instead of the all-knowing dispassionate observer I was trying to be. Would I have made mental pronouncements about what did and didn't belong, for example? Would I have been surprised when the server could not understand my garbled Thai request?

It is difficult even to suggest examples of this kind of attitude in action, because they are, by their very nature, deeply contextual; what's playful in one context might be arrogant in another. Given a world in which hierarchical subject/object dynamics shape virtually every interaction that takes place, the danger of any given interaction shifting back to that dynamic (despite the best intentions of everyone) seem high. Disclaimer issued, it seems important to offer at least one illustration. The one I've chosen comes from an essay by Bob Sehlinger, called "Etiquette Soup," that tells the story of being a Vietnam-era soldier in San Francisco at the point at which northern Chinese cuisine was just making its presence known in that city.

Sehlinger describes himself and his eating habits in terms that sound familiar to me. Having grown up in a small southern town with virtually nothing but barbecue, fried chicken, and catfish to eat, he entered the world of Chinese cuisine with interest but grave caution: "Wishing to make a good impression, I approached the experience with diplomatic reserve more in keeping with a Papal audience. I was ever alert for customs and protocols to honor, was exceedingly polite, bowed a lot (because I had seen it done in *The King and I*), and whispered in the manner of people in libraries."[33] When his parents came to visit him, they took the opportunity to hook up with some old college friends—an occasion that called for a big dinner at the Mandarin, a new northern Chinese restaurant in town.

He continues, "All of us, including our Oakland hosts (well practiced in Cantonese fare), were dumbfounded by the strange preparations listed by the dozen on our menus. Worse than hopeless, it was like trying to order dinner from the Dead Sea Scrolls. Confused and muddled but nevertheless enthusiastic, we elected to place ourselves in the hands of the chef" (129). What followed was a wonderful two-hour feast. At its conclusion, as Sehlinger sat silently congratulating himself for having committed no (known) faux pas during dinner, the waiter appeared with a large cut glass bowl full of ice and water. He returned with an individual bowl and two silver spoons for each guest. He spoke. No one understood him, and no one asked him to repeat himself. He went away.

The diners, knowing something was expected of them, proceeded to theorize on the meaning and purpose of the water. For a while, they threw out potted theories of the meaning of water in Chinese culture: "Theories incorporating baptism, rebirth, and cleansing of course, came immediately to mind, followed by a 'communion of the waters' hypothesis, as well as some convoluted ideas involving reincarnation and the Ming Dynasty, the Oriental reverence for elders, and metaphors of earth as the 'water planet'" (131). After this went on for some time, the diners began, tentatively at first, to ladle out some of the water and ice into their small bowls and to slurp, drink or wash with it. Tentativeness soon gave way to boisterousness:

> Before long we had abandoned the spoons altogether and were swirling our fingers in the translucent bowls and splashing gaily with our hands in the now depleted reservoir of the cut glass bowl.
>
> It was this scene, eight American diners flailing like starlings in a fountain, that stopped our waiter more certainly than cardiac arrest as he swooped into the room with a platter of hot, glazed bananas: bananas that under nor-

mal circumstances would have been dipped immediately into ice water to harden the glaze before serving. I'll bet they would have been good. (132)

I still laugh out loud when I read this story. It appeals to me, and illustrates a moment of nonsubjecthood because of the way that the diners cope when they lose control of their situation. When they arrive at the restaurant, the eight companions are ignorant, but in control nevertheless. They direct the waiter to have the chef prepare a meal for them, and they sit back to eat it. Sehlinger congratulates himself for remaining in control at the end of this first portion of the meal; he behaves as if he knows what he is doing, even though he doesn't.

When first confronted with the mysterious icewater bowl, the eight make a valiant attempt to maintain control by making sense of it; they come up with all manner of bizarre but erudite-sounding explanations that make use of what "we" know to be true about "them." But eventually, the allure of a big bowl of water and a lot of spoons grows too great, and, like small children in the kitchen sink, they go at it for all they're worth, forgetting their worries about decorum, not bothering about their ignorance, setting aside their anxiety about creating an International Scene.

I am in awe of this moment. These eight neophytes know they don't know what to do, know that what they are doing makes no sense whatsoever, and yet manage to transcend that potentially paralyzing knowledge and make complete and utter fools of themselves. Happily. They are, momentarily, foolish nonsubjects.

Sehlinger doesn't tell us what happens next. I like to imagine that the foolishness has reached such a pitch that, at the appearance of the waiter, there is no way for the eight to regain control of their situation, and they are left to be smilingly, unabashedly foolish in front of one of Them.

In the final chapter, I turn to contextualism, the other element of an attitude I advocate for anticolonialist food adventurers to develop. This aspect of the attitude particularly addresses the other two features of the cultural food colonialist attitude that have been the focus of this work—the quest for the exotic and the obsession with authenticity. I begin with what may seem an extended digression—a discussion of authenticity used strategically.

*Chapter 11*

# Eating in Context

<small>The following item appeared in *Chile Pepper*, a small magazine devoted to</small> chiles, hot sauces, and other hot foods:

> Being absolutely politically correct now apparently applies to food, as we see from the clipping from the *Santa Fe New Mexican* . . . , where John Roberts of Chimayo writes: "Equally disturbing are the increasing number of chile contests and cook-offs where Anglos continuously are awarded prizes for dishes that are not authentic Mexican Indian or native New Mexican. Mexican Indian and native foods of the Rio Grande Valley Pueblo Indians are ancient native cuisines of the Southwest and should not be exploited." Give us a break John—how does preparing and eating traditional foods, or non-traditional, for that matter, exploit them? How does the home cook exploit food, anyway? And who are those generic Mexican Indians? Do you mean the Maya? How about the Tarahumaras and the Zapotecs? Yeah![1]

The first time I read this small item, I was drawn up short by its author's juvenile response to John Roberts's concerns about exploitation—and the feeling hasn't gone away after repeated readings. Rather than seriously considering how food could be exploited, the author simply dismisses the notion as another shot in the political correctness wars—and then goes on to challenge Roberts's credibility by attacking his use of the term "Mexican Indians." "Ha" the author shoots back, "unlike you, I know the actual *names* of several Mexican Indian nations!" In other words, authenticity doesn't matter—but I know more about it than you do. *Nyah.*

This response fits a familiar food-adventurer pattern: I appeal to authenticity in a way that scores cultural sophistication points off someone else. Roberts, the author of the original item, appeals to authenticity in a different kind of way, however. He suggests that there is something problematic about the fact that Anglos are once again profiting off the cultural creations of Indian peoples—and they are doing so in ways that explicitly disregard the histories of those creations.

I've argued that when outsiders insist that a cuisine must abide by certain (outsider-chosen) rules in order to be authentic, authenticity works in the service of colonialism. In the first three parts of this book, I've described food adventurers' desire for authenticity as something to be gotten over. I've noted the connection between authenticity and false notions of culinary purity, its role as a link between exoticism and otherness, and, over all of this, the tendency for colonizers to usurp the power to decide what is authentic in a culture. But I've also suggested at various points that authenticity might play useful roles in developing an anticolonialist attitude. In this last chapter, I put some flesh on the bones of that suggestion, by exploring the idea of strategic authenticity—something John Roberts uses in his piece quoted in *Chili Pepper* magazine.

Then I will return to a suggestion I considered in part 3: What if we disconnected authenticity from novelty and exoticism? What if we understood an authentic cuisine as one that responds deeply to the context in which it presently finds itself? Could I satisfy the desire for some deep connection with something real—a desire that has sent me on one exotic quest after another—by attending to the context of my foods? I believe I can, if I begin by remembering that food is, first and foremost, an agricultural product; the most important context in which to situate food is therefore the agricultural one. The sustainable agriculture movement provides an ideal framework within which to think about the agricultural context of food; I conclude by suggesting ways that we might enlist sustainable agriculture to address issues of culture and ethnicity.

## Strategic Authenticity

When insiders appeal to the integrity and authenticity of their cuisine in an attempt to control others' access to their culture—and when outsiders support these appeals—then authenticity can challenge the colonizing relationship. When insiders to a cuisine claim the right to decide when a cuisine is being misappropriated, the very act of claiming that right has anticolonizing potential. And when outsiders who would be food anticolonizers pay attention to such claims—when we take them seriously (and, yes, also critically and reflectively)—we can contribute to that anticolonizing effort.

To call such appeals to authenticity "strategic" highlights the fact that these are cases in which insiders appeal to authenticity as a situation-specific way to control access to their cuisine, rather than as a general approach to it. Strategic authenticity is a means of defying colonizing appropriation—a means that colonized people initiate.[2] Anticolonizing outsiders can also play supporting roles by recognizing and honoring the rights of insiders to make decisions about how their cuisine will be taken up. This might be the role John Roberts is playing by pointing out the exploitation of indigenous food traditions, assuming he is not himself a member of one of the Native nations in question. When insiders claim authority with regard to questions of authenticity in a cuisine—and when food adventurers acknowledge that authority—"normal" power relations shift just a bit. Insiders and outsider allies upset the expected pattern in which outsiders take it upon themselves to decide what is authentic about a cuisine and prescribe that to others—including even those inside the cuisine in question.

"Strategic" also emphasizes the tactical, situational way in which authenticity is employed. To use authenticity strategically is to enlist the notion that cuisines have essential characters, but to do so in a temporary, stopgap kind of way. A strategic user of authenticity doesn't really believe that cuisines have fixed, immutable essences that cannot be violated, but she might sometimes speak and act as if she does when doing so will impress upon an outsider the seriousness of the matter.

The strategic user begins from an understanding that, with respect to her cuisine's tradition, *not* everything goes. A cuisine is not infinitely flexible (or it is no longer a cuisine), and at any given time, it might be necessary to say of some aspect of it, "No, this cannot be changed. You cannot do that to a recipe, to a style of preparation, to a list of ingredients, and still call it a dish in my cuisine." Relations of domination and subordination render such moves necessary; if one's cuisine (and one's culture more generally) were not threatened with exploitation and appropriation, strategic authenticity wouldn't be strategic.

This understanding of authenticity gives us an anticolonialist way to reconsider Claudia Roden's comments about variation in Middle Eastern cooking—when is it appropriate and when is it not? Recall her assertion that "It is tragic when food writers add or take away an ingredient to make a lifted recipe 'their own', and pass it off as authentic. They are falsifying tradition. This is how a culture ends up garbled and destroyed in the lap of another."[3]

This Roden puts her foot down, declaring "no more." This Roden writes, of Middle Eastern cuisines as deeply rooted in traditional practice, not open to change or alteration ("although there are no *standard* recipes in countries where they don't use cookery books . . . and although there are many versions of a dish—there are just so many and no more" [Barr and Levy, 112]). This Claudia Roden talks as if cuisines *do* have a fixed, unchanging essence. But this Roden is responding to the wave of Middle Eastern cookbooks that have been produced by Euroamerican cookbook writers, and that threaten (to her eyes, at least) to engulf and devour the indigenous traditions of Middle Eastern cooking.

Another Claudia Roden describes Middle Eastern recipes as almost infinitely flexible. This other Roden writes to individual cooks working in our kitchens, and encourages us to try recipes as they are written—at least once—and then to vary them according to our own tastes. This other Roden would not see the destruction of her cuisine in the fact that my friend Kristi serves tabouli together with salsa and tortilla chips; she might well applaud it as a creative use of a flexible Middle Eastern dish.

Using authenticity strategically is extremely tricky if one is not to end up sounding completely self-contradictory, a criticism I in fact made of Roden. Consider some of the traps that insiders and outsiders alike must avoid in attempting to use authenticity in anticolonialist ways. There is the notion that all insiders' claims to authenticity must be adhered to by all outsiders *just because they are insiders*, and the related notion that insiders always have the last word with respect to their own cuisine, regardless of their own knowledge of cooking. There is the belief that one can always actually establish, clearly and definitively, who is an insider and who is an outsider—and thereby ascertain who has the right to make strategic claims about authenticity. And there is the idea that cuisines actually *do* have fixed, unchanging essences that must never be tampered with under any circumstances. Given these traps, it would be easy for strategic authenticity to revert to authenticity in the service of colonialism—to mummify colonized cultures just as colonization itself does, and to reinforce the division between Us and Them.

Resistant potential exists, however, and when food adventurers acknowledge the authority and power of culturally colonized peoples to make decisions about how their cuisines will or will not be shared with others, such a shift in power can challenge a food adventurer's belief in the legitimacy of their uncritical adventuring.[4] So while it is undeniably tricky, strategic authenticity might still be a tool worth using by food adventurers who wish to become anticolonialist eaters, as well as by insiders to a cuisine.

We can find additional insights into strategic authenticity by considering other cultural arenas. Literary theorists have identified it in postcolonial literature. Diana Brydon, for example, observes that, although much postcolonial literature is devoted to exploring the hybrids formed when various cultures meet and intersect, "some Native writers in Canada resist what they see as a violating appropriation, to insist on their ownership of their stories and their exclusive claim to an authenticity that should not be ventriloquized or parodied."[5] In a world filled with cross-pollinations, borrowings, and stealings, there is tremendous power in marginalized people claiming the right to say, "No. These are our stories. You cannot tell them this way." And when colonizing outsiders pay attention to this "No," when we acknowledge its legitimacy and authority, the colonizing structure of the relationship suffers a small but important blow.

This example illustrates the fact that appeals to authenticity are strategic when they are employed by marginalized people to protect their cultural productions—but not when they are used to protect the power of dominant culture productions. Think about how different the scenario would be if it involved Euroamericans insisting on the ownership of their stories, and forbidding Native parodies of them. Such a move would not be at all anticolonialist—although Native Americans' refusal to abide by such a demand well could be. (Indeed, parody is one important literary tool that marginalized cultures can use to challenge the dominance of mainstream literatures. I think parody is used this way with food. Many countries around the world, responding to being invaded by U.S.-based franchises, develop fast food restaurants that bear a distinct, often tongue-in-cheek resemblance to chains such as McDonald's and Wimpy's. One of my favorites [in Switzerland, of all places] was named "McCheaper"; it capitalized on the fact that it served the same foods as the McDonald's down the street, but for a lot less money. In Bogota, I encountered a place called Benny's, painted in familiar black and white Holstein splotches, that served ice cream. No doubt Ben and Jerry would not be as amused as I was.)

In another example from literature, bell hooks points to a strategic use of authenticity in Langston Hughes's poem "You've taken my blues," which she describes as a "critical commentary on appropriation." Hughes writes,

> You've taken my blues and gone—You sing 'em on Broadway—And you sing 'em in Hollywood Bowl—And you mixed 'em up with symphonies—And you fixed 'em—So they don't sound like me. Yep, you done taken my blues and gone."

hooks describes Hughes's poem as expressing a "longing for ongoing cultural recognition of the creative source of particular African American cultural productions that emerge from distinct black experience. . . ."[6] She argues that Hughes is not calling for some essentialist ethnic purity in this poem, although others have interpreted it in this way—a fact that illustrates the trickiness of trying to employ authenticity strategically. (One always runs the risk of being labeled an essentialist.) Rather, Hughes calls for the *right* of Black artists to have a say in the ways Black cultural creations get taken up in other cultures—and for the *responsibility* of those borrowing cultures never to forget their Black origins.

Hughes's poem reveals the consequences of losing all control over one's own art forms: they stop "sounding like me." His could be the lament of members of any number of cultures whose cuisines have been fast food-ized or foil-packeted by the American consumerist machinery. The foods of many parts of Mexico, China, and India have stopped "tasting like me" to millions of Americans of Mexican, Chinese, and Indian descent as a result of these ubiquitous foil packets that bear so little resemblance to their origins. Uma Narayan puts in writing what countless other immigrants and ethnic Americans have felt or said about the food in "their" ethnic restaurants in the United States: "Eating in these restaurants, I taste India only faintly via a complex nostalgia of associations, something hard to explain to Western friends who seem oddly disappointed to learn that my acquaintance with, say, *tandoori* chicken is as shallow as theirs, being limited to such restaurant-related contexts."[7] I think again of Madhur Jaffrey, who wrote her recipe book in "self-defense" as a way to make sure that at least some of her American friends experienced food that "tasted like her."

Joanna Kadi illustrates a strategic use of authenticity in music, in an example that explores a potential role for outsiders. She notes that, for several reasons, she wants to share her cultural traditions with others, despite the obvious risks involved. Nevertheless, she notes, "I also believe some things should never be shared. For starters, sacred instruments, rhythms, and rituals."[8] She tells of two white women who decided to use a sacred Australian aboriginal instrument in a concert, despite the explicit objections of an Aboriginal woman present. In such a context, Kadi argues, the objections of an insider to a culture constitute a sufficient argument for *not* using a ritually significant instrument—whether or not the user believes in sacredness. And like John Roberts, who worries about the fact that Anglos are winning all the prizes at chili cook-offs, she calls for an end to the state of affairs in which "white people get the praise, money, and publicity from public performance" of the music of colonized people (125). Resistance to colonialism in this context requires white women to relinquish their use of a sacred instrument, and to acknowledge the rights of an insider to decide how and where her culture is to be employed by others.

Does Kadi's example go beyond strategic authenticity, to some absolutist, essentialist notion of authenticity of the sort to which I object? Here again we see the tension inherent in the nature of strategic authenticity, a tension that always threatens to pull it over into some other domain. Kadi, after all, argues that some things ought *never* to be shared, that some aspects of a culture ought to be inviolate. Such a position runs the risk of making certain parts of cultures beyond criticism—at least criticism by outsiders. Can this ever be a wise claim to make? Doesn't this simply create a situation in which cultures become stagnant, reified, and (ultimately) oppressive even to those inside of them?

Kadi likely states her position somewhat more strongly than she intends. We could read her comment in a larger context, noting that given the current exploitive climate in which capitalist consumerism treats every cultural creation from Native American spirituality to Australian sacred instruments as a commodity to be marketed—given this climate, certain things ought never to be shared. This reading takes away the sense that some strands of a tradition are, by definition, untouchable, and replaces it with the acknowledgement that colonialist exploitation is an undeniable fact that must figure into any current assessment of how cultural exchange can go on.

But even under that more liberal reading, Kadi still must be understood as seeking to preserve the sacredness of threatened sacred traditions. In contrast, Uma Narayan seeks to challenge certain kinds of religiously inspired traditions, precisely because those traditions themselves are antidemocratic. The fact that such traditions may be threatened by outside colonizing forces is, to her way of thinking, not necessarily a bad thing. As an example of such repressive traditions, Narayan identifies the dietary rules governing Brahmins under which she lived while growing up. She writes, "Growing up in a context where food was intimately connected to caste status and various regimes of 'purity,' it is 'food parochialism' that tends to strike me as dangerous, while a willingness to eat the food of Others seems to indicate at least a growing democracy of the palate" (180).

The contrast between Narayan and Kadi—admittedly a contrast between women of different cultures addressing different kinds of cultural creations— nevertheless can illustrate the balance that must be struck when one seeks to employ authenticity strategically. Kadi illustrates the power that insiders can claim by naming parts of their tradition off limits to outsiders, or by stipulating the precise conditions under which outsiders may participate in them. But Narayan's principled rejection of her own strict Brahmin eating traditions reminds us that, to be anticolonialist, such an appeal to authenticity must always be only a temporary, tactical appeal. We have too many examples of the ways that rigid adherence to traditions harms its practitioners to think that authenticity can be liberatory when it becomes essentialized.

In sum, strategic appeals to the authenticity of a cuisine can usefully, if only temporarily and locally, challenge food colonizers' authority to exploit and alter that cuisine however they see fit. To be effective in challenging colonizing relations, such appeals should be initiated by insiders to that cuisine. Food adventurers who stand outside the cuisine, but who wish to participate in resisting colonial relations, have an obligation to listen carefully to the prescriptions and demands of insiders in all their diversity, and to act in response to them, recognizing that it is always an open question which Them should be attended to. (It is inappropriate, for example, for outsiders to treat all the claims of an insider as sacrosanct. Recall that self-questioning, in Sandra Harding's sense of becoming a traitor, requires one to reflect critically on the perspectives of Others, not just mechanically accept them.)

But strategic authenticity is just that—a single strategy. Used exclusively, it becomes cultural separatism—a position that I've criticized from various angles already in this section. And strategic authenticity only operates effectively if we assume there is a sharp division between Us and Them—but this dichotomy is one of the very things that underlies my ability to turn Them into resources for *my* use. Furthermore, cultural exchange is not optional; none of us can decide to stop participating in it, no matter our place in the framework of colonialism (and our place may indeed be a complicated one). Finally, there *are* virtues to cultural exchange—although those virtues generally cannot be realized within the bounds of a colonizing relationship.

I find strategic authenticity inadequate for another kind of reason as well. It does not speak to the desires that send many adventurers in search of authenticity in the first place—desires that are well summed up in Vine Deloria's observation, quoted earlier, that "White people in this country are so alienated from their own lives and so hungry for some sort of real life that they'll grasp at any straw to save themselves. But high tech society has given them a taste for the 'quick fix.'"[9]

There is no question that food adventurers, like the religious "adventurers" of whom Deloria writes, have tried to satisfy our hunger in "quick fix" ways—ways that attempt to forge some kind of automatic connection to a context that we find alluring/exotic/novel. Such fixes won't last. But the hunger for some kind of nonrandom connection to food will remain. I see it in the feelings of rootlessness, in the arbitrariness that seems to characterize adventurers' culinary choices. I see it in the ways that we romanticize others' food traditions (traditions they themselves might find narrow and oppressively constricting). I see it in our nostalgia for our own childhood foods. Many adventurers long for some kind of sustainable connections with and through food.

I want to address this desire for connection in a way that will also work in the service of anticolonizing, and that will acknowledge the complicatedly cross-cultural nature of the world we inhabit (a world where divisions between Us and Them, insider and outsider are not at all unambiguous). I want to forge connections to contexts in which neither connection nor context is (entirely) arbitrary.

Agriculture—in particular, the movement known as sustainable agriculture—provides a way to create such linkages. In the final section of this chapter I'll explore how a sustainable agricultural concept known as the "foodshed" can enable the food adventurer to attend to the contexts of their food in a way that challenges the rootlessness of colonizer. Conversely, I'll also show how thinking as a cultural food anticolonialist can add new dimensions of meaning to the foodshed and can provide the sustainable agriculture movement with more satisfactory ways to attend to ethnicity and culture than it has employed up until now.

The sort of attention to context I am describing makes way for an alternative notion of authenticity, one I've hinted at elsewhere. This is authenticity conceived as attention to place—where place is understood not just in its agricultural senses, but also in its cultural ones. The question this kind of authenticity asks us to pursue is "How ought we—here, now—cook and eat?"

## Recontextualizing Food

If you walked down the aisles of a supermarket, watched commercial television for a few days, drove around the vicinity of a shopping mall, browsed the "restaurants by ethnicity" section of the yellow pages, and then used the perceptions you gathered as the basis for a description of the relationship between food and context in the United States, you'd probably characterize the relationship as "all food, all the time." The variety of foods that persons of even moderate means may purchase (at any time of the day or night) is staggering, and seems to be governed by nothing other than the sheer physical possibility of getting it to the consumer. Observe the ways in which food is advertised, and it often seems that there are no social, cultural, ethical, or agricultural contexts in which particular foods are at home, no particular claims or restrictions on anyone's palate. Not even the seasons or the climate (those seemingly intractable forces of nature) bear any (particularly obvious) relevance to what we actually eat; trucks, container ships, and airplanes make it possible for me to eat fresh foods year-round that wouldn't grow in southern Minnesota in July, let alone January. Food adventurers, we have seen, take advantage of this decontextualizing of food insofar as we graze from cuisine to cuisine in endless search for a new eating experience, and with the expectation that the foods we eat will use all and only authentic ingredients, no matter their provenance.

But certainly one context *is* extremely relevant to our diet today—the market. As rural sociologists Jack Kloppenburg, John Hendrickson, and G. W. Stevenson describe it, "We are embedded in a global food system structured around a market economy that is geared to the proliferation of commodities and the destruction of the local. We are faced with transnational agribusinesses whose desire to extend and consolidate their global reach implies the homogenization of our food, our communities, and our landscapes. We live in a world in which we are ever more distant from each other and from the land, and so we are increasingly less responsible to each other and to the land."[10] The global food system functions as a kind of anticontext context, one whose goal is the antithesis of strengthening connection—among people, between people and their food, people and the land.

Yet while people of means may be able to buy virtually any food (any food the market decides is profitable, that is) at virtually any time—and while the consumer machinery busily blares out information about where to buy frozen Thai entrees and fresh tropical fruits (in Fargo at 3:00 A.M.)—we need only scratch the surface to realize that things are not as they appear. Many people locate themselves (by birth, by heritage, by choice, by force of moral argument) in food contexts in which such open-ended, market-defined choices are neither desirable nor available, and in which such capitulation to the dubious charms of the global food system is not an option. Perhaps they are ethically committed to vegetarianism, or to safe working conditions and fair wages for farm workers. They are culturally committed to retaining ties with the dishes of their homelands or of their grandmothers' homelands. They are environmentally committed to reducing pollution and waste. They are religiously committed to preparing foods according to specific ritual requirements. Despite evidence to the contrary (evidence courtesy of the global food system, marketing division), they insist upon seeing foods as inhabiting particular cultural, agricultural, political, social contexts, they value those contextual relationships for all sorts of reasons, and they seek to preserve and promote them.

Food adventurers can find means for addressing (and redirecting) their hunger for authenticity by expressly and intentionally thinking about our food as inhabiting contexts. While many kinds of contexts present themselves as obviously relevant to this task, I believe that agriculture provides us with the most important, nonarbitrary one in which to forge relationships to and through food.

## Why Agriculture?

As a food adventurer, I have often been troubled by the capriciousness with which I turn my attention to a new cuisine. Nothing particularly compels me one way or another—other than novelty itself. I've described myself as feeling culinarily rootless—a feeling I have found disturbing and have sought to eliminate (ironically enough) through my ethnic adventuring. At such times I don't see myself as situated in any contexts that I could use to inform my decisions about what to eat and why.

As part of the work of becoming an anticolonizing adventurer, I want to locate myself in some nonarbitrary context—not a context I've chosen for its exotic glamour or its ability to net me sophistication points, but one that has concrete, material claims on my existence. I think agriculture can be such a context—in fact, I think that the agricultural context *should* fundamentally shape the food decisions of every eater, cook, or food writer—particularly those of us who live in the so-called developed world. The fact that it doesn't shape the decisions of many of us is, I submit, a very bizarre feature of the very bizarre food world we inhabit.

The agricultural context has come to *seem* completely arbitrary and irrelevant—a recent turn of events (and one that still has not affected much of the world's population). In my grandmother's day, the United States was an agriculture-based economy, most people lived in rural regions, and a vast portion of virtually anyone's diet consisted of food they grew themselves or bought from someone else who grew it themselves. One's immediate agricultural context largely determined what one ate. Today, most of us don't know *any* of the people who grow *any* of our foods—unless we deliberately (and with no small effort) set out to eat locally grown foods and to cultivate relationships with growers. I can stop a conversation dead by telling people about my friend Marti, who grows, gathers or barters about 80 percent of her own food, living in Bloomington, Indiana. Three generations ago, Marti would have been an ordinary farm woman; today she is an exotic specimen, the cultural equivalent of a genetic sport. What's amazing today is not that it's possible *not* to eat locally, but that, in the United States, it's nearly *impossible to do so*.

Of course, someone is growing and harvesting our food, whether or not we know who that someone is. And, of course, oranges don't really grow in Minnesota, even though I can always find several varieties of them fresh in my grocery store. It is not that food has no agricultural context, it's that its context doesn't matter, given the possibilities of the food transport system. Humans have not transcended the fact that foods require certain conditions in order to grow; rather, thanks to planes, trains, trucks and ships, we have transcended the need for most of us to think about those conditions most of the time. Indeed, it is this very system that has made it possible for food adventurers to come to know and demand authentic varieties of dishes from all over the world; why wouldn't the ingredients be available here?

Yet while ignoring the agricultural context of food is entirely possible for many eaters in the United States today, that context does not go away through inattention. We cannot transcend the fact that food is an agricultural product; we can only modify it in ways that may not at all be in our interest. Consider just a few of the outgrowths of living in a world food system that acts as if the agricultural context is simply an obstacle to be transcended: widespread degradation of soil and water resources, depletion of fossil fuel reserves, concentration of agribusinesses in places where labor costs are low and there is little protection for workers' rights, the deflavoring of fresh foods (a side effect of efforts to make them transportable), the erosion of foods' nutritional value (a result of increased processing, packaging, and transportation), the disappearance of the small family farm, and the companion destruction of rural communities. It is also easy to identify the ways in which this system contributes to neocolonization—for instance, through its creation of banana republics in which hired workers grow luxury crops for export on land they formerly owned and on which they grew staple crops.

Wendell Berry notes that consumers (he calls us "industrial eaters") are remarkably ill-equipped to recognize the realities of this food system—to say nothing of challenging them: "The industrial eater is, in fact, one who does not know that eating is an agricultural act, who no longer knows or imagines the connections between eating and the land, and who is therefore necessarily passive and uncritical—in short, a victim."[11] For Berry, this passivity is dangerous, because it leaves us unequipped to ask the questions he thinks are critical: "How fresh is [my food]? How pure or clean is it, how free of dangerous chemicals? How far was it transported. . . ? When the food product has been manufactured or 'processed' or 'precooked,' how has that affected its quality or price or nutritional value?" (374) Our ignorance leaves us at the mercy of a market that may not at all have the wellbeing of eaters as an important goal.

Food adventurers can begin to attend to the context of our eating by grounding our adventuring in Berry's recognition that eating is an agricultural act (and, negatively, by grappling with the degree to which it has become an industrial act). We can return to noticing that foods are connected the literal dirt and sun and rain and wind of *places*—and to *times*—to seasons, times of day. This attention to context will ground our decisions about what to eat and how; it will serve as a framing guide for our adventuring.

The sustainable agriculture movement is one important alternative agricultural and environmental movement that is at least implicitly supportive of this approach to adventuring. Sustainable agriculture pairs a commitment to producing food in ways that are environmentally sustainable with a commitment to promoting the health of human communities. Sustainable agriculturalists argue that one of the most important means of promoting such sustainability is by producing food for consumption locally—by creating, according to Kloppenburg, Hendrickson, and Stevenson, "self-reliant, locally or regionally based food systems comprised of diversified farms using sustainable practices to supply fresher, more nutritious foodstuffs to small-scale processors and consumers to whom producers are linked by the bonds of community as well as economy" (2).

The sustainable agriculture movement has spawned or encouraged a host of grassroots and hands-on projects. Community supported agriculture, farmers' markets, restaurants featuring local produce, community gardens, and other similar efforts reflect the movement's emphasis on linking food growers, cooks, and eaters with each other, in the pursuit of high-quality, sustainably produced, affordable foodstuffs. In short, I think the sustainable agriculture movement already stands in position to give adventuring anticolonialists the opportunity to forge the kinds of deep, significant links to our food that many of us have been seeking in our ethnic food forays.

Furthermore, sustainable agriculture challenges and undercuts the sharp division traditionally drawn between material concerns and cultural ones, by drawing out the consequences of material choices (to use fossil-fuel intensive methods of farming, for example) for cultural life (the concentration of agribusiness in places where labor is cheap, due to the relatively low cost of shipping goods, for instance), and vice versa. As such, it seems an ideal place to locate a conversation about cultural food colonialism.

In fact, the sustainable agriculture movement would be well served by deeper consideration of some of the social and cultural concepts of sustainability—in particular, creative ways to value the ethnic diversity of a community. "Ethnic diversity" is an explicit goal of many advocates of sustainability, but one that warrants much more critical development. Food adventurers can make a meaningful contribution to the sustainable agriculture movement, by thinking creatively about the ways in which culinary ethnic diversity complements and supports the move to the local.

### The Foodshed as a Site for Cultural Food Anticolonialism

One of the conceptual tools of the sustainable agriculture movement that I have found most useful for articulating a meaningful context for my eating is the notion of the "foodshed."[12] The foodshed, like the watershed, is defined as the physical area reached by a food supply. Thinking in terms of a foodshed (doing what Kloppenburg, and colleagues call "foodshed analysis") encourages me to think about the pathways food travels to reach my location (How far? By what means? At whose expense—monetary, environmental, social?), and to envision more sustainable ways for me to feed myself (ways that require food to travel less, for example). Thinking of ourselves as inhabiting foodsheds, then, can give us concrete guidance about how to move from the global food system to a more sustainable system. The foodshed gives us a methodical way to decide what and how to eat.

Furthermore, as Kloppenburg, Hendrickson, and Stevenson suggest, the term "connects the cultural ('food') with the natural ('. . . shed'). The term 'foodshed' thus becomes a unifying and organizing metaphor for conceptual development that starts from a premise of the unity of place and people, of nature and society" (2). Because it explicitly recognizes this intertwining of cultural and natural, the foodshed also serves as an ideal tool for thinking about how the projects of cultural food anticolonialism and sustainable agriculture might support and inform each other.

A commitment to thinking from the foodshed can help us reduce our participation in *cultural* food colonialism—whether we are food adventurers interested in eating nonexploitatively, food writers looking to combat our tendency to objectify those about whom we write, or ethnic restaurant owners and workers interested in resisting various effects of colonization on our cuisine. To show the connections, I'll make use of two of the principles that Kloppenburg, Hendrickson, and Stevenson say should guide our thinking as we work to move from the global food system to multiple foodsheds: first, "foodsheds are socially, economically, ethically, and physically embedded in particular places" (6) and second, "a foodshed will be embedded in a moral economy that envelopes and conditions market forces" (4).

### Location, Location, Location

What does it mean to say that a foodshed should be embedded in a particular place? Within the sustainable agriculture movement, one can find a variety of answers to this question. The strictest interpretation of bioregionalism argues that we ought to grow and eat all and only foods indigenous to our particular bioregion—a prescription that rules out exotic plants, where "exotic" is understood to include anything that arrived after a particular (very early) date. Others are less concerned about the pedigree of all plants (after how many centuries does a plant earn the title "indigenous?"), but nevertheless argue that regions ought to be self-sufficient in food, not relying on external trade at all. Kloppenburg, Hendrickson, and Stevenson, in contrast, eschew notions of locality and regionality and base their definition of location on the more flexible idea of proximity—an idea that also moves beyond the purely agricultural features of a locale to include the cultural as well: "The extent of any particular foodshed will be a function of the shapes of multiple and overlapping features such as plant communities, soil types, ethnicities, cultural traditions, and culinary patterns" (6). They advocate self-reliance rather than the more stringent self-sufficiency, recognizing, as they do, that sometimes external trade may be a highly desirable element of a foodshed. They further note that self-reliance "is closely linked to both social and environmental sustainability. A community that depends upon its human neighbors, neighboring lands, and native species to supply the majority of its need must ensure that the social and natural resources it utilizes to fulfill those needs remain healthy" (6–7).

The emphasis on proximity or locality is perhaps the best-known aspect of the sustainable agriculture movement. Many people otherwise unfamiliar with the movement know about (and shop at) farmers' markets, farmstands, and food co-ops offering local produce; some even join community supported agriculture projects that offer subscribers a weekly allotment of whatever vegetables are in season. Recently, the visibility of these projects has grown considerably, thanks to the efforts of a number of chefs, entrepreneurs, and cookbook authors who have made important contributions to raising public awareness of the value of eating locally.

In the past twenty years—and with increasing frequency in the last ten—locally owned restaurants have sprung up around the country that feature locally grown or gathered foods in season. Probably the most famous of these is Chez Panisse. Chef-owner Alice Waters was one of the first U.S. chefs to return to locally grown foods, and one of the most articulate spokespersons for the virtues and pleasures of eating local. She has since been joined by such chef superstars as Charlie Trotter and Rick Bayless in publicly advocating the virtues of the local and featuring local ingredients in their restaurants.

Many recent cookbooks also include discussions of the importance of using seasonal foods, supporting local farmers' markets and food cooperatives, and avoiding produce that has had to travel thousands of miles in a ship in order to reach your dinner table. The *Blue Moon Cookbook*, for example, chronicles the menus of a restaurant by that name in Vermont, dedicated to serving local, seasonal meals. This book is notable for being among the small number of works devoted to local foods in cold climates. Rick Bayless's cookbooks also emphasize the importance of buying local ingredients—even when that means substitution for a traditional Mexican ingredient.[13] As early as 1973, Jaffrey argued that, while it was possible to get fresh vegetables from all over the world, authentic Indian cuisine is deeply seasonal and local.[14] (Translation: just because you can get the ingredients a Bengali cook would use doesn't mean you should.)

Chefs and cookbook writers add to the ecological and economic arguments for bioregionalism their own *aesthetic* arguments for eating locally; locally grown food is fresher, and because it doesn't need to be engineered to travel cross-country, can be bred for flavor, not durability. Being able to work directly with local growers means that one can have a say in the foods they grow, and the ways they are harvested and processed. (It also means that local growers are ensured of a reliable market for their crops—and thus a steady income for themselves.) All of these elements affect how good food tastes when it reaches your table in a restaurant—especially if we, with Berry, understand eating as an "extensive pleasure."

The emphasis on locally grown, seasonal foods provides a nonarbitrary, meaningful way for cooks, restaurateurs, and other food makers or sellers to make choices about the foods they offer—and for food adventurers to think about the foods they can legitimately seek: Did this food get produced in a sustainable manner—or did it have to travel thirteen hundred miles to land on my plate?[15] We've seen why adventurers ought to suspect our insatiable desires for food novelty—and why we ought to explore ways to rein in those desires. The goal of food self-reliance provides an additional motivation, as well as a guide, for doing so.

But as those of us in northern regions know, the meaningful limit presented by seasonality and locality can be restrictive indeed. Eating locally can be a rather grim business in the winter in Minnesota—even if you rely heavily on preserved foods. (It does not escape Minnesotans' notice that Alice Waters' restaurant is in California.) Even in the height of summer, the variety of foods that one can grow, sustainably, in any given region is dramatically smaller than the variety that I have become accustomed to finding in the fresh produce section of my not-even-very-good local supermarket. Indeed, this is a common complaint about eating locally; it's boringly restrictive.

This is precisely the point at which food adventurers' approach to eating can make an important contribution to sustainable agriculture. Sustainable agriculture theorists assert that we need to think of locality in terms of *people and their cuisines* as well as the land itself. If that is the case—if we take that assertion seriously—then my foodshed can become a much less restrictive place than it first appears to be, for along with its fairly limited vegetable palate, it contains significant ethnic diversity. Likewise, if, according to the principles of bioregionalism, the social resources of one's community must remain healthy, then the culinary diversity present in one's foodshed becomes something we must foster and nourish. And what better way to do so than for all of us living in a foodshed to bring our various culinary heritages to bear on the foods that grow in our region?

In my community, that would mean sharing my recipes for how to use those endless supplies of potatoes and squash with my friends from El Salvador, Colombia, France, Somalia and Japan, my coworkers whose heritages are German, European Jewish, Hmong, or Mexican. My foodshed (understood culturally *and* agriculturally) may be a dismal, barren place from the tropical-fruits standpoint, but it has riches of its own that can help us entertain ourselves with our limited selection of stored and preserved foods from November until late April, when the first edible things start to present themselves in the earth.

Recognizing that a foodshed is embedded in a place that is constituted not only in terms of its climate and soil conditions but also in terms of the social and cultural heritages of the people living there provides a meaningful way for anticolonialist food adventurers both to ground our adventuring (by focusing our cooking and eating on proximately produced food items) and to contribute to a fuller fleshing out of the meaning of the foodshed (fostering the various ethnic heritages present in a foodshed by encouraging conversations among culinary traditions about how to use the foods of the region).

## The Moral Economy

I move now to the second principle that should guide our move to the foodshed. Kloppenburg, Hendrickson, and Stevenson write that foodsheds should be governed not by the economy of the market, but by a moral economy in which "mutuality, reciprocity and equity" hold sway. They suggest that "the moral economy of a foodshed will be shaped and expressed principally through communities" that they call "commensal communities" (5). Food can serve as a useful force that "could be the basis for the reinvigoration of familial, community, and civic culture" (4–5)—but they go on to note that this is an extremely difficult principle to realize.

The three theorists point to community supported agriculture (CSA) programs, in which growers and eaters share in the financial risks and rewards of the growing season through the sale of garden "shares" as one example of reinvigorated community culture. Having participated in CSAs in several different Midwestern towns and cities, I can attest to the fact that they do encourage the growth of community. Harvesting and delivering food with fellow CSA members, and talking with other CSA members about how they used that grocery bag full of kale we all got last week are undoubtedly community-building activities. Newsletters share growers' and shareholders' recipes for whatever's ripe, as well as tips about how to shift to a way of cooking based on the season rather than the supermarket. Often the grow-

ing season begins and ends with a potluck at which shareholders and growers get a chance to mingle and talk food with each other.

But clearly we need other ways to build our foodshed communities—
ways that address, for example, a greater diversity of economic positions,
family situations, and work schedules within which people organize their
lives. In particular, the sustainable agriculture movement needs help thinking about how to recognize, valorize, and develop the ethnic diversity of
communities. As I've noted, ethnic diversity often appears in sustainable
agriculturalists' laundry list of things we are to value—but there is often little specificity about what it would mean to value the variety of ethnicities
that live in the shed.

The question that this feature of the foodshed poses for the food adventurer is How can we understand the preference for proximity in a way that
also values the ethnic diversity present in our local communities? What
would it mean to cultivate the multiple ethnic heritages of a region as a way
to cultivate the overall health of the foodshed? To answer these questions we
will need to think about what it means for a *cuisine* to be local (as opposed to
a plant), and what it means for cooking techniques and recipes to be local.

Cuisines belong in a foodshed so long as they are the home cuisines of
people now living in that foodshed. On those terms, Vietnamese, Mexican,
and Ethiopian foods are (or are becoming) as local to my southern Minnesota bioregion as Swedish and German recipes, as are the Dakota and
Ojibwe foods that preceded *all* of us immigrants.

Such a definition of "local" is necessary unless advocates of sustainable
agriculture also want to become anti-immigrationists and ethnic purists. Some
versions of bioregionalism have been criticized precisely because they seem
to live right next door to such ethnocentrism. Their praise of the local, the
small, the self-contained can sound terrifying to people whose history includes being drummed out of small, local, and homogeneous communities.[16] Sometimes sustainable agriculturists can focus on the local in a way
that makes attention to the concerns of larger regions seem extrinsic and artificial—as simply holdovers from a global food network model. Such a narrow reading of "local" can make it look as if immigrant people, like alien
plants, are not welcome in a region. And some advocates of sustainability
argue for preserving ethnic diversity along the same lines as preserving biodiversity, namely because every culture is valuable and ought to flourish—

but in its own corner, where it belongs. Helena Norberg-Hodge, for example, writes that "Cultural diversity is as important as diversity in the natural world and, in fact, follows directly from it. Traditional cultures mirrored their particular environments, deriving their food, clothing, and shelter primarily from local resources. . . . The cuisines of different cultures still reflect local food sources, from the olive oil prevalent in Mediterranean cooking to the oatmeal and kippered herring on the Scotsman's breakfast table. Without retreating into cultural or economic isolationism, we can nourish *the traditions of our own region.*"[17]

Advocates of sustainable agriculture are well aware of one set of arguments concerning the potential provincialism of their philosophy—namely, arguments about the gossipy, inbred nature of small towns. They counter with arguments that show the richness of small-town life. However, their responses don't tend to address the heart of my concern, which has to do not with the smallness of small-town life so much as the tendency of small towns to exclude outsiders, perhaps most particularly racial and ethnic outsiders. Insofar as they talk about the challenges of promoting racial and ethnic heritage at all, they tend to talk about recognizing and valuing the peoples who have lived in a region for centuries—the indigenous ones.

I would agree that valorizing cultures that have learned well how to live in a region is necessary—but it is not sufficient in world full of migrants. Even if the indigenist versions of bioregionalism can make good arguments for why plants and animals should not be transplanted to regions other than the ones in which they originated, their arguments will not work when applied to people—indeed, they become deeply racist when so applied. An expanded bioregionalist vision must include a deep, well-integrated commitment to ethnic diversity—and must regard this diversity not simply as a thing to be "dealt with" but as a fundamental feature of the environment that is every bit as important to it as is the diversity of its plant life.

I think the foodshed as defined by Kloppenburg, Hendrickson, and Stevenson explicitly allows for this expanded vision. I want to participate in building a foodshed that is inherently antiracist and nonethnocentric, and is committed to promoting the growth of all human cultures within a given locale. We need to understand the local to comprise all the foods *and all the eaters* within a given region. This means that national and global issues are of necessity *also* local issues—and not only environmental issues, but social and political ones as well. In my own foodshed, the problems and concerns of migrant workers from Mexico—and thus also the problems of the Mexican economy—are of necessity local problems, because some of the members of my foodshed are Mexicans who are or were migrant farmworkers. Similarly, Somalia's struggles to rebuild its society become local problems here in south central Minnesota, as significant numbers of Somalis become my neighbors.

Cosmopolitanism begins at home in the contemporary world; the food-shed is of necessity both deeply local and deeply international. To under-stand oneself as a part of such a foodshed requires one to cultivate a deep understanding of the foods one grows, cooks, and eats. Where were these foods originally grown? Where else are they grown now? How have they been prepared and eaten? Can they be grown sustainably in this region? How do others in my bioregion prepare and eat them? (Can we swap recipes?) What significance do they have in my culture or in the culture of my neigh-bors? In the foodshed, questions about the ethnicities of foods are interwo-ven with all kinds of other more "soil-based" questions about foods. These cultural questions are no more important than questions about the growing conditions of a particular plant variety—but they are no less important either.

## Another Authenticity

I want to suggest—briefly—how the attention to context that I have been advocating might give rise to an alternative conception of authenticity, one that speaks to the desire for a connection to something real that has haunted this work. I'll define this form of authenticity as "foodshed fidelity."

The food adventurer seeking fidelity to the foodshed cooks and eats in ways that attempt to "meet the expectations of the foodshed" (to paraphrase Wes Jackson)[18] in all its facets—social, economic, ethical, and physical. Such fidelity can be an extensive pleasure—a source of the radical joy I discussed in chapter 10.

The adventurer's understanding of the scope and limits of her foodshed, as well as her understanding of what counts as meeting its expectations, emerge from (and are continually revised and deepened through) conversa-tions among foodshed inhabitants. Does my foodshed include cooperatively grown (though imported) coffee? Can a dish exhibit "foodshed fidelity" even if it tastes bad? Am I promoting or harming the social fabric of the foodshed if I refuse to eat at the neighborhood Mexican restaurant because its local Chicana owners say they can't afford to use local produce in their cooking? Disagreements will arise because members of the foodshed differently situated will regard different features of it as important, will define its expectations in ways that privilege different commitments—ethnic diversity, soil health, local self-sufficiency, community participation. There is no single, "correct" image of the foodshed, its relations and its expectations—there are many well-grounded understandings of it, and thus many ways to approach one's relationships to it. Indeed, conversation, even argument, about what the expectations of the foodshed are, and how best to reach them, may be among its most important resource and *is* absolutely necessary for its continued health. As John Dewey might observe, the good itself (by which, in this case, we mean the expectations of the foodshed) is not a fixed, immutable goal toward which we humans aim, but is itself under constant revision in light of new evidence, new understandings. Neither the goal nor the methods of attaining it are givens. They are achievements, the results of debate and discussion among members of the relevant community.

Foodshed fidelity rejects authenticity understood as lockstep devotion to the way They do it "over there," but that does not mean it dismisses the importance of attending to, cultivating, and even sometimes preserving (unchanged) different cuisines. In the foodshed, these concerns become topics of conversation, as members think and argue with each other about how to ensure the continued health of the ethnic diversity within the foodshed. Rather than a single answer to the question—namely, "do it exactly the way it's done in the country of origin"—there may be any number of answers because there are any number of ways that cultures and their cuisines will choose to enter into the foodshed, any number of ways they and others around them will define their flourishing in that foodshed.

Radical joy and extensive pleasure may not be everyday occurrences—in our current food system, they may barely be annual events—but they can serve as meaningful goals by which the adventurer can shape her relationships to food.

There's a connection between my concept of authenticity and what philosopher of music Peter Kivy has called "the other authenticity"—"personal authenticity."[19] Personal authenticity, which Kivy advocates, is fidelity to the performer's own best sense of what the (aesthetically) best performance of a work would be. The success of a performance will be judged by audiences, who will apply their own best sense of what a good performance of the work would sound like. The performer has an obligation—both aesthetic and moral, for Kivy—to try to realize their own best sense through her performance; the audience has a similar obligation to employ its best sense in judging it.

Although Kivy doesn't discuss the matter in *Authenticities,* he would no doubt agree that a performer's best sense of what makes for an aesthetically valuable performance is not something that she plucks out of the air at random, but rather something that emerges as a result of reasoned listening, playing, thinking, reading, and talking with knowledgeable others. We would expect the same of an audience member's sense—at least if we were planning to take her opinion seriously. This is not to say that performer and audience will always or even usually agree, or that there is no place for innovation in one's approach, but it is to say that deciding what counts as good is not an arbitrary act. It is rooted in a conversation—a long, deep conversation in which there is no unanimity, but in which there is frequent convergence. (Note also that it would be perfectly possible for a performer to turn out a personally authentic performance that an audience declared awful; personally authentic does not mean "good;" it means "faithful to what the performer takes to be good.")

In other words, personal authenticity is not really so much fidelity to one's private (read: utterly idiosyncratic) performance goals as it is fidelity to a set of goals that have emerged in a context of discussion and debate. Yes, these goals are still "unique" to an individual performer—if they are more than just a cookie-cutter replica of another performer, that is—but they are not sui generis.

If we understand Kivy's notion of the aesthetically good/great/worthy/worthwhile performance as an "extensive" concept in the sense Wendell Berry describes in chapter 10, then personal authenticity can also stand as a model for fidelity to the foodshed.

## Moving to the Foodshed

My first year in graduate school, I lived in a giant apartment building for graduate students at Northwestern University. My next-door neighbor there was a Thai woman who was working on her degree in linguistics. Every once in a while, she'd come over and ask me if I could read one of her papers, to check the English for grammatical errors. As a gesture of appreciation for my time, she would always make me a Thai dish to sample. One day she brought me a kind of custard of a dull orange color that she said was made from winter squash of a variety very familiar to me. It was delicious. It reminded me just a bit of pumpkin pie, but no, it was in fact quite different. I've thought about that dish (and tried to find a recipe for it) for more than fifteen years now. If only I'd thought to ask her for it then!

While I've longed for the recipe, it wasn't until I began working on this chapter that I really thought about my neighbor and her gifts of Thai food— ironic, given how often I've thought and written about Thai food in the last fifteen years. In giving my ethnic food autobiography, I'd always described my trip to the Thai Star cafe as my first exposure to Thai food. I think my memory lapse speaks volumes about the extent to which I continue to live my life in the global food system, a system in which the moral economy is subsidiary to the marketplace. Thinking about my relationship to Thai food through the cultural/agricultural medium of the foodshed caused me to tell a significantly different story about my eating history—a story that begins not with me as consumer, but with me as a neighbor, a colleague, and a fellow resident of the kind of state where nothing grows outside between October and April.

# Returning to the Garden

THREE YEARS AGO, I JOINED A GROUP OF LOCAL RESIDENTS TO CREATE A COMMUNITY garden in our small town. The "efficient cause" of this effort—the most immediate factor motivating it—was the recent arrival of a group of Somali families. They joined a small, very low-profile group of Latinos (mostly former migrant workers who decided to put down roots) and a few African-American, Asian and Latino professors' families to comprise the entire population of color in the town.

Local English-as-a-second-language (ESL) teachers and volunteers, casting about for ways to get these new residents involved in their community, hit upon the idea of a community garden. I think we had the idea that everyone who lives in Somalia lives in the country and thus knows how to farm; gardening would be a "natural" for them, and they'd be able to experience a lot of success with it, as opposed to their struggles with virtually all other things American. Furthermore, it would be an inexpensive project to launch, and people would (hopefully) have food at the end of it. Last, and perhaps most important, it would give new St. Peter residents and longer-term residents a pleasant field (literally) on which to engage with each other.

I was eager to be a part of a project that was actually using food to facilitate intercultural communication and connection. I saw it as another opportunity to put into action some of my theories about how to become anticolonialist food adventurers. Here was a way for our community to invest in our local foodshed while also investing in the lives of its residents.

The experiences of the first three years of gardening have been yet another series of lessons in the difficulties of actually engaging in sincere, effective anticolonialist and antiracist work. Viewed from one angle, the project has been an overwhelming success; I feel happy every time I visit the garden to check on my potato patch. The garden represents a wonderful cooperative effort among college, school district, county extension office and individual citizens—financed on a shoestring. The number of gardeners has increased significantly each year. Last year, one Somali man grew gorgeous watermelons, despite everyone's dire predictions of failure.

Switch the perspective just slightly, and the reviews are decidedly more mixed. The garden coordinating committee remains overwhelmingly white, despite well-intentioned efforts to make it otherwise, and the percentage of gardeners of color participating has actually dropped in the last year.

In its first year of existence, the garden got off to a late start. Planting took place on an impossibly hot, dry day in June. With donated land, plants, and seeds we recruited ten families to garden a tiny plot of land. All the families were Somali. They had some success with the garden (at least with the crops rabbits don't like), but it didn't exactly meet the goals of intercultural communication. Also, it turns out that a lot of the Somalis in St. Peter came from Mogadishu; they knew no more about gardening than the average apartment dweller in New York City. They were not necessarily excited to stand in the sweltering midwestern sun to tend a patch of vegetables they could buy for little more money at the local food warehouse.

The end of the growing season was perhaps its highlight; all of us who had been involved in the garden (meaning the white organizers and the Somali gardeners) shared a potluck lunch at one of the Somali gardeners' apartments. Everyone brought a dish from their own repertoire of "home cooking"—many with ingredients grown in the garden—and we shared recipes and compliments on each other's cooking. We talked over the year's successes and planned for the next year; the Somali gardeners were full of good ideas about what they'd like to grow next year, and what support they'd need. The white organizers vowed to work to make the committee more diverse—particularly racially.

The next year, an astounding number of people showed up on garden-planting day; we repeatedly ran out of plants, necessitating several return trips to the garden centers in town, and resulting in more than a few tense moments among gardeners worried they wouldn't get their fair share. That year, with more lead time, we'd prepared more thoughtfully. We'd spent time in ESL classes, interviewing the Somali women and Latinas who attend them about what vegetables they like to grow, and had tried to order the corresponding seeds. (It turns out that everyone seemed to gravitate toward a pretty familiar set of food crops—tomatoes, onions, garlic, peppers, beans.) We'd done extensive recruiting in locations where Euroamerican and Latino residents were more likely to notice it. The result was a garden both more ethnically and more botanically diverse. But whether that apparent diversity was resulting in much actual cultural interchange was unclear; were there more than a few scattered conversations among gardeners of different ethnicities? The garden committee struggled with what I think of as our "persistent whiteness"; recruiting efforts failed to turn up any Somali gardeners who were able to commit to being on the committee. Furthermore, our efforts to be multilingual had difficulty going beyond the barest minimum. A volunteer made us a lovely garden sign in English, Somali, and Spanish. But the monthly newsletter was printed only in English, as were the seed packets (they bore no pictures).

The year was summed up for me by the disastrous potluck that ended it. At the appointed hour, a tiny group of gardeners—all of us white, all of us members of the committee—met at the appointed place (an obscure building at the college, for which I'd provided no map). We met, ate our meager dinner (none of us had outdone ourselves in the food department—three of us brought bread, and one man brought candy coated pretzels), and went home. An hour later I received a panicked call from a colleague; he'd just come upon a group of Somali gardeners who had been sitting for hours in the student cafeteria, waiting for the potluck to begin. They'd brought the food—giant pans of delicious Somali specialties—but by then there was no one there to eat it. Somehow, the beautiful garden sign that said "welcome" in three languages seemed like a sham. How welcoming was the garden if its organizers didn't even make sure that people knew how to find its events? How intercultural was the effort if there were no Euroamericans present to sample the Somali women's dishes?

As I write this, the garden beds are mostly still in their early-summer stage of healthiness. We've managed to coax a few Latinos to garden—an accomplishment, since immigration worries force many of them to fly under the radar screen. White gardeners span a larger economic and generational distance than in the past. I regularly receive calls from community organizations, eager to donate time to the garden; volunteers just built a wheelchair-accessible garden bed. But the Somali gardening population is down. And it was a lot easier to find people interested in building the garden bed than it is to make sure that all the signs posted in the garden are trilingual.

But I have hopes. I hope that, with another year (and some grant money), we might come up with more creative ways to realize some of the potential of this growing space—agricultural, but more importantly, cultural. I hope next year that *ten* middle schoolers will sign up to be "Garden Buds," instead of one. I hope that more people will start talking to each other across racial lines about how to produce those big, beefy looking tomato plants or how to control those funny white bugs without pesticides. About the plants they grew back home—or the plants their grandmother grew back in her home—that just might survive this short, hot burst of summer we endure.

And I hope that everyone will get to the potluck at the same time.

# Notes

## Introduction

1. I have an overwhelming desire to put quotation marks around the word "ethnic" every time it appears in the text, to indicate that this term is inaccurate, presumptuous, and problematic in any number of other ways. But I know how annoying it gets to read words with quotation marks around them, so I will not do so. But I will hope that readers come to understand, through the course of reading this book, why I find the word troublesome, with its underlying assumptions that some foods are ethnic and some are not.

2. Sara Paretsky, in her 1985 book *Killing Orders* (New York: Ballantine, 1985), writes, "I stopped for a breakfast falafel sandwich at a storefront Lebanese restaurant. . . . The decimation of Lebanon was showing up in Chicago as a series of restaurants and little shops, just as the destruction of Vietnam had been visible here a decade earlier. If you never read the news but ate out a lot you should be able to tell who was getting beaten up around the world" (36).

3. On the term "third world," cultural theorist Trinh T. Minh-ha writes in *Woman Native Other: Writing Postcoloniality and Feminism* (Bloomington: Indiana University Press, 1989), "To survive, [it] must necessarily have negative *and* positive connotations: negative when viewed in a vertical ranking system—'underdeveloped' compared to over-industrialized, 'underprivileged' within the already Second sex—and positive when understood sociopolitically as a subversive, 'non-aligned' force. Whether 'Third World' sounds negative or positive also depends on *who* uses it. Coming from you Westerners, the word can hardly mean the same as when it comes from Us members of the Third World. Quite predictably, you/we who condemn it most are both we who buy in and they who deny any participation in the bourgeois mentality of the West" (97–98). I am uncomfortable with this term, but I have chosen to use it anyway—primarily because none of the alternatives is any better. I do not encase the term in quotation marks, but that doesn't mean that I take it to be unproblematic.

4. For an analysis of Burton's much-aided journey to the headwaters of the Nile, see Mary Louise Pratt, *Imperial Eyes: Travel Writing and Transculturation* (New York: Routledge, 1992). For an analysis of Schoolcraft's use of Ojibwe experts to locate the headwaters of the Mississippi, see Gerald Vizenor, *The People Named the Chippewa* (Minneapolis: University of Minnesota Press, 1984).

5. Paul Gauguin, *The Writings of a Savage: Paul Gauguin,* ed. Daniel Guerrin, trans. Eleanor Levieux (New York: Viking, 1978), 48.

6. For a detailed account of the modern Western food system, with attention to the colonialist relations it establishes between north and south, see David Goodman and Michael Redclift, *Refashioning Nature: Food, Ecology and Culture* (London: Routledge, 1991).

7. Marjorie Ireland, personal correspondence, June 28, 1991.

8. This is obviously a very truncated and simplified definition of cultural imperialism. For an interesting discussion of the complexity of this concept, see John Tomlinson, *Cultural Imperialism: A Critical Introduction* (Baltimore: Johns Hopkins University Press, 1991).

9. On the term "Middle East," Joanna Kadi has noted to me that the term "is problematic, as it gives power to a worldview of particular imperialists standing in a particular point and moving/colonizing toward a particular point. I use the term 'Arab world,' or 'Arab food.' This term is also somewhat problematic, as it excludes Turkey, Iran (Persia), and Israel [and, I would add, Greece]. But to me it's less problematic than 'Middle East.'" I appreciate this objection. I have chosen to continue to use the term, however, because it is the one that is used by the restaurants, cookbooks, and restaurant reviews I will be discussing.

10. For an excellent summary of the contributions made by the Indians of the Americas to the diet of the world, see Jack Weatherford, *Indian Givers: How the Indians of the Americas Transformed the World* (New York: Fawcett Columbine, 1988). See also Raymond Sokolov, *Why We Eat What We Eat: How the Encounter Between the New World and the Old Changed the Way Everyone on the Planet Eats* (New York: Summit, 1991).

11. Claudia Roden, *A Book of Middle Eastern Food* (New York: Vintage, 1974), 12.

12. Nicholas Thomas notes, in *Colonialism's Culture: Anthropology, Travel and Government* (Princeton, N.J.: Princeton University Press, 1994), that "Colonizers have . . . frequently been divided by strategic interests and differing visions of the civilizing mission. . . . Colonizing projects were . . . frequently split between assimilationist and segregationist ways of dealing with indigenous peoples; between impulses to define new lands as vacant spaces for European achievement, and a will to define, collect and map the cultures which already possessed them; and in the definition of colonizers' identities, which had to reconcile the civility and values of home with the raw novelty of sites of settlement" (2–3).

    What Thomas claims for colonialism in general I would also claim for cultural food colonialism in particular.

13. In *Reading National Geographic* (Chicago: University of Chicago Press, 1993), Catherine Lutz and Jane Collins identify "the melting-pot norm that sees immigrants as gradually shedding, perhaps over generations, their cultural veneers on the way to becoming simply modern people. We might say that Americans see themselves as no longer in possession of a culture but as holding on to history through their scientific advancements and their power to influence the evolutionary advance of other peoples to democracy and market economies" (109).

14. This view of culture contrasts sharply and interestingly with the view of culture that prevailed, e.g., in European and American anthropology until this century. Under this view, European culture *was* culture, the *only* culture. Other societies tended to be analyzed in terms of the degree to which they approached this "ideal."

    In contrast, for many contemporary white Christian-raised persons, "cultures" are what other people have. The particular productions of our people are simply the productions of humans as humans. At the same time, the earlier notion of culture prevails in such expressions as "being cultured," or "getting culture," where it is understood that "to be cultured" is to be enculturated in European culture.

15. Eaters for whom these "exotic" foods are a daily occurrence also may long to spice up their diets with the foods of Middle America. Abby Wilkerson related the story of her

friend Cayo, a Euroamerican who grew up in the Philippines. While Cayo had her pick of tropical fruits every morning, what she, too, longed for was cold cereal and milk. "When she did have the much-prized boxed cereal, she couldn't send in the box tops for prices because she was overseas! She had all the 'exotic' she wanted and . . . longed for American consumer normalcy" (personal correspondence).

16. Jane Stern and Michael Stern, *American Gourmet* (New York: Harper Collins, 1991), 64.

17. Joanna Kadi, *Thinking Class* (Boston: South End Press, 1996), 122.

18. National Restaurant Association, *Ethnic Cuisines: A Profile* (Washington, D.C.: National Restaurant Association, 1995), 56.

19. In this regard, Pierre Bourdieu writes, "Finally, the teachers, richer in cultural capital than in economic capital, and therefore inclined to ascetic consumption in all areas, pursue originality at the lowest economic cost and go in for exoticism (Italian, Chinese cooking etc.) and culinary populism (peasant dishes). They are thus almost consciously opposed to the (new) rich with their rich food, the buyers and sellers of *grosse bouffe*, the 'fat cats', gross in body and mind, who have the economic means to flaunt, with an arrogance perceived as 'vulgar', a life-style which remains very close to that of the working classes as regards economic and cultural consumption." See his *Distinction: A Social Critique of the Judgment of Taste,* trans. Richard Nice (Cambridge: Harvard University, 1984), 185.

20. Peg O'Connor has pointed out in conversation the interesting ways in which experimentation and danger intertwine, here and elsewhere in my account.

21. Books include Susan Bordo, *Unbearable Weight* (Berkeley and Los Angeles: University of California Press, 1993); Jeremy Iggers, *The Garden of Eating: Food, Sex, and the Hunger for Meaning* (New York: Basic Books, 1996); Carolyn Korsmeyer, *Making Sense of Taste* (Ithaca, N.Y.: Cornell University Press, 1999); and Elizabeth Telfer, *Food for Thought: Philosophy and Food* (New York: Routledge, 1996). Other important work in the philosophy of food includes that of Ray Boisvert, Glenn Kuehn, and Paul Thompson. The activities of Convivium: The Philosophy and Food Roundtable may be viewed at http://www.gustavus.edu/Groups/convivium.

22. For an earlier account of the relation between philosophy and food see Deane Curtin and Lisa Heldke, *Cooking, Eating, Thinking: Transformative Philosophies of Food* (Bloomington: Indiana University Press, 1992).

23. This has actually gone on even longer, if one considers turn-of-the-century writers Jane Addams and Charlotte Perkins Gilman. See, e.g., Jane Addams, *The Newer Ideals of Peace*, online at paradigm.soci.brocku.ca/lward/Addams/Addams__atoc.htm (accessed July 3, 2001); and Charlotte Perkins Gilman, *Women and Economics: A Study of the Economic Relations between Women and Men* (reprint, New York: Prometheus, 1994).

24. See, e.g., Bordo, *Unbearable Weight*; Hilde Bruch and Catherine Steiner-Adair, *The Golden Cage: The Enigma of Anorexia Nervosa* (Cambridge, Mass.: Harvard, 1978); and Kim Chernin, *The Obsession: Reflections on the Tyranny of Slenderness* (1984; reprint, New York: Harper Perennial, 1994).

25. On domestic science, see Laura Shapiro, *Perfection Salad: Women and Cooking at the Turn of the Century* (New York: Henry Holt, 1986); for women, food, and popular culture, see Sherrie A. Inness, ed., *Dinner Roles: American Women and Culinary Culture* (Iowa City: University of Iowa Press, 2001); Sherrie A. Inness, ed., *Pilaf, Pozole and Pad Thai* (Amherst: University of Massachusetts, 2001); and Sherrie A. Inness, ed., *Kitchen Culture*

*in America: Popular Representations of Food, Gender and Race* (Philadelphia: University of Pennsylvania, 2000); for medieval religious history, see Carol Walker Bynum, *Holy Feast and Holy Fast: The Religious Significance of Food to Medieval Women* (Berkeley and Los Angeles: University of California Press, 1988); and for the history of eating disorders, see Joan Jacobs Brumberg, *Fasting Girls: The Emergence of Anorexia Nervosa As a Modern Disease* (Cambridge, Mass.: Harvard University Press, 1988).

26. Ruth Frankenberg, *White Women, Race Matters: The Social Construction of Whiteness* (Minneapolis: University of Minnesota, 1993), 1, 6.

27. John Dewey and James Hayden Tufts, *Ethics*, vol. 7 of *John Dewey: The Later Works, 1925–1953* (Carbondale: Southern Illinois University Press, 1985), 169.

## Part One Introduction

1. It's true that when it comes to global immigration, the United States is often involved, even if indirectly. Because of this country's breathtakingly pervasive role in world politics and economics, it does often play some kind of role in the immigration and dislocation of populations from one country to another. Search back a few steps, and you may find the United States somehow involved in the journey that a Thai family made to Kenya. But such U.S. involvement is a contingent fact, not a necessary one; cultures can and do interact with each other independently of the United States all the time. My mental image is simply wrong in this regard.

2. John Dewey, "Outlines of a Critical Theory of Ethics," in vol. 3 of *John Dewey: The Early Works, 1882–1898* (Carbondale: Southern Illinois University Press, 1969), 247.

3. John Dewey and James Hayden Tufts, *Ethics*; vol. 7 of *John Dewey: The Later Works, 1925–1953* (Carbondale: Southern Illinois University Press, 1985), 173. Such a move, he argues, successfully undercuts the debates between "those who hold that motives are the only thing which count morally and those who hold that consequences are alone of moral import" (173)—in short, between those, following Immanuel Kant, who believe that we assess the moral worth of an action in terms of the intentions of an actor, and those who follow the utilitarians Jeremy Bentham and John Stuart Mill in making the results of our actions the only morally relevant thing. By calling character and conduct two faces of the same coin, Dewey shows the disagreement to be based on a spurious distinction.

4. John Dewey, "The Study of Ethics: A Syllabus," in vol. 4 of *John Dewey: The Early Works, 1882–1898* (Carbondale: Southern Illinois University Press, 1971), 242.

5. In Ira Shor and Paolo Freire, *A Pedagogy for Liberation: Dialogues on Transforming Education* (New York: Bergin and Garvey, 1987), 13. Dewey and Tufts also provide illuminating insight into the relation between the individual and the culture-wide when they write that "it is a fact that a vast network of relations surrounds the individual: indeed, 'surrounds' is too external a term, since every individual lives in the network as a part of it. The material of personal reflection and of choice comes to each of us from the customs, traditions, institutions, policies, and plans of these large collective wholes. They are the influences which form his character, evoke and confirm his attitudes, and affect at every turn the quality of his happiness and his aspirations"; (*Ethics*, 317–18).

6. Anthropologist Mary Weismantel, in *Food, Gender, and Poverty in the Ecuadorian Andes* (Philadelphia: University of Pennsylvania Press, 1998), points out that ideological con-

flict "is frequently not . . . the European battlefield with flags flying and lines clearly drawn, but a guerilla warfare taking place in the interstices of unimportant incidents." In particular, "The emergence of certain foodstuffs as topics of discussion, as rebukes, insults, punchlines, snubs, wishes, and 'somedays,' is the creation of an arena of conflict, but it is an arena dispersed into the atmosphere of everyday life" (17).

7. See Chandra Mohanty's essay "Under Western Eyes" in *Third World Women and the Politics of Feminism,* ed. Chandra Mohanty, Ann Russo and Lourdes Torres (Bloomington: Indiana University Press, 1991). Mohanty provides a description and analysis of the problems that result when one tries to create universal analytic categories, into which one then attempts to squeeze and wedge all the experiences of particular cultures. Mohanty discusses such universal terms as "woman" and "patriarchy", but her discussion could also extend to the term "colonialism".

As a way out of such universalizing, Mohanty does not demand an end to all generalizations, but rather argues that generalizations ought to emerge from careful analysis of concrete, specific contexts. I am attempting to follow her prescription, by focusing my account on contemporary Euroamerican food adventurers.

## Chapter 1

1. Claudia Roden, *A Book of Middle Eastern Food* (New York: Vintage, 1974), 19.

2. The story is considerably more complicated than this in any specific case. As anthropologist Richard Wilk points out in the case of Belize, class and racial divisions combined to dictate that poor, freed slaves ate lobsters because they were cheap and available; wealthy persons of European descent ate them because they were high-class food in Europe, and only middle-class people of European origin rejected them as "trash fish." See "Food and Nationalism: The Origins of 'Belizean Food'" (paper presented at the Conference on Food and Drink in Consumer Societies, Wilmington, Del., 1999), 5.

3. National Restaurant Association, *Ethnic Cuisines: A Profile* (Washington D.C.: National Restaurant Association, 1995), 52, 54; emphasis in the original; hereafter, page numbers cited parenthetically in the text.

4. Calvin Trillin, *American Fried,* 1974, reprinted in *The Tummy Trilogy* (New York: Noonday, 1994), 35.

5. Food adventurers probably do not usually create economic hardships with our questing; we don't, for example, probably close down many restaurants when we abandon them for new venues. When a food adventurer loses interest in a restaurant because it is no longer at the cutting edge, chances are good that his place is taken up by another eater who now feels comfortable patronizing it, because he has had enough exposure to the cuisine that it no longer feels completely alien. As one kind of food colonialist stops being interested in it, another kind starts.

6. Steve Ettlinger with Melanie Falick, *The Restaurant Lover's Companion* (Reading, Mass.: Addison-Wesley, 1995), xv.

7. Michael Gorra, "Questions of Travel: At Dusk, the Margins of Empire Blur. Enter the Travel-Writer," *Transition* 64 (1994): 63.

8. *Merriam-Webster's Collegiate Dictionary*, 10th ed., 407; hereafter, page numbers cited parenthetically in the text.

9. Are "American" foods like hamburgers "exotic" or "native"? Is Hopi tikki bread native or exotic? The Hopi have been making tikki bread on this continent for many more centuries than McDonalds has been manufacturing hamburgers, and yet I'm certain that Euroamericans would tend to define the former as the "exotic" foodstuff, the latter as the "native." Perhaps cuisines, like persons, can become "naturalized," so that they are no longer exotic—and perhaps the reverse is also true. This realization points us in the direction of meanings of exotic that take us beyond the notion of not-native.

10. Catherine Lutz and Jane Collins, *Reading National Geographic* (Chicago: University of Chicago Press, 1993), 89, 90.

11. Lutz and Collins make this same point in an anecdote about clothing and dance. They report the following conversation with a Westerner, about a photograph in the magazine:

    "They're just dancing, I mean, it's not any special kind of dance, they're just, like, having a party." [Interviewer: What makes you think it's not a special dance?] "Well, they would probably be more dressed in, you know—whatever native thing that they wear . . . you know, more the native wear that, you know, and they would be dancing with all makeup on and stuff like that."

    The young people were then doing "just" a dance, which is to say the unmarked, unremarkable Western style of dancing rather than a "special dance," presumably a more ritualized, non-Western, cultural dance. Here, "non-Western" clothing, as with all other markers of the exotic, stands for culture while the Western version of these things, the modern, stands outside of culture, representing the natural standard. (*Reading National Geographic,* 248)

    Note that the interview subject in this passage doesn't have any particular ideas about what to expect of this Other culture; he or she just "knows" that it should be something different from "ordinary" dancing and dressing—where ordinary is assumed to mean "the kind of dancing I would do."

12. For more on the problems with viewing colonized cultures as completely powerless in the face of Western forces, see Uma Narayan, *Dislocating Cultures: Identities, Traditions, and Third World Feminism* (New York: Routledge, 1997).

13. Graham Huggan, "The Postcolonial Exotic: Salman Rushdie and the Booker of Bookers," *Transition* 62 (1994): 26.

## Chapter 2

1. National Restaurant Association, *Ethnic Cuisines: A Profile* (Washington, D.C.: National Restaurant Association, 1995), 50; hereafter, page numbers cited parenthetically in the text.

2. Peter Kivy, *Authenticities: Philosophical Reflections on Musical Performance* (Ithaca, N.Y.: Cornell University Press, 1995), 1; hereafter, page numbers cited parenthetically in the text.

3. Uma Narayan uses the case of sati—the immolation of women on their husbands' funeral pyres—to explore the question of how expectations of both insiders and outsiders determine which aspects of a culture get coded as authentic. Uma Narayan, *Dislocating Cultures: Identities, Traditions, and Third World Feminism* (New York: Routledge, 1997), chapter 2.

4. John Urry understands the components of authenticity and difference in the reverse order. He argues that, at least in the case of tourism, tourists *seek* difference—that is the

goal of their tourism—and they believe they are most likely to find that difference in the authentic elements of another culture. See *The Tourist Gaze* (London: Sage, 1992),11.

5.  Vine Deloria quoted in Ward Churchill, *Indians R Us? Culture and Genocide in Native North America* (Monroe, Maine: Common Courage, 1994), 286, emphasis in the original.

6.  It bears noting that authenticity, conceived in terms of novelty, functions as a consumer good—something that can be purchased in a spirituality weekend, a meal, a compact disc, or a shirt. Virtually anything can *become* a consumer good or service in the present consumer climate. Authenticity is captured in these goods, and sold or exchanged.

7.  Jeffrey Steingarten, *The Man Who Ate Everything* (New York: Random House, 1997), 243; hereafter, page numbers cited parenthetically in the text.

8.  Djoko Wibisoni and David Wong, *The Food of Singapore: Authentic Recipes from the Manhattan of the East* (Singapore: Periplus, 1995), 25.

9.  In his article on the emergence of a Belizean national cuisine, Richard Wilk provides a useful taxonomy of the ways in which cuisines affect each other; they include mixing, substitution, wrapping, compression, and alternation. See "Food and Nationalism: The Origins of 'Belizean Food' " (paper presented at the Conference on Food and Drink in Consumer Societies, Wilmington Del., 1999), 7–8.

10. An essay by Audre Lorde famously declares in its title "The Master's Tools Will Never Dismantle the Master's House." In *This Bridge Called My Back: Writings by Radical Women of Color*, ed. Cherríe Moraga and Gloria Anzaldúa (New York: Kitchen Table/Women of Color, 1984).

11. Keith Floyd, *Far Flung Floyd: Keith Floyd's Guide to South-East Asian Food* (New York: Carol, 1994), 35.

12. Jennifer Brennan, *The Original Thai Cookbook* (New York: Perigee, 1981); hereafter, page numbers cited parenthetically in the text.) "If you think it odd that ketchup is used, believe me, it is authentic and used widely in Thailand today. It is even bottled locally" (103).

13. Mecke Nagel, personal correspondence with author.

14. Those who want to tell this tale can go at least one more round. Jeffrey Steingarten notes that while the word "ketchup" may well have either Malaysian or Chinese roots, "the history of a word is not the history of a dish. Ketchup is not a Chinese sauce of fermented fish brine, a sickly sweet soy from Java, or a British oyster juice. Everybody knows what ketchup is." It is a tomato sauce that has been made, in one form or another, at least since the early eighteenth century. Steingarten here introduces yet another wrinkle into the matter of authenticity, with his *Alice in Wonderland*-style distinction between a word and a thing. See *The Man Who Ate Everything*, 97–98.

15. The *Oxford English Dictionary* is among those sources. Uma Narayan notes the OED definition: "A preparation of meat, fish, fruit or vegetables, cooked with bruised spices and turmeric, and used as a relish with rice." Narayan, who speaks Tamil, notes that she "had the perfect postcolonial moment" when she "discovered" this word's origin; *Dislocating Cultures*, 164.

16. Madhur Jaffrey, *An Invitation to Indian Cooking* (New York: Vintage, 1973), 5; hereafter, page numbers cited parenthetically in the text.

17. *The Diner's Dictionary*, by John Ayto, provides a purportedly factual account that is actually quite similar to Jaffrey's; it too makes curry "essentially a British dish. . . . It became

popular in the eighteenth century with employees of the East India Company, who would vie with each other to see who could eat the fieriest one (still a test of machismo in some quarters)"; (Oxford: Oxford University Press, 1993), 107.

18. *Breakfast, Dinner and Tea: Viewed Classically, Poetically, and Practically* (New York: D. Appleton, 1859), 254–55.

19. Fannie Merritt Farmer, *The Boston Cooking-School Cookbook* (Boston: Little, Brown, 1896), 204.

20. R. A. P. Hare, *Tasty Dishes of India* (Bombay: D. B. Taraporevala, 1958), 91.

21. Heidi Haughy Cusick, *Soul and Spice: African Cooking in the Americas* (San Francisco: Chronicle), 53; hereafter, page numbers cited parenthetically in the text.

22. Narayan, *Dislocating Cultures,* 164.

23. Steve Ettlinger with Melanie Falick, *The Restaurant Lover's Companion* (Reading, Mass.: Addison-Wesley, 1995), 13.

24. She notes, for example, that "The Chinese, who insist on the freshest herbs and vegetables for all their own food, use some of the stalest curry powder for the curried dumplings they serve in Hong Kong's best tea rooms" (7).

What is interesting about this passage is the way in which she sets curried dumplings apart from the Chinese's "own foods." Implicitly, Jaffrey is suggesting that curried dumplings are Indian, and the fact that the Chinese do not treat her food with the same care they treat their own is a kind of cultural slight to her cuisine. But why are curried dumplings Indian and not Chinese? Jaffrey seems to want to both claim and reject curry.

25. Tami Hultman, eds., *The Africa News Cookbook: African Cooking for Western Kitchens* (New York: Viking, 1986), 45.

26. As anthropologist Wilk points out, diners from outside the culture may play an absolutely crucial, even definitive role in the way that a cuisine develops. He points to the example of Belize, which has developed a national cuisine only very recently. He identifies three separate versions and notes that "one version of national food was developed in America by Belizeans for Americans. Another was developed partially by Americans in Belize, for Belizeans. But a third version . . . [was] developed by Belizean and foreign entrepreneurs to feed tourists with a taste for something authentic and local"; "Food and Nationalism," 11. Wilk, for his part, makes no evaluative comments about the incredibly large role played by outsiders—tourists, Peace Corps workers, and others—in this evolution.

27. Trinh T. Minh-ha, *Woman Native Other: Writing Postcoloniality and Feminism* (Bloomington: Indiana University Press, 1989), 88; hereafter, page numbers cited parenthetically in the text. It is important to note that Trinh uses the word *postcoloniality* in the title of her book, and I believe, would characterize the relationship she describes in this passage as a postcolonial one. Thus, for example, her use of the notion of "difference," as opposed to some older, colonialist notion such as exoticism. Nevertheless, what she reveals in this passage is the ways in which the new, postcolonial regime is still based on power and domination—the power of (post)colonizers to define and appropriate the Other for their/our purposes. Thus, I think it is appropriate to use her work in the context of a project to examine a relationship I am still describing as colonialist.

28. Through the Other's acknowledgement and validation of us, we become authentic. Consider the related observation from John Berger's essay "Why Look at Animals?" in which he notes, "The pet completes [the owner], offering responses to aspects of his character

which would otherwise remain unconfirmed. He can be to his pet what he is not to any-body or anything else. Furthermore, the pet can be conditioned to react as though it, too, recognizes this. The pet offers its owner a mirror to a part that is otherwise never re-flected"; in Berger, *About Looking* (New York: Vintage, 1991), 14. The pet, in the owner's eyes, "authenticates" the owner, "completes" him.

29. For an exhaustive discussion of the way in which Europeans constructed the "Oriental," see Edward Said, *Orientalism* (New York: Vintage, 1978).


## Chapter 3

1. For most Euroamerican eaters to imagine what it would mean for our food to be injured by the practices of some other culture, we must turn to the arena of the health and safety of our food supply. There, we have very vivid ideas about the susceptibility of our food to the influences of others. Recall when U.S. inspectors found traces of cyanide in some grapes in a shipment from Chile. The response to Chilean fruit imports was immediate, and nearly hysterical.

   The fact that we have trouble thinking of harms to our food practices that are not health-related is no virtue, on my view, but represents the degraded relationship to food that many of us in the United States now experience. For more on this general relation-ship, see Jeremy Iggers, *The Garden of Eating: Food, Sex, and the Hunger for Meaning* (New York: Basic Books, 1996).

2. Ward Churchill, *Marxism and Native Americans* (Boston: South End Press, 1983), ii.

3. Edward Said, *Orientalism* (New York: Vintage, 1979), 7; hereafter, page numbers cited parenthetically in the text.

4. bell hooks, *Black Looks: Race and Representation* (Boston: South End Press, 1992), 26; hereafter, page numbers cited parenthetically in the text.

5. Dean MacCannell provides insight into this aspect of the colonizing attitude by way of an analysis of modernity. In his book *The Tourist: A New Theory of the Leisure Class* (New York: Schocken, 1976), MacCannell discusses the modern worldview in terms of the way it defines a distinction between modern and non-modern peoples, and points out that this distinction has been accorded tremendous significance in modern western cul-ture: "No other major social structural distinction . . . has received such massive rein-forcement as the ideological separation of the modern world from the nonmodern world. International treaties and doctrines dividing the world into multinational blocs serve to dramatize the distinction between the developed nations and the lesser ones which are not thought to be capable of independent self defense. Modern nations train development specialists. . . . The giving of this and other forms of international aid is a *sine qua non* of full modern status, as dependence on it is a primary indicator of a society trying to modernize itself" (8).

   Considered in terms of the present chapter, MacCannell's distinction highlights the way in which modern societies define nonmodern ones as those who *cannot* do for themselves. Implicit in the modern notion is that nonmodern societies cannot do so in principle; they aren't temporarily down on their luck, but backward, undeveloped or underdeveloped—perhaps genetically so. Indeed, racism plays a central role in modern societies' description of other societies as nonmodern.

6. Asian Women United of California, *Making Waves: An Anthology of Writings by and about Asian American Women* (Boston: Beacon Press, 1989), 17.

7. This belief is sometimes used by collectors as a justification for removing cultural artifacts from third world nations. See Gillette Griffin, "Collecting Pre-Columbian Art," in *The Ethics of Collecting Cultural Property: Whose Culture? Whose Property?* ed. Phyllis Mauch Messenger (Albuquerque: University of New Mexico Press, 1989). Peter Kivy makes a similar observation about authenticity in music when he notes that members of a particular epoch may not be in the best position to appreciate the music of that epoch. See *Authenticities: Philosophical Reflections on Musical Performance* (Ithaca, N.Y.: Cornell University Press, 1995), 151.

8. John Berger, "Why Look at Animals?" in *About Looking* (New York: Vintage, 1991), 16.

9. Thanks to Peg O'Connor for this observation.

10. John Thorne, with Matt Lewis Thorne, *Outlaw Cook* (New York: North Point Press, 1992), 152–53; hereafter, page numbers cited parenthetically in the text.

11. For a more bizarre example of this attitude, one in which nature plays the role of Other, consider the fugu fish fad. This fish is highly poisonous—unless prepared in a very specific, very difficult way. Diners in Japan, and (for a brief time) the United States would pay exorbitant sums of money to eat this fish—always running some risk that they would die as a result of it. Certainly part of what is at work in the minds of such diners is a desire to flirt with death. But I think the practice also manifests a desire to prove to nature that "she" can't hold out on us like this; we *can* outsmart her and eat this fish, despite the fact that nature has equipped it with deadly poison. Eating this potentially deadly fish is not something that is done simply because people are hungry and it was available, or even because the fish tastes particularly good. (It apparently doesn't.) It became a tremendously high-status thing to do *because* it was dangerous, *because* it was perceived as involving going where we don't belong. Defying a perceived threat from nature—ignoring an imagined "no trespassing" sign—gives the activity at least part of its cachet. (I'll explore the allure of danger more in part 2.)

12. Trinh T. Minh-ha, *Woman Native Other: Writing Postcoloniality and Feminism* (Bloomington: Indiana University Press, 1989), 89; hereafter, page numbers cited parenthetically in the text.

13. On a more positive note, many Middle Eastern restaurant operators also reported that their restaurants were visited by many Euroamerican diners, who felt solidarity with Arab Americans and Arabs, and who saw their own presence in public restaurants as one very visible way to show that solidarity.

## Part Two Introduction

1. Rena Diamond, "Become Spoiled Moroccan Royalty for the Evening: The Allure of Ethnic Eateries," *Bad Subjects* 19 (english-server.hss.cmu.edu/BS/19/default.htm), March 17, 1995; hereafter, page numbers cited parenthetically in the text.

2. Tim Zagat, forward to *The Restaurant Lover's Companion*, by Steve Ettlinger with Melanie Falick (Reading, Mass: Addison-Wesley, 1995), xi.

3. Paul Levy, *Out to Lunch* (New York: Harper and Row, 1986), 19; hereafter, page numbers cited parenthetically in the text.

4. Ali Behdad, *Belated Travelers: Orientalism in the Age of Colonial Dissolution* (Durham, N.C.: Duke University Press, 1994), 44; hereafter, page numbers cited parenthetically in the text.

5. The term "foodie" was coined, somewhat simultaneously, by Levy and Ann Barr—with whom he wrote *The Foodie Handbook*—and Gael Greene, who used it in *New York* magazine. See Ann Barr and Paul Levy, *The Foodie Handbook* (New York: Timber House, 1984), 11.

6. For an illuminating analysis of the aesthetics of taste—*literal* taste—see Carolyn Korsmeyer, *Making Sense of Taste* (Ithaca, N.Y.: Cornell University Press, 1999).

7. Eve Zibart, Muriel Stevens, and Terrell Vermont, *The Unofficial Guide to Ethnic Cuisine and Dining in America* (New York: Macmillan, 1995), 179; hereafter, page numbers cited parenthetically in the text.

8. Steve Ettlinger with Melanie Falick, *The Restaurant Lover's Companion* (Reading, Mass: Addison-Wesley, 1995), xix; hereafter, page numbers cited parenthetically in the text.

9. In the democratizing effort to get their readers involved in the knowledge-collecting process, Ettlinger and Falick are also actually behaving as good Cartesians. In his *Discourse on Method*, René Descartes notes that the task of completing scientific knowledge is a substantial one that he cannot accomplish on his own, and he encourages his readers to undertake experiments themselves, and report their results back to him.

10. Diamond, commenting on a review that suggests that a Vietnamese restaurant resembles a Vietnamese village, asks, "Would this alleged village be from before or after the war?" See "Become Spoiled," 4.

## Chapter 4

1. Ali Behdad, *Belated Travelers: Orientalism in the Age of Colonial Dissolution* (Durham, N.C.: Duke University Press, 1994), 47.

2. Relevant to this point, Jane and Michael Stern note that, while *Jean Brillat-Savarin,* the nineteenth-century author of *The Physiology of Taste*, preferred chicken to pheasant, "among most gourmets, pheasant became the ultimate symbol of epicureanism, mostly because it was game and therefore more scarce than any domestic fowl"; Jane Stern and Michael Stern, *American Gourmet* (New York: Harper Collins, 1991), 25.

3. Meat is not alone in this regard. Corrinne Bedecarré has noted to me that rare, exotic plants—or rare forms of plants—hold the same kind of allure: truffles, morels, fiddle-head ferns. She notes the irony of the fact that local folks with real knowledge of their area but not much money end up eating these same luxury foods that wealthy people eat in restaurants. A friend who grew up in central Florida told about being taken out to dinner at a very elegant restaurant in Miami for the first time. She was encouraged to try the hearts of palm salad, which she did, despite its outrageous price. When it arrived, she blurted out to the server and her dining companion, "But that's swamp cabbage!"—a food she regularly gathered with her grandfather.

4. See Carol Adams, *The Sexual Politics of Meat* (New York: Continuum, 1990); Nick Fiddes, *Meat: A Natural Symbol* (London: Routledge, 1992) and Marvin Harris, *Good to Eat: Riddles of Food and Culture* (New York: Simon and Schuster, 1985) for three different explorations of the meanings and roles of meat.

5. The contemporary illustrator Sue Coe's work well documents the brutal conditions under which workers and animals suffer and die. See *Dead Meat* (New York: Four Walls, Eight Windows, 1995).

6. Jane and Michael Stern point out that in the 1950s and '60s in the United States, a meat dish featuring lots of bones would have been described as "a real man-pleaser, presumably because men derive special pleasure from gnawing on bones"; *American Gourmet*, 28.

7. This might be a path by which people otherwise disinclined to vegetarianism could conceptually explore it. By reflecting on the qualities that make certain animals "inedible"— animals one cannot imagine eating—and by coming to recognize those qualities in the animals one routinely eats, one can begin to "defood" the animals in the latter category. One transforms them from something that is a food into something that is quite explicitly not a food the way that your pet cat isn't food. Of course the thought experiment might work in other direction just as well; someone might see the same qualities in the two groups of animals and decide on that basis that pets and zoo animals are also appropriate as food.

8. Spices are also hyperexotic, I think. This is due in part to their often very pronounced flavors and odors, but also to the history of the spice trade, a multistranded history of imperialism of glamorous tales of adventure.

9. Adams, *The Sexual Politics of Meat*, 91–94.

10. Adam Gopnik, "The Politics of Food: Is There a Crisis in French Cooking?" *New Yorker* (April 28/May 5, 1997), 158.

11. Mary Weismantel, using a semiotic analysis, notes that "the sign 'potato' [or, we might say, piece of meat] in a specific food system is largely defined by its position relative to the signs around it." Mary Weismantel, *Food, Gender, and Poverty in the Ecuadorian Andes* (Philadelphia: University of Pennsylvania Press, 1998), 15.

12. Paul Levy, *Out to Lunch* (New York: Harper and Row, 1986), 93; hereafter, page numbers cited parenthetically in the text.

13. Charles Koczka, "The Need for Enforcing Regulations on the International Art Trade," in *The Ethics of Collecting Cultural Property*, ed. Phyllis Mauch Messenger (Albuquerque: University of New Mexico Press, 1989), 190–91.

14. For a contrasting approach to the role of food writer (one also trained as a philosopher), see the work of Jeremy Iggers. Iggers regularly addresses ethical, social and political issues in his food reviews for the Minneapolis *Star Tribune*, and his book *The Garden of Eating* places questions of individual responsibility at its center. Jeremy Iggers, *The Garden of Eating: Food, Sex, and the Hunger for Meaning* (New York: Basic Books, 1996).

15. Rena Diamond, "Become Spoiled Moroccan Royalty for the Evening: The Allure of Ethnic Eateries, *Bad Subjects* 19 (englishserver.hss.cmu.edu/BS/19/default.html), March 17, 1995, 5.

16. Calvin Trillin, *The Tummy Trilogy* (New York: Noonday, 1994), x; hereafter; page numbers cited parenthetically in the text.

17. Jane Stern and Michael Stern, *Road Food* (1978) and *Good Food* (1983), reprinted as *Road Food and Good Food* (New York: Alfred A. Knopf, 1986).

18. Lucy Long, "Culinary Tourism: A Folkloristic Perspective on Eating and Otherness," *Southern Folklore* 55, no. 3 (1998): 193.

19. This discussion makes me think about how perplexing—and how permeable—is the border between ethnic food and regional food. How long will it be before the cuisines of

various Asian cultures come to have regional varieties in the United States, the way that we now have Tex-Mex food, or Creole food? We now recognize the category of Chinese-American food, but typically such food is regarded with disdain as simply being a watered-down version of "real" Cantonese food, whereas Tex-Mex and New Mexican foods have come to occupy a culinary niche of considerable cachet.

20. Trinh T. Minh-ha, *Woman Native Other: Writing Postcoloniality and Feminism* (Bloomington: Indiana University Press, 1989), 88; hereafter, page numbers cited parenthetically in the text.

21. I think of the fact that, at my own predominantly-white college, the African-American students often choose to dine together in the student cafeteria. White students regularly ask me, "Why do they always segregate themselves?" Resisting the urge to give the flippant answer ("Why do *you* always segregate yourselves? All the white students eat together, too!") my response often is that mealtime presents a time each day when those students can take a small break from the task of Representing Their Race, a task they are called upon to carry out in their classes, on the sports fields, and in their dorms.

    For a critique of the view that it is always the obligation of the racialized Other to educate mainstream culture about themselves, see Andre Lorde, "The Master's Tools Will Never Dismantle the Master's House," in *This Bridge Called My Back: Writings by Radical Women of Color,* ed. Cherríe Morggaand Gloria Anzaldúa (New York: Kitchen Table/Women of Color, 1984).

22. Christy Hohman-Caine, "Commentary: Part I," in Messenger, ed., *The Ethics of Collecting Cultural Property,* 89.

## Chapter 5

1. This is not the place for a full-blown critique of the definition of objectivity as neutrality. I would simply note here that the ideal of neutrality is both impossible and undesirable as a goal for objectivity. For a critique of such a notion of objectivity, and the development of an alternative model, see Lisa Heldke and Stephen Kellert, "Objectivity as Responsibility," *Metaphilosophy* 26, no. 4 (1995): 360–78.

2. Keith Floyd, *Far Flung Floyd: Keith Floyd's Guide to South-East Asian Food* (New York: Carol, 1994); hereafter, page numbers cited parenthetically in the text. I've cheated a bit in this chapter by including *Far Flung Floyd,* a work that is actually part cookbook as well as part food adventure tale, interspersing stories of his dining exploits with recipes for the foods he cooked while he traveled. His work illustrates some of the central ways the food aristocrat establishes and maintains a sharp, clear, hierarchical boundary between himself and the Other he consumes.

3. At least part of that "piece to the camera" was in fact shown on the television show—though what difference Floyd perceives between its being shown on television and his discussing it in print is not entirely clear to me. Furthermore, we must regard as disingenuous his suggestion that it is not in his power to decide whether or not this scene will survive the cutting room ("I hope to God. . . .") He has made it abundantly clear throughout the book that he is the final authority on matters concerning the show.

4. It is notable that Floyd reserves all his most virulent racism for the Chinese. In nearly every country he visits, he recounts an ugly encounter with someone of Chinese descent—an encounter that not infrequently brings him to release some anti-Chinese invective.

5. Jean-François Revel, *Culture and Cuisine* (1982), excerpted in *Cooking, Eating, Thinking,* ed. Deane Curtin and Lisa Heldke (Bloomington: Indiana University Press, 1992), 245, emphasis in the original; hereafter, page numbers cited parenthetically in the text.

6. Elsewhere, I suggest that Revel's argument here can be read as an attempted refutation of Plato's assertion, in the *Gorgias*, that cooking is a mere knack, unlike medicine, which is a genuine art. Revel responds to Plato's claim that cooking involves no genuine knowledge by asserting that the highest form of cooking is in fact organized according to a set of general principles. See my "Do You Really Know How to Cook?" *Philosophy Now* 31 (2001): 12–15.

7. International cooks are also, apparently, always men—"men who understand its basic principles . . . men who tirelessly seek to exploit these bases to create new dishes." Revel does admit there exists an intermediate cuisine, "bourgeois cuisine," of which women are capable. It developed as a result of the appearance of several cookbooks designed for the "housewife", which "nonetheless applied the fundamental methods of Grand Cuisine with regard to essential points." Bourgeois cuisine rests on the "know-how" of international cuisine and the "heritage" of regional. Revel, *Culture and Cuisine,* 245, 248.

8. Regarding developing the resources of a culture along lines dictated by the colonizer: Philosopher, leader of the Ghanaian independence movement, and first president of Ghana, Kwame Nkrumah quotes Jules Ferry, Premier of France, in an 1885 speech before the Chamber of Deputies:

   "The nations of Europe desire colonies for the following three purposes: (i) in order that they may have access to the raw materials of the colonies; (ii) in order to have markets for sale of the manufactured goods of the home country; and (iii) as a field for the investment of surplus capital." See Nkrumah, *Towards Colonial Freedom* (London: Heinemann, 1962), 3.

**Part Three Introduction**

1. Jennifer Brennan, *The Original Thai Cookbook* (New York: Perigee, 1981), 3, 4; hereafter, page numbers cited parenthetically in the text.

2. *The Compleat Cook: Expertly Prescribing the Most Ready Wayes, Whether Italian, Spanish or French, for Dressing of Flesh, and Fish, Ordering of Sauces, or Making of Pastry.* (London: Angel in Corn-hill, 1655).

3. In making this my focus, I will unfortunately ignore other very interesting, often disturbing aspects of these books: their tendency to regard all Americans as living in large cities with excellent grocers; to refer to all home cooks as women and all professional cooks as men; to hide the work done by servants (coffee is "served"—by an agent unspecified); to describe the diet in the country of which they write in a way that studiously avoids any references to hunger or malnutrition; and in fact to avoid all talk of politics whatsoever. Cookbooks, as a whole, tend to be strikingly apolitical. Exceptions exist; see, for example, Emily Hahn, *The Cooking of China* (New York: Time-Life, 1968); Claudia Roden, *A Book of Middle Eastern Food* (New York: Vintage, 1974); and Joan Rowland, *Good Food from the Near East: Five Hundred Favorite Recipes from Twelve Countries* (New York: M. Barrows, 1950). Hahn's work includes a discussion of the efforts to save Chinese cuisine that took place outside of China, when the cultural revolution in China

declared Chinese cuisine to be bourgeois. The anticommunist tone of this cookbook is very pronounced—at least in contrast to the blandly apolitical nature of most other works.

4. *Betty Crocker's Good and Easy Cookbook* (New York: Simon and Schuster, 1954).

## Chapter 6

1. The Lily Library collection at Indiana University counts several examples among its holdings. See New Yorking Suomaliaisten Naisten Osuuskoti, *Keittorkirja*. (Fitchburg, Mass.: Suomalaisen Sosialistinen Kustannusyhtiv, 1918); and Marie Rosicka, *Narodni Domaci Kucharka: Cesko-Amerika* (Omaha, Neb.: Narodni Tiskorna 1904).

2. Joan Nathan, *The Jewish Holiday Kitchen* (New York: Schocken, 1988).

3. John Thorne, with Matt Lewis Thorne, *Outlaw Cook* (New York: North Point Press, 1992), 342.

4. Exceptions to this include books like *Cooking Thai Food in American Kitchens*. The author, Malulee Pinsuvana, describes the work this way: "[This book] is written for the many Americans who have been to Thailand and still remember Thai food. It is written also for many Thais who are studying or living in the United States"; (Bangkok: Thai Watana Panic, 1992), "From the Author," unpaginated introduction; hereafter, page numbers cited parenthetically in the text). As might be expected, the book is written in both Thai and English, to accommodate both her audiences.

5. Madhur Jaffrey, *An Invitation to Indian Cooking* (New York: Vintage, 1973), 3; hereafter, page numbers cited parenthetically in the text.

6. Tariq Ansari, "Fed up of Punjabi Moghali," *Epicurious Forums: Thought for Food* (food4.epicurious.com/HyperNews/get/eating/320.html), July 18, 1997.

7. Ardashes H. Keoleian, *The Oriental Cookbook: Wholesome, Dainty and Economical Dishes of the Orient, Especially Adapted to American Tastes and Methods of Preparation* (New York: Sully and Kleinteich, 1913), 6.

8. Claudia Roden, *A Book of Middle Eastern Food* (New York: Vintage, 1974).

9. Keith Floyd, *Far Flung Floyd: Keith Floyd's Guide to South-East Asian Food* (New York: Carol, 1994); hereafter, page numbers cited parenthetically in the text.

10. Jennifer Brennan, *The Original Thai Cookbook* (New York: Perigee, 1981). Edward Said might have been describing such a cookbook writer when he wrote of Edward William Lane's 1836 book *An Account of the Manners and Customs of the Modern Egyptians*: "Lane [saw himself as] able to submerge himself amongst the natives, to live as they did, to conform to their habits, and 'to escape exciting, in strangers, any suspicion of . . . being a person who had no right to intrude among them.' Lest that imply Lane's having lost his objectivity, he goes on to say that he conformed only to the *words* (his italics) of the Koran, and that he was always aware of his difference from an essentially alien culture." For Said, "Lane's power was to have existed amongst them as a native speaker, as it were, and also as a secret writer. And what he wrote was intended as useful knowledge, not for them, but for Europe. . . . As narrator, Lane is both exhibit and exhibitor, winning two confidences at once, displaying two appetites for experience: the Oriental one for engaging companionship (or so it seems) and the Western one for authoritative, useful knowledge." Edward Said, *Orientalism* (New York: Vintage, 1979), 160.

11. Ann Barr and Paul Levy, *The Official Handbook: Be Modern—Worship Food* (New York: Timber House, 1984), 110.

12. Jessica B. Harris, foreword to *Soul and Spice: African Cooking in the Americas,* by Heidi Haughy Cusick (San Francisco: Chronicle Books, 1995), 8.

13. Mimi Ouei, *The Art of Chinese Cooking* (New York: Random House, 1960), ix; hereafter, page numbers cited parenthetically in the text.

14. Carmen Aboy Valldejuli, *Puerto Rican Cookery* (Gretna: Pelican, 1983), x; hereafter, page numbers cited parenthetically in the text.

15. Janet Richards and Charles Richards, *Classic Chinese and Japanese Cooking* (San Francisco: City Lights, 1958), 1.

16. In contrast, authors like Jeff Smith (the "Frugal Gourmet") and Sheila Lukins (coauthor of the Silver Palate cookbooks, and author of the *All Around the World Cookbook*), are regularly and roundly criticized for the shallow and trivial ways that they describe cuisines. In a market filled with English-language texts about many of the world's cuisines, their approaches seem absurdly cursory to the adventuring food colonizer. While their cookbooks do not present recipes so baldly "Americanized" as those in *Betty Crocker,* neither are they regarded as "authentic" by the critical food adventurer. A review of Lukins's book notes, among other things, that "it is a whirlwind tour on the order of 'If It's Tuesday This Must Be Belgium.' Or Tunisia. Or Jamaica. Or Thailand." The reviewer notes, charitably, that Lukins does not intend the book to be a "substitute for books by such authorities as Madhur Jaffrey [or] Paula Wolfert" but points out that the recipes are "personalized interpretations" in which "titles [sometimes] suggest a more authentic link to the country than the recipes deliver." Kathie Jenkins, "Sheila Lukins, on Her Own, Travels World for Cookbook," *Los Angeles Times,* May 12, 1994, sec. H, p. 9).

17. Peter Kivy carefully outlines several ways that the demands for various forms of musical authenticity come into conflict with each other. See, in particular, his discussion of the conflict between "historical authenticity" and "sensible authenticity" in his *Authenticities: Philosophical Reflections on Musical Performance* (Ithaca, N.Y.: Cornell University Press, 1995), 231.

18. I am also reminded of an article I recently saw about the nation's first all-organic restaurant, in Washington D.C. "All-organic" here means that the servers wear organic cotton clothing that is washed using organically produced soaps, among other things. After reading the article, I started wondering about the building; was it a new building? Were its materials all organically and sustainably produced? (I was also rather surprised to learn that the restaurant served meat—veal, no less.)

19. The idea that authenticity demands "exact" replication raises an interesting parallel between cookbooks and ethnographic films, as that genre has been described by Elliot Weinberger in "The Camera People," *Transition* 55 (1992): 24–54; Weinberger doesn't use the term *authenticity,* but he covers related ground with his use of the words "Reality" and "objectivity." He notes that ethnographic filmmakers "worship a terrifying deity known as Reality, whose eternal enemy is its evil twin, Art" (24). (For cooking, the evil twin might be "interpretation" or "adaptation.") He identifies Margaret Mead as the first to argue that, in "the field" the problem of objectivity can be solved by simply setting up a tape recorder in the midst of those one wants to document, and leaving it there indefinitely (38). The ethnographic filmmaker can enter "the field" unnoticed, and take away a

"true" picture of what "the people" are really like. All that is needed, the ethnographic filmmaker seems to suggest, is the right piece of (mirror-like) technology, and we can grasp "real life." Similarly, the cookbook writer I've just been describing seems to hold that strict replication counts, ipso facto, as authenticity.

20. Tami Hultman, ed., *The Africa News Cookbook: African Cooking for Western Kitchens* (New York: Viking, 1986), xiv; hereafter, page numbers cited parenthetically in the text.

21. David Spoerri, *Mythology and Meatballs: A Greek Island Diary Cookbook,* trans. Emmett Williams (Berkeley: Aris Books, 1982).

22. John Thorne, with Matt Lewis Thorne, *Outlaw Cook* (New York: North Point Press, 1992), 277.

## Chapter 7

1. Not all cookbooks are meant for cooking. Historical cookbooks are sometimes reprinted for their scholarly value. And other cookbooks may be *meant* for cooking, but may in fact be almost impossible for the ordinary cook to use in that manner because of the difficulty and complexity of the recipes; this is often true of the cookbooks of celebrity restaurant chefs.

2. Pearl Buck and Lyle Kenyon Engel, *Pearl Buck's Oriental Cookbook* (New York: Simon and Schuster, 1972); hereafter, page numbers cited parenthetically in the text.

3. Jennifer Brennan, *The Original Thai Cookbook* (New York: Perigee, 1981); hereafter, page numbers cited parenthetically in the text.

4. Keith Floyd, *Far Flung Floyd: Keith Floyd's Guide to South-East Asian Food* (New York: Carol, 1994); hereafter, page numbers cited parenthetically in the text.

5. Heidi Haughy Cusick, *Soul and Spice: African Cooking in the Americas* (San Francisco: Chronicle Books, 1995), 16.

6. Graham Huggan, "The Postcolonial Exotic: Salman Rushdie and the Booker of Bookers," *Transition* 62 (1994), 26.

7. There is something more than a little odd about the name of this cookbook. What does it mean for a Westerner to lay a claim to the "territory" of Thai food, by describing as "original" a book that records a culture not her own? The book jacket explains the meaning "original" is to have in this context; this is the first Thai cookbook published in English in the United States. This explanation tends to invite the conclusion that something comes into existence only when it does so in the United States.

8. As such, they might be candidate sites for engaging in what Maria Lugones has called "playful world travelling." See her "Playfulness, World-Travelling and Loving Perception," *Hypatia* 2, no. 2 (1987): 3–19.

9. N.A., *Cooking Hawaiian* (Dallas: International, 1979), 1; hereafter cited in text.

10. Yael Raviv, "The Hebrew Banana: Local Food and the Performance of National Identity," paper presented at the Association for the Study of Food and Society/Agriculture, Food and Human Values joint conference, New York University, 2000, 6.

11. Stuart Griffin, *Japanese Food and Cooking* (Rutland, Vt.: Charles E. Tuttle, 1959), xii; hereafter, page numbers cited parenthetically in the text.

12. Claudia Roden, *A Book of Middle Eastern Food* (New York: Vintage, 1974), 59, 46, 423; hereafter, page numbers cited parenthetically in the text.

13. George Mardikian, *Dinner at Omar Khayyam's* (New York: Viking, 1944).

14. Cora Rose Brown and Bob Brown, *Four-in-One Book of Continental Cookery* (London: Arco, 1956). A 1936 cookbook includes a different sort of example of an invitation to normalize an exotic ingredient—an example that contemporary readers will no doubt find quite amusing. In a vignette entitled "The Sauce that Mother Made (Anne Learns a Secret)," the Anglo Anne learns how to please her Italian husband Joe by putting garlic in her spaghetti sauce. For Anne, garlic is a smelly food, probably associated in her mind with an inferior grade of people. (A 1914 cookbook refers to the "lower class foreigners [who] eat it on bread, making a meal of dark bread, garlic and red wine. It is offensive to sensitive nostrils. . . ." See Clarence Edwards, *Bohemian San Francisco: Its Restaurants and Their Most Famous Recipes* [San Francisco: Paul Elder, 1914], 108–9.) But here she is, married to an Italian, and she must find a way to please his (and her own) taste buds with the flavors familiar to him from his childhood. Here, the cookbook author is not attempting to preserve the exoticism of this "exotic" ingredient, but rather is attempting to decriminalize it, to make it the sort of thing that clean-living women named Anne can eat without embarrassment, and can use to blend into their new families. This is quite a different challenge from the one that faces the food adventurer, I believe. Anne wants to become a part of a tradition. This cookbook, I think, was written for her—thus suggesting another category of insider-to-outsider cookbooks than those I've already mentioned. See Mary Carmen Riello, *Italian Cook Book Written in English* (New Haven, Conn., 1936).

15. Elizabeth Gili, Introduction to *Tia Victoria's Spanish Kitchen,* by Victoria Serra (South Brunswick, N.Y.: A. S. Barnes, 1963), 7.

16. They would most certainly shy away from *That Man in the Kitchen*, a 1946 cookbook that includes a chapter entitled "A Cook's World Tour," in which we are informed, in no uncertain terms, that "The Chinese cuisine is indeed weird and peculiar, involving the use of such things as birds' nests, sharks' fins, water lilies, sea weed, putrefied fish, smoked ducks, lotus seeds, preserved eggs, and soya bean sauces. These classical Chinese creations bear about the same relationship to our American type Chinese food as Mexican cookery bears to the Texas style *tamales* and *chili con carne*. Only experienced travelers should experiment with native Chinese cookery when visiting our Celestial friends of the Far East"; see Malcolm LaPrade, *That Man in the Kitchen: How to Teach a Woman to Cook* (Boston: Houghton Mifflin, 1946), 235. This text appears opposite a cartoon drawing of two ambiguous "natives" with bones through their noses and big, bushy hair, who are standing behind a huge iron pot, sizing up a nervous looking American anthropologist-type man with pith helmet and notebook.

17. Roana Schindler and Gene Schindler, *Hawaii Kai Cookbook* (New York: Hearthside, 1970), 12.

18. I cannot help but wonder how Floyd would respond to the battery cages in which most chickens raised in the U.S. spend their lives, or the feed lots in which many cattle are raised. I do not mean to condone the practice of keeping animals in small cages—and then killing them—but I find it more than a bit suspicious that Floyd's moral outrage emerges in this "exotic" context. It seems likely that the animals he saw caged in a restaurant spent little of their time there, whereas a cage is the only place most U.S. chickens ever live.

## Chapter 8

1. Mary Louise Pratt, *Imperial Eyes: Travel Writing and Transculturation* (New York: Routledge, 1992), 163.

2. Nor is there anything even slightly utopian about the ways in which many of these authors describe the people and cultures that are the subjects of their study. I encounter repeated references to the "dirtiness" of Mexicans and Chinese, the simplicity of Pacific Islanders, and other similar comments in a cookbook such as Clarence Edwards' Bohemian San Francisco: Its Restaurants and their Most Famous Recipes (San Francisco: Paul Elder, 1914). I hope I am not overly naive in believing that such baldly racist talk would have difficulty finding a publisher today.

3. Myra Waldo, The Art of South American Cookery (Garden City, N.Y.: Doubleday, 1961), 9.

4. Caroline Weiss, A Collection of Creole Recipes (New Orleans: Peerless, 1941), 5.

5. Freda DeKnight, A Date with a Dish: A Cook Book of American Negro Recipes (New York: Hermitage, 1948), xiii.

6. R. A. P. Hare, Tasty Dishes of India (Bombay: D. B. Taraporevala, 1958), 9.

7. Ann Barr and Paul Levy, The Official Foodie Handbook: Be Modern—Worship Food (New York: Timber House, 1984), 110; hereafter, page numbers cited parenthetically in the text.

8. Claudia Roden, A Book of Middle Eastern Food (New York: Vintage, 1974), unpaginated acknowledgments; hereafter, page numbers cited parenthetically in the text.

9. Paul Levy describes Elizabeth David as the inspiration for—and the original example of—a group of people he names "scholar cooks;" see Levy, Out to Lunch (New York: Harper and Row, 1986), 31. Among the scholar cooks, presumably, the anthropologist cooks are just one subspecies. Other scholar cooks include diplomat-turned-fish-specialist Alan Davidson, and Jane Grigson.

10. Madhur Jaffrey, An Invitation to Indian Cooking (New York: Vintage, 1973), 4.

11. John Thorne, with Matt Lewis Thorne, Outlaw Cook (New York: North Point Press, 1992), 323.

12. Lutz and Collins examine the similar ways that National Geographic transforms the individuals in its photographs into "types", nearly-interchangeable members of the group known as Other. See Catherine Lutz and Jane Collins, Reading National Geographic (Chicago: University of Chicago Press, 1993), esp. chapter 4.

13. Jack Kloppenburg Jr. and Daniel Lee Kleinman, "Seed Wars: Common Heritage, Private Property, and Political Strategy," Socialist Review 95 (1987): 28.

14. Not all recipes change; some foods are temperamental enough that cooks feel disinclined to change them for fear that they will fail. Not all cooks feel comfortable modifying recipes either. In my own family, my mother and I are much more likely to tinker with a recipe than are my two sisters. (Interestingly enough, both of them are trained as scientists.) For one philosophical discussion of the processes of recipe creation and exchange see my "Recipes for Theory Making" in Cooking, Eating, Thinking, ed. Deane Curtin and Lisa Heldke (Bloomington: Indiana University, 1991).

15. Anthropologist Mary Douglas is the first to have used the term "decipher" to characterize the process one might carry out to understand the "encoded messages" that food contains. Those messages, Douglas argues, are "about different degrees of hierarchy, inclusion and exclusion, boundaries and transactions across the boundaries"; Douglas, "Deciphering a Meal," in Food and Culture: A Reader, ed. Carole Counihan and Penny Van Esterik (New York: Routledge, 1997), 37.

16. Philosopher Otto Neurath constructed the following thought experiment: suppose sailors set to sea in a ship. While they were out to sea, they systematically had to replace

each plank in the ship, so that, when they returned home, not an original plank remained. Did they return in the same ship?

17. Such an interpretation isn't entirely beyond the realm of possibility, as is evidenced by the taco. As Andrew Smith points, out, "In Mexico, the word taco was a generic term like the English word sandwich. Mexican tacos are basically any food rolled, folded or fried into tortillas that are consumed by hand." "Re: Tacos" (<lgasfs@listproc.umbc.edu> via <owner-asfs@lisstproc.umbc.edu> July 25, 2001).

18. Joanna Kadi, *Thinking Class* (Boston: South End Press, 1996), 121.

19. Consult wysiwyg://38/http://www.brown.edu/Students/Brown__Hawaii\__Club/About__Hawaii/spam.htm for more Hawaiian Spam nuggets.

20. Jennifer Brennan, *The Original Thai Cookbook* (New York: Perigee, 1981); hereafter, page numbers cited parenthetically in the text.

21. Quoted in Aimée Cesaire, *Discourse on Colonialism,* trans. Joan Pinkham (New York: Monthly Review Press, 1972), 17.

22. Gerald Vizenor offers a similar description of the "discovery" of the headwaters of the Mississippi by Henry Schoolcraft. See Vizenor, *The People Named the Chippewa* (Minneapolis; University of Minnesota Press, 1984), 37–55.

23. On the emergence in the United States of cookery as a "science" governed by "rational" principles, see Laura Shapiro, *Perfection Salad: Women and Cooking at the Turn of the Century* (New York: Henry Holt, 1986).

24. Erna Fergusson, *Mexican Cookbook* (Santa Fe: Rydal, 1934), 3; hereafter cited in text.

25. Fergusson's comments draw attention to a tension between a certain kind of development and authenticity, similar to the tension between exoticism and authenticity I pointed out earlier. If recipes are rendered too scientifically accurate, they may cease to be "authentic" and lose much of their cultural capital. *The Africa News Cookbook: African Cooking for Western Kitchens* confronts this tension in the introduction: "If you're a person who wants instructions and exact measurements in a recipe, *The Africa News Cookbook* should be reassuring. . . . But cooking 'by the book' is not the African way. So we urge you to discover how easily these recipes can be shaped to your own preferences"; Tami Hultman, ed., *The Africa News Cookbook: African Cooking for Western Kitchens* (New York: Viking, 1986), xiii.

26. Jean-François Revel, *Culture and Cuisine* (1982), excerpted in *Cooking, Eating, Thinking,* ed. Deane Curtin and Lisa Heldke (Bloomington: Indiana University Press, 1992), 246.

27. This explanation makes particular sense if you agree with John Thorne's conception of the cookbook as "the original kitchen machine. . . . Recipes collapse the fullness of lived experience into a mechanical succession of steps that—once parsed small enough—can be followed by anyone. But the result—the made dish—is only a copy, a simulacrum, whose true meaning lies somewhere else"; Thorne, 342.

**Part Four Introduction**

1. Ward Churchill, *Indians R Us? Culture and Genocide in Native North America* (Monroe, Maine: Common Courage, 1994), 285.

2. Jane Stern and Michael Stern, *Road Food and Good Food* (New York: Alfred A. Knopf, 1986), 412.

## Chapter 9

1. See "The Baker's Apprentice" in John Thorne, with Matt Lewis Thorne, *Outlaw Cook* (New York: North Point Press, 1992).
2. Christopher Kimball, "From the Editor," *Cook's Illustrated,* March/April 1995, 3; hereafter, page numbers cited parenthetically in the text.
3. Weismantel points out that, in the Andean highlands, "the Spaniards came as conquerors, and the relations of domination established in the colonial period were represented by the stigmatizing of certain indigenous foods as 'Indian,' and hence unfit for consumption by non-Indians. This practice of denigration, evident in early sources . . . , is still very much a part of Andean life." Mary Weismantel, *Food, Gender, and Poverty in the Ecuadorian Andes* (Philadelphia: University of Pennsylvania Press, 1998), 9.
4. Yael Raviv, "The Hewbrew Banana: Local Food and the Performance of National Identity," paper presented at the Association for the Study of Food and Society/Agriculture, Food and Human Values Joint Conference, New York University, 2000, 8.
5. Krishnendu Ray, "Migrant Practices (Again)," online posting, Association for the Study of Food and Society, February 11, 2000.
6. Krishnendu Ray, "Migrant Food Practices," online posting, Association for the Study of Food and Society, February 10, 2000.
7. Arlene Voski Avakian, "Re: Migrant Practices (Again)" (<asfs@listproc.umbc.edu> via <owner-asfas@listproc.umbc.edu>), February 11, 2000).
8. Churchill's view of cultural exchange is also too stark in the way that it describes precontact Native nations as having had "homogeneous histories and traditions"; Churchill, *Indians R Us?* 285. Were there not exchange, trade, war among Native nations long before Europeans invaded these continents? Such preinvasion interaction points to the possibility of exchange that is not always or simply born of domination, *and* moves us away from the idea that pure cultures are a desirable and attainable goal.
9. For a discussion of the ways in which Native cultures shaped U.S. culture, and also cultures worldwide, see Jack Weatherford, *Indian Givers: How the Indians of the Americas Transformed the World* (New York: Fawcett Columbine, 1988).
10. Madhur Jaffrey, *An Invitation to Indian Cooking* (New York: Vintage, 1973), 11.
11. Aimé Cesaire, *Discourse on Colonialim,* trans. Joan Pinkham (New York: Monthly Review Press, 1972), 11.
12. bell hooks, *Black Looks: Race and Representation* (Boston: South End Press, 1992), 32; hereafter, page numbers cited parenthetically in the text.

## Chapter 10

1. Peg O'Connor, *Oppression and Responsibility: A Wittgensteinian Approach to Social Practices and Moral Theory* (University Park: Pennsylvania State University Press, 2002), 136.
2. See especially O'Connor's essay "Moving to New Boroughs: Transforming the World by Inventing Language Games" in her *Oppression and Responsibility.*
3. For a similar examination of motives, in this case motives for doing theory across cultural boundaries, see Maria Lugones and Elizabeth V. Spelman, "Have We Got a Theory For You! Feminist Theory, Cultural Imperialism and the Demand for 'The Woman's Voice,'" *Hypatia* 2, no. 2 (1987), especially 577 and 580–81.

4. John Dewey and James Hayden Tufts, *Ethics;* vol. 7 of *John Dewey: The Later Works, 1925–1953* (Carbondale: Southern Illinois University Press, 1985), 173.

5. Sandra Harding, *Whose Science? Whose Knowledge?* (Ithaca, N.Y.: Cornell University Press, 1991), 289.

6. I have used Harding's notion of traitorous identities to develop an alternative conception of objectivity, objectivity as responsibility. Recall that in chapter 4 I rejected the definition of objectivity as neutrality. Responsibility is here my alternative to neutrality. See Lisa Heldke and Stephen Kellert, "Objectivity As Responsibility," *Metaphilosophy* 26, no. 4 (1995): 360–78; and Lisa Heldke, "On Being a Responsible Traitor: A Primer," in *Daring to be Good: Essays in Feminist Ethico-Politics,* ed. Ann Ferguson and Bat-Ami Bar On (New York: Routledge, 1998).

7. For an articulation of this view and the problems with it, see Uma Narayan, *Dislocating Cultures: Identities, Traditions, and Third World Feminism* (New York: Routledge, 1997), chapter 4.

8. Clifford Geertz, quoted in Trinh T. Minh-ha, *Woman Native Other: Writing Postcoloniality and Feminism* (Bloomington: Indiana University Press, 1989), 88; hereafter, page numbers cited parenthetically in the text.

9. Jeff Smith, *The Frugal Gourmet Cooks Three Ancient Cuisines* (New York: Avon, 1989), 56; hereafter, page numbers cited parenthetically in the text.

10. Dolores Botafogo, *The Art of Brazilian Cookery: A Culinary Journey through Brazil* (Garden City, N.Y.: Doubleday, 1960), 25.

11. Lugones and Spelman suggest that it is only through friendship that such cross-cultural dialogue can genuinely emerge. Such friendships can grow in a restaurant, but surely it will be exceedingly difficult.

12. Maria Lugones speaks of the virtues of traveling to other "worlds" as a way to love across racial and cultural lines. She writes, "Through travelling to other people's 'worlds' we discover that there are 'worlds' in which those who are the victims of arrogant perception are really subjects, lively beings, resistors, constructors of visions even though in the mainstream construction they are animated only by the arrogant perceiver and are pliable, foldable, file-awayable, classifiable" (Maria Lugones "Playfulness, 'World'-Travelling and Loving Perception, *Hypatia,* 2, no. 2 [1987]), 18). I am suggesting something similar here, although Lugones speaks of travel to actually existent worlds, while I am thinking of worlds that may or may not presently exist.

13. bell hooks, *Black Looks: Race and Representation* (Boston: South End Press, 1992), 26; hereafter, page numbers cited parenthetically in the text.

14. I agree with hooks that cross-racial (and cross-cultural) encounters can only take place in a climate of mutual recognition of racism—which is why I chose the term "anticolonialism," rather than something like "multiculturalism", to characterize my food-adventuring aims. Barry Troyna characterizes the difference between the "anti" (in his case, "antiracist") and the "multi" positions thus: "A multicultural perspective prioritizes the inclusion and promotion of ethnic minority lifestyles and cultures. . . . The rationale for this approach derives from the assumption that it encourages white[s'] empathy with (and tolerance of) ethnic minority groups. . . . On the other hand, there has been the more recent emergence and gradual diffusion of antiracist concepts. . . . Here the concern is with white institutions rather than with black groups. That is to say, 'us' rather than

'them.' In this model we find . . . greater attention to structures which produce, sustain and legitimate values and practices which help to maintain racial inequality"; Troyna, quoted in Peter Erickson, "What Multiculturalism Means," *Transition* 55 (1992), 106.

15. "Ghenet," *Gourmet*, March 1999, 38.

16. Helen Mendes, *The African Heritage Cookbook* (New York: Macmillan, 1971), 11–17.

17. Howard Paige, *Aspects of Afro-American Cookery* (Southfield, Mich.: Aspects, n.d.), 9–13.

16. Vertamae Smart-Grosvener, *Vibration Cooking, or Travel Notes of a Geechee Girl* (New York: Ballantine, 1986), xviii. See also Anne E. Goldman, *Take My Word: Autobiographical Innovations of Ethnic American Working Women* (Berkeley and Los Angeles University of California Press, 1996), chapter 2, for a discussion of the African-American "culinary autobiography."

19. See Celestine Eustis, *Cooking in Old Creole Days: La Cuisine Creole a L'Usage des Petits Menages,* introduction by S. Weir Mitchell (New York: R. H. Russell, 1903), xiii; hereafter cited in text.

20. Caroline Weiss, *A Collection of Creole Recipes* (New Orleans: Peerless, 1941), 5.

21. Rick Bayless, with Deann Groen Bayless and JeanMarie Brownson, *Rick Bayless's Mexican Kitchen* (New York: Scribner's 1996), 14.

22. For an extended discussion of the relation between aesthetic and moral appreciation of food, see Lisa Heldke, "The (Extensive) Pleasures of Food," paper presented at the Building Bridges Conference, Carbondale, Ill., 2000.

23. Wendell Berry, "The Pleasures of Eating," in *Cooking, Eating, Thinking,* ed. Deane Curtin and Lisa Heldke (Bloomington: Indiana University Press, 1992), 378; hereafter, page numbers cited parenthetically in text.

24. Alix Kates Shulman, *Drinking the Rain* (New York: Penguin, 1996), 145.

25. Yvonne Dion-Buffalo and John Mohawk, quoted in Frederique Apffel-Marglin, "Development or Decolonization in the Andes?" (unpublished manuscript, 1994), 1.

26. Arturo Escobar similarly discusses alternatives *to* development, as opposed to alternative development—by which he means "a rejection of the entire paradigm." This is "a historical possibility already underway in innovative grassroots movements and experiments"; Escobar, "Imagining a Post-Development Era? Critical Thought, Development and Social Movements," *Social Text* 31/32 (1991): 27.

27. Apffel-Marglin, "Development," 2.

28. Mary Louise Pratt describes a similar approach to contact in *Imperial Eyes*: autoethnographic activity. Autoethnographic instances are those "in which colonized subjects undertake to represent themselves in ways that *engage with* the colonizer's own terms. If ethnographic texts are a means by which Europeans represent to themselves their (usually subjugated) others, autoethnographic texts are those the others construct in response to or in dialogue with those metropolitan representations." As an example of an autoethnographic activity, she points to the arpillera made by Peruvian women. Arpilleras are a "product of the contact zone" between indigenous people and Euroamerican colonizers. The arpillera maker takes the images of her culture, her landscape that are produced and presented to her as fact by outsiders, and recreates them so that they say something about her world as she sees it. "Is the *arpillera*-maker depicting the vertical archipelago as she knows it, or as she knows the agronomists knew it, or against the way she knows the agronomists knew it? Is she reproducing a Peruvian national myth? A

product of the contact zone, the *arpillera* perhaps makes . . . an autoethnographic gesture, transculturating elements of metropolitan discourses to create self-affirmations designed for reception in the metropolis. In such autoethnographic representations, subjugated subjects engage, and seek to engage, the metropolis's constructions of those it subjugates"; Pratt, *Imperial Eyes: Travel Writing and Transculturation* (New York: Routledge, 1992), 8, 142. On PRATEC terms, she digests that image and keeps what she needs of it. This example goes on to talk about the "return" direction as well—the direction in which the arpillera maker makes her own contribution to the dialogue, her own response to the west.

29. For the cake story, see Pico Iyer, *Video Night in Kathmandu* (New York: Alfred Knopf, 1988).

30. Similarly, George Yúdice points out the dangers of current multiculturalist tendencies to rewrite all cultural exchanges, no matter the circumstances under which they take place, as positive. See "We Are *Not* the World," *Social Text* 31/32 (1991): 203–216.

31. Apropos this point, Lugones offers a relevant distinction between two senses of play. "An agonistic sense of playfulness is one in which *competence* is supreme. You better know the rules of the game. In agonistic play there is risk, there is *uncertainty*, but the uncertainty is about who is going to win and who is going to lose." Alternatively, in the playfulness she advocates, "We may not have rules, and when we do have rules, *there are no rules that are to us sacred*. We are not worried about competence. We are not wedded to a particular way of doing things." Lugones, "Playfulness," 15, 16.

32. Being silly is a horrifying prospect for philosophers raised on A. J. Ayer, who dismissed all philosophical entities he did not believe in by saying that the statements describing them were not even false but *meaningless*—trifling, foolish.

33. Bob Sehlinger, "Etiquette Soup," in *Travelers' Tales: Food—A Taste of the Road*, ed. Richard Sterling (San Francisco: Travelers' Tales, 1996), 129; hereafter page numbers cited parenthetically in the text.

## Chapter 11

1. "PodPourri," *Chili Pepper*, March/April, 1995, 9.

2. I am indebted to Chris Atmore for the term "strategic authenticity."

3. Roden quoted in Ann Barr and Paul Levy, *The Official Foodie Handbook: Be Modern—Worship Food* (New York: Timber House, 1984), 112; hereafter, page numbers cited parenthetically in the text.

4. On a somewhat related note, Nicholas Thomas writes, "'Primitivist' idealizations are advanced . . . by some Aborigines and some Maori, and their evident strategic value in advancing the recognition of indigenous cultures clearly precludes any categorical rejection of the whole discourse"; Thomas, *Colonialism's Culture: Anthropology, Travel and Government* (Princeton, N.J.: Princeton University Press, 1994), 172. Likewise, calls for the preservation of an authentic cuisine might have strategic value for advancing the survival and recognition of that cuisine—strategic value that precludes our initial tendency to want to toss out the entire notion of authenticity as too deeply mired in colonialism itself.

5. Diana Brydan, quoted in Graham Huggan, "Postcolonialism and Its Discontents," *Transition* 62 (1993), 132.

6. bell hooks, *Black Looks: Race and Representation* (Boston: South End Press, 1992), 30.

7. Uma Narayan, *Dislocating Cultures: Identities, Traditions, and Third World Feminism* (New York: Routledge, 1997), 175.

8. Joanna Kadi, *Thinking Class* (Boston: South End Press, 1996), 124; hereafter, page numbers cited parenthetically in the text.

9. Vine Deloria, quoted in Ward Churchill, *Indians R Us? Culture and Genocide in Native North America* (Monroe, Maine: Common Courage, 1994), 94.

10. Jack Kloppenburg, John Hendrickson, and G. W. Stevenson, "Coming in to the Foodshed," *Agriculture and Human Values* 13, no. 3 (1996); 4; hereafter, page numbers cited parenthetically in the text.

11. Wendell Berry, "The Pleasures of Eating," in *Cooking, Eating, Thinking*, ed. Deane Curtin and Lisa Heldke (Bloomington: Indiana University Press, 1992), 375; hereafter, page numbers cited parenthetically in the text.

12. I use the formulation of the foodshed developed by Kloppenburg, Hendrickson, and Stevenson. They, in turn, point to Arthur Getz for their inspiration. See "Urban Foodsheds," *The Permaculture Activist* 24 (October 1991), 26–27.

13. Some cookbooks, in their exuberance to jump on the fresh/local/seasonal bandwagon, make pronouncements that leave sustainable agriculturists cringing and leave the rest of us wondering what those words even mean anymore. For example, while *Perla Meyer's Art of Seasonal Cooking* is filled with passages in which she reports things like "I am more interested in creating a robust onion and potato dish, a hearty ragout, or a custardy bread pudding than in celebrating the globality of fresh foods by serving asparagus or raspberries in winter," she follows them with passages in which she announces "happily, over the past few years, the winter kitchen has become increasingly varied due to the growing selection of cool weather vegetables—celery root, broccoli rape, fennel, Belgian endive, and other winter greens" (ed. Judy Knipe; New York: Simon and Schuster, 1991, 351), or reports that "the abundance of fresh fruits and vegetables that spans several seasons makes our lives as cooks and chefs more exciting and creative. I can't imagine a winter now without fennel, broccoli rape, or celery root, and when it comes to salads, even radicchio and frisee are almost commonplace. And how about fruits such as fresh figs, golden raspberries, fresh currants, and even sour cherries?" (12). On this definition of seasonality, if we can find it in our grocery stores, it must be in season!

14. Madhur Jaffrey, *An Invitation to Indian Cooking* (New York: Vintage, 1973), 147.

15. According to Kloppenburg et al., ". . . food in the United States travels an average of 1300 miles and changes hands half a dozen times before it is consumed" (2).

16. Thanks to Stephen Kellert for addressing this concern with me in conversation on numerous occasions.

17. Helena Norberg-Hodge, *Ancient Futures: Learning from Ladakh* (San Francisco: Sierra Club, 1991), 182–183, emphasis added.

18. Wes Jackson, *Meeting the Expectations of the Land: Essays in Sustainable Agriculture and Stewardship* (San Francisco: North Point Press, 1985).

19. Peter Kivy, *Authenticities: Philosophical Reflections on Musical Performance* (Ithaca, N.Y.: Cornell University Press, 1995), 7.

# Bibliography

Adams, Carol. *The Sexual Politics of Meat: A Feminist-Vegetarian Critical Theory.* New York: Continuum, 1990.

Addams, Jane. *The Newer Ideals of Peace.* Online at paradigm.soci.brocku.ca/lward/Addams/ Addams_atoc.htm. Accessed July 3, 2001. Originally published 1907.

Ansari, Tariq. "Fed up of Punjabi Moghali." *Epicurious Forums: Thought for Food.* Online at food4.epicurious.com/HyperNews/get/eating/320.html. July 18, 1997.

Apffel-Marglin, Frederique. "Development or Decolonization in the Andes?" Unpublished manuscript, 1994.

Asian Women United of California, ed. *Making Waves: An Anthology of Writings by and about Asian American Women.* Boston: Beacon Press, 1989.

Avakian, Arlene Voski. "Re: Migrant Practices (Again)." <asfs@listproc.umbc.edu> via <owner-asfs@listproc.umbc.edu> February 11, 2000.

Ayto, John. *The Diner's Dictionary.* Oxford: Oxford University Press, 1993.

Bailey, Alison. "Privilege: Expanding on Marilyn Frye's 'Oppression.'" *Journal of Social Philosophy* 29, no. 3 (1998): 4–119.

Barr, Ann and Paul Levy. *The Official Foodie Handbook: Be Modern—Worship Food.* New York: Timber House, 1984.

Bayless, Rick, with Deann Groen Bayless and JeanMarie Brownson. *Rick Bayless's Mexican Kitchen.* New York: Scribner's, 1996.

Behdad, Ali. *Belated Travelers: Orientalism in the Age of Colonial Dissolution.* Durham, N.C.: Duke University Press, 1994.

Belasco, Warren J. *Appetite for Change: How the Counterculture Took on the Food Industry 1966–88.* New York: Pantheon, 1989.

Bellin, Mildred Grosberg. *The Jewish Cookbook: According to the Jewish Dietary Laws.* New York: Bloch, 1941.

Berger, John. "Why Look at Animals?" In *About Looking.* New York: Vintage, 1991.

Berry, Wendell. "The Pleasures of Eating." In *Cooking, Eating, Thinking: Transformative Philosophies of Food,* ed. Deane Curtin and Lisa Heldke. Bloomington: Indiana University Press, 1992. Originally published in Berry, *Home Economics.* Berkeley: North Point Press, 1987.

*Betty Crocker's Good and Easy Cookbook.* New York: Simon and Schuster, 1954.

Boahen, A. Adu. *African Perspectives on Colonialism.* Baltimore: Johns Hopkins University Press, 1987.

Boisvert, Ray. "Food Transforms Philosophy," *The Maine Scholar* 14 (2001): 1–14.

———. "Philosophy Regains Its Senses," *Philosophy Now* 3 (2001): 9–11.

Bordo, Susan. *Unbearable Weight.* Berkeley and Los Angeles: University of California Press, 1993.

———. "Feminism, Postmodernism and Gender-Scepticism." In *Feminism/Postmodernism,* edited by Linda J. Nicholson. New York: Routledge, 1990.

Botafogo, Dolores. *The Art of Brazilian Cookery: A Culinary Journey through Brazil*. Garden City, N.Y.: Doubleday, 1960.

Bourdieu, Pierre. *Distinction: A Social Critique of the Judgment of Taste*. Trans. Richard Nice. Cambridge: Harvard University Press, 1984.

*Breakfast, Dinner and Tea: Viewed Classically, Poetically, and Practically*. New York: D. Appleton, 1859.

Brennan, Jennifer. *The Original Thai Cookbook*. New York: Perigee, 1981.

Brown, Cora Rose and Bob Brown. *Four-in-One Book of Continental Cookery*. London: Arco, 1956.

Bruch, Hilde and Catherine Steiner-Adair. *The Golden Cage: The Enigma of Anorexia Nervosa*. Cambridge, Mass., Harvard University Press, 1978.

Brumberg, Joan Jacobs. *Fasting Girls: The Emergence of Anorexia Nervosa as a Modern Disease*. Cambridge, Mass., Harvard University Press, 1988.

Bynum, Caroline Walker. *Holy Feast and Holy Fast: The Religious Significance of Food to Medieval Women*. Berkeley and Los Angeles: University of California Press, 1988.

Buck, Pearl and Lyle Kenyon Engel. *Pearl Buck's Oriental Cookbook*. New York: Simon and Schuster, 1972.

Césaire, Aimé. *Discourse on Colonialism*. Trans. by Joan Pinkham. New York: Monthly Review Press, 1972.

Chernin, Kim. *The Obsession: Reflections on the Tyranny of Slenderness*. 1981. Reprint, New York: Harper Perennial, 1994.

Churchill, Ward. *Fantasies of the Master Race: Literature, Cinema and the Colonization of American Indians*. Ed. M. Annette Jaimes. Monroe, Maine: Common Courage, 1992.

———. *Indians R Us? Culture and Genocide in Native North America*. Monroe, Maine: Common Courage, 1994.

———. *Marxism and Native Americans*. Boston: South End Press, 1983.

Clifford, James. *The Predicament of Culture: Twentieth-Century Ethnography, Literature, and Art*. Cambridge, Mass.: Harvard University Press, 1988.

Coe, Sue. *Dead Meat*. New York: Four Walls, Eight Windows, 1995.

Collins, Patricial Hill. *Black Feminist Thought*. New York: Routledge, 1990.

*The Compleat Cook: Expertly Prescribing the Most Ready Wayes, Whether Italian, Spanish or French, for Dressing of Flesh, and Fish, Ordering of Sauces, or Making of Pastry*. London: Angel in Corn-hill, 1655.

*Cooking Hawaiian Style*. Dallas: International, 1979.

Counihan, Carole and Penny Van Esterik. *Food and Culture: A Reader*. New York: Routledge, 1997.

Covington, Dennis. *Salvation on Sand Mountain: Snake Handling in Southern Appalachia*. New York: Penguin, 1996.

Curtin, Deane and Lisa Heldke, eds. *Cooking, Eating, Thinking: Transformative Philosophies of Food*. Bloomington: Indiana University Press, 1992.

Cusick, Heidi Haughy. *Soul and Spice: African Cooking in the Americas*. San Francisco: Chronicle, 1995.

David, Elizabeth. *A Book of Mediterranean Food*. London: John Lehman, 1950.

———. *French Country Cooking*. London: John Lehman, 1951.

DeKnight, Freda. *A Date With a Dish: A Cook Book of American Negro Recipes*. New York: Hermitage, 1948.

Deloria, Vine. *Custer Died for Your Sins: An Indian Manifesto.* 1969. Reprint, Oklahoma City: University of Oklahoma Press, 1988.

DeVault, Marjorie. *Feeding the Family: The Social Organization of Caring as Gendered Work.* Chicago: University of Chicago Press, 1991.

Dewey, John. "Outlines of a Critical Theory of Ethics." In vol. 3 of *John Dewey: The Early Works, 1882–1898.* Carbondale: Southern Illinois University Press, 1969.

———. *The Quest for Certainty: A Study of the Relation of Knowledge and Action.* Vol. 4 of *John Dewey: The Later Works, 1925–1953.* Carbondale: Southern Illinois University Press, 1984.

———. "The Study of Ethics: A Syllabus." In vol. 4 of *John Dewey: The Early Works, 1882–1898.* Carbondale: Southern Illinois University Press, 1971.

Dewey, John and James Hayden Tufts. *Ethics.* Vol. 7 of *John Dewey: The Later Works, 1925–1953.* Carbondale: Southern Illinois University Press, 1985.

Diamond, Rena. "Become Spoiled Moroccan Royalty for the Evening: The Allure of Ethnic Eateries." *Bad Subjects* 19. Online at english-server.hss.cmu.edu/BS/19/default.html. March 17, 1995.

Douglas, Mary. "Deciphering a Meal." In *Food and Culture: A Reader,* ed. Carol Counihan and Penny Van Esterik. New York: Routledge, 1997. Originally published in Mary Douglas, *Implicit Meanings: Selected Essays in Anthropology.* New York: Routledge, 1984.

Edwards, Clarence. *Bohemian San Francisco: Its Restaurants and Their Most Famous Recipes.* San Francisco: Paul Elder, 1914.

Erickson, Peter. "What Multiculturalism Means." *Transition* 55 (1992): 105–14.

Escobar, Arturo. "Imagining a Post-Development Era? Critical Thought, Development and Social Movements." *Social Text* 31/32 (1991): 20–56.

Ettlinger, Steve with Melanie Falick. *The Restaurant Lover's Companion.* Reading, Mass.: Addison-Wesley, 1995.

Eustis, Celestine. *Cooking in Old Creole Days: La Cuisine Creole a L'Usage des Petits Menages.* Introduction by S. Weir Mitchell. New York: R. H. Russell, 1903.

Fanon, Frantz. *Toward the African Revolution.* Trans. Haakon Chevalier. 1967. Reprint, New York: Monthly Review, 1980.

Farmer, Fannie Merritt. *The Boston Cooking-School Cookbook.* Boston: Little, Brown, 1896.

Fergusson, Erna. *Mexican Cookbook.* Santa Fe: Rydal, 1934.

Fiddes, Nick. *Meat: A Natural Symbol.* London: Routledge, 1992.

Finkelstein, Joanne. *Dining Out: A Sociology of Modern Manners.* New York: New York University, 1989.

Floyd, Keith. *Far Flung Floyd: Keith Floyd's Guide to South-East Asian Food.* New York: Carol, 1994.

Frankenberg, Ruth. *White Women, Race Matters: The Social Construction of Whiteness.* Minneapolis: University of Minnesota Press, 1993.

Freire, Paolo. *Pedagogy of the Oppressed.* 1973. Reprint, New York: Continuum, 1988.

Gauguin, Paul. *The Writings of A Savage: Paul Gauguin.* Ed. Daniel Guerin. Trans. Eleanor Levieux. New York: Viking, 1978.

Gendzier, Irene L. *Frantz Fanon: A Critical Study.* New York: Pantheon, 1973.

Getz, Arthur. "Urban Foodsheds." *The Permaculture Activist* 24 (October 1991), 26–27.

"Ghenet." *Gourmet,* March, 1999: 38.

Gili, Elizabeth. Introduction to *Tia Victoria's Spanish Kitchen,* by Victoria Serra. South Brunswick, N.Y.: A. S. Barnes, 1963.

Gilman, Charlotte Perkins. *Women and Economics: A Study of the Economic Relations between Women and Men*. 1898. Reprint, New York: Prometheus, 1994.

Goldman, Anne E. *Take My Word: Autobiographical Innovations of Ethnic American Working Women*. Berkeley and Los Angeles: University of California Press, 1996.

Goodman, David and Michael Redclift. *Refashioning Nature: Food, Ecology and Culture*. London: Routledge, 1991.

Goodwin, Andrew and Joe Gore. 1980. "World Beat and the Cultural Imperialism Debate." *Socialist Review* 20, no. 3 (1980): 63–80.

Gopnik, Adam. "The Politics of Food: Is There a Crisis in French Cooking?" *New Yorker*, April 28/May 5 1997, 150–61.

Gorra, Michael. "Questions of Travel: At Dusk, the Margins of Empire Blur. Enter the Travel-Writer." *Transition* 64 (1994): 53–67.

Grewel, Inderpal. *Home and Harem: Nation, Gender, Empire and the Cultures of Travel*. Durham, N.C.: Duke University Press, 1996.

Griffin, Gillette. "Collecting Pre-Columbian Art." In *The Ethics of Collecting Cultural Property: Whose Culture? Whose Property?* Ed. Phyllis Mauch Messenger. Albequerque: University of New Mexico Press, 1989.

Griffin, Stuart. *Japanese Food and Cooking*. Rutland, Vt.: Charles E. Tuttle, 1959.

Hafner, Dorinda. *A Taste of Africa: With over 100 Traditional African Recipes Adapted for the Modern Cook*. Berkeley: Ten Speed, 1994.

Hahn, Emily. *The Cooking of China*. Foods of the World Series. New York: Time-Life, 1968.

Harding, Sandra. *Whose Science? Whose Knowledge?* Ithaca, N.Y.: Cornell University Press, 1991.

Hare, R.A.P. *Tasty Dishes of India*. Bombay: D. B. Taraporevala Sons, 1958.

Harris, Jessica B. Foreword to *Soul and Spice: African Cooking in the Americas*, by Heidi Haughy Cusick. San Francisco: Chronicle, 1995.

Harris, Marvin. *Good to Eat: Riddles of Food and Culture*. New York: Simon and Schuster, 1985.

Heldke, Lisa. "Coresponsible Inquiry: Objectivity from Dewey to Feminist Epistemology." Ph.D. diss., Northwestern University, 1986.

———. "Do You Really Know How to Cook? A Discussion of Plato's Gorgias." *Philosophy Now*, 31 (2001), 12–15.

———. "The (Extensive) Pleasures of Eating: Or, Why Did This Meal Suddenly Become Less Delicious When I Found Out My Server Has No Health Insurance, the Cook Worked 90 Hours Last Week, and the Recipes Were Published in a Cookbook Whose Author Collected Them from the Women of South India, Whom She Fails to Credit Even in Her Acknowledgments?" Keynote address at Building Bridges: A Graduate Student Conference. Southern Illinois University, Carbondale Ill., 2000.

———. "On Being a Responsible Traitor: A Primer." In *Daring to be Good: Essays in Feminist Ethico-Politics*. Ed. Ann Ferguson and Bat-Ami Bar On. New York: Routledge, 1998.

———. "Recipes for Theory Making." 1989. In *Cooking, Eating, Thinking: Transformative Philosophies of Food*, ed. Deane Curtin and Lisa Heldke. Bloomington: Indiana University Press, 1992. Originally published in *Hypatia* 3, no. 2 (1988): 15–30.

Heldke, Lisa and Stephen Kellert. "Objectivity as Responsibility." *Metaphilosophy* 26, no. 4 (1995): 360–78.

Hillerman, Tony. *A Thief of Time*. New York: Harper Collins, 1988.

Hohman-Caine, Christy. "Commentary: Part I." In *The Ethics of Collecting Cultural Property: Whose Culture? Whose Property?* Ed. Phyllis Mauch Messenger. Albuquerque: University of New Mexico Press, 1989.

hooks, bell. *Black Looks: Race and Representation*. Boston: South End, 1992.

———. *Talking Back: Thinking Feminist, Thinking Black*. Boston: South End, 1989.

Huggan, Graham. "The Postcolonial Exotic: Salman Rushdie and the Booker of Bookers." *Transition* 64 (1994): 22–29.

———. "Postcolonialism and Its Discontents." *Transition* 62 (1993): 130–35.

Hultman, Tami, eds. *The Africa News Cookbook: African Cooking for Western Kitchens*. New York: Viking, 1986.

Iggers, Jeremy. *The Garden of Eating: Food, Sex, and the Hunger for Meaning*. New York: Basic Books, 1996.

Inness, Sherrie, A., ed. *Dinner Roles: American Women and Culinary Culture*. Iowa City: University of Iowa Press, 2001.

———, ed. *Kitchen Culture in America: Popular Representations of Food, Gender and Race*. Philadelphia: University of Pennsylvania Press, 2000.

———, ed. *Pilaf, Pozole and Pad Thai: American Women and Ethnic Food*. Amherst: University of Massachusetts, 2001.

Ireland, Marjorie. Personal correspondence with Jeremy Iggers, Minneapolis *Star Tribune,* June 28, 1991.

Iyer, Pico. *Video Night in Kathmandu*. New York: Alfred A. Knopf, 1988.

Jenkins, Kathie. "Sheila Lukins, On her Own, Travels World for Cookbook." *Los Angeles Times,* May 12, 1994, sec. H, p. 9.

Jackson, Wes. *Meeting the Expectations of the Land: Essays in Sustainable Agriculture and Stewardship*. San Francisco: North Point Press, 1985.

Jaffrey, Madhur. *The Flavors of India*. New York: Carol Southern, 1995.

———. *An Invitation to Indian Cooking*. New York: Vintage, 1973.

———. *Worlds-of-the-East Vegetarian Cooking*. New York: Alfred A. Knopf, 1988.

Kadi, Joanna. *Thinking Class*. Boston: South End Press, 1996.

———, ed. *Food for our Grandmothers: Writings by Arab-American and Arab-Canadian Feminists*. Boston: South End Press, 1994.

Kappeler, Susanne. "Why Look at Women?" In *The Pornography of Representation*. Minneapolis: University of Minnesota Press, 1986.

Keoleian, Ardashes H. *The Oriental Cook Book: Wholesome, Dainty and Economical Dishes of the Orient, Especially Adapted to American Tastes and Methods of Preparation*. New York: Sully and Kleinteich, 1913.

Kimball, Christopher. "From The Editor." *Cook's Illustrated*, March/April 1995, 3.

Kivy, Peter. *Authenticities: Philosophical Reflections on Musical Performance*. Ithaca, N.Y.: Cornell University Press, 1995.

Kloppenburg, Jack Jr. "No Hunting! Scientific Poaching and Global Biodiversity." *Z Magazine*, September 1990, 104–8.

Kloppenburg, Jack Jr., John Hendrickson, and G. W. Stevenson. "Coming in to the Foodshed." *Agriculture and Human Values* 13, no. 3 (1996): 1–10.

Kloppenburg, Jack Jr. and Daniel Lee Kleinman. "Seed Wars: Common Heritage, Private Property, and Political Strategy." *Socialist Review* 95 (1987): 7–41.

Klug, John. "Benihana of Tokyo." HBS case 9-673-057, *Harvard Business Review*, 1972, 1–16.

Koczka, Charles. "The Need for Enforcing Regulations on the International Art Trade." In *The Ethics of Collecting Cultural Property: Whose Culture? Whose Property?* ed. Phyllis Mauch Messenger. Albuquerque: University of New Mexico Press, 1989.

Korsmeyer, Carolyn. *Making Sense of Taste: Food and Philosophy.* Ithaca, N.Y.: Cornell University Press, 1999.

Kuehn, Glenn. "Tasting the World: An Aesthetic of Food." Ph.D. diss., Southern Illinois University at Carbondale, 2001.

Lamm, Nomy. "It's a Big Fat Revolution." In *Listen Up: Voices from the Next Feminist Generation.* Ed. Barbara Findlen. Seattle: Seal, 1995.

LaPrade, Malcolm. *That Man in the Kitchen: How to Teach a Woman to Cook.* Boston: Houghton Mifflin, 1946.

Levy, Paul. *Out to Lunch.* New York: Harper and Row, 1986.

Long, Lucy. "Culinary Tourism: A Folkloristic Perspective on Eating and Otherness." *Southern Folklore* 55, no. 3 (1998): 181–204.

Lorde, Audre. "The Master's Tools Will Never Dismantle the Master's House." In *This Bridge Called My Back: Writings by Radical Women of Color,* ed. Cherríe Moraga and Gloria Anzaldúa. New York: Kitchen Table/Women of Color, 1984.

Lugones, Maria. "Playfulness, 'World'-Travelling, and Loving Perception." *Hypatia* 2, no. 2 (1987): 3–19.

Lugones, Maria and Elizabeth V. Spelman. 1983. "Have We Got a Theory for You! Feminist Theory, Cultural Imperialism and the Demand for 'The Woman's Voice.'" *Women's Studies International Forum* 6, no. 6 (1983): 573–81.

Lutz, Catherine A. and Jane L. Collins. *Reading National Geographic.* Chicago: University of Chicago Press, 1993.

MacCannell, Dean. *The Tourist: A New Theory of the Leisure Class.* New York: Schocken, 1976.

Mardikian, George. *Dinner at Omar Khayyam's.* New York: Viking, 1944.

McClary, Susan. *Feminine Endings: Music, Gender, and Sexuality.* Minneapolis: University of Minnesota Press, 1991.

———. "Terminal Prestige: The Case of Avant-Garde Music Composition." *Cultural Critique* 12 (1989): 57–81.

McIntosh, Peggy. "White Privilege and Male Privilege: A Personal Account of Coming to See Correspondences Through Work in Women's Studies." Wellesley, Mass.: Wellesley Center for Research on Women Publication 189 (1988).

Medaris, Angela Shelf. *The African-American Kitchen: Cooking from Our Heritage.* New York: Dutton, 1994.

Mehta, Gita. *Karma Cola: Marketing the Mystic East.* New York: Fawcett Columbine, 1979.

Memmi, Albert. *The Colonizer and the Colonized.* Translated by Howard Greenfield. New York: Orion, 1965.

Mendes, Helen. *The African Heritage Cookbook.* New York: Macmillan, 1971.

Messenger, Phyllis Mauch, ed. *The Ethics of Collecting Cultural Property: Whose Culture? Whose Property?* Albuquerque: University of New Mexico Press, 1989.

Meyer, Perla. *Perla Meyer's Art of Seasonal Cookery.* Ed. Judy Knipe. New York: Simon and Schuster, 1991.

Mohanty, Chandra. "Under Western Eyes." In *Third World Women and the Politics of Feminism*, ed. Chandra Mohanty, Ann Russo, and Lourdes Torres. Bloomington: Indiana University Press, 1991.

Moosewood Collective. *Sundays at Moosewood Restaurant*. New York: Simon and Schuster, 1990.

Mowat, Farley. *People of the Deer*. Rev. Ed., 1975. Reprint, Toronto: McClelland and Stewart, 1980.

Munro, J. Richard. "Good-Bye to Hollywood: Cultural Imperialism and the New Protectionism." *Vital Speeches of the Day* 56, no. 17 (1990), 524–27.

Nagel, Mecke. Personal correspondence with the author, April 8, 1999.

Narayan, Uma. *Dislocating Cultures: Identities, Traditions, and Third World Feminism*. New York: Routledge, 1997.

Nathan, Joan. *The Jewish Holiday Kitchen*. New York: Schocken, 1988.

National Restaurant Association. *Ethnic Cuisines: A Profile*. Washington, D.C.: National Restaurant Association, 1995.

New Yorkin Suomalaisten Naisten Osuuskoti. *Keittokirja*. Fitchburg, Mass.: Suomalaisen Sosialistinen Kustannusyhtiv, 1918.

Nkrumah, Kwame. *Consciencism*. New York: Monthly Review Press, 1970.

———. *Neocolonialism: The Last Stage of Imperialism*. New York: International, 1965.

———. *Towards Colonial Freedom*. London: Heinemann, 1962.

Norberg-Hodge, Helena. *Ancient Futures: Learning from Ladakh*. San Francisco: Sierra Club, 1991.

O'Connor, Peg. *Oppression and Responsibility: A Wittgensteinian Approach to Social Practices and Moral Theory*. University Park: Pennsylvania State University Press, 2002.

Ouei, Mimie. *The Art of Chinese Cooking*. New York: Random House, 1960.

Paige, Howard. *Aspects of Afro-American Cookery*. Southfield, Mich.: Aspects, n.d.

Parasecoli, Fabio. "Post-Revolutionary Chowhounds: Pleasure, Food and the Italian Left." Paper presented at the Association for the Study of Food and Society/Agriculture, Food and Human Values Joint Conference. New York University, New York, 2000.

Paretsky, Sara. *Killing Orders*. New York: Ballantine, 1985.

Perrault, Jeanne. "White Feminist Guilt, Abject Scripts, and (Other) Transformative Necessities." *West Coast Line* 13/14 (1994): 226–38.

Pinsuvana, Malulee. *Cooking Thai Food in American Kitchens*. Bangkok: Thai Watana Panich, 1992.

"PodPourri." *Chili Pepper*, March/April, 1995, 9.

Pratt, Mary Louise. *Imperial Eyes: Travel Writing and Transculturation*. New York: Routledge, 1992.

Rauber, Paul. "Conservation á la Carte." *Sierra*, November/December 1994, 42–49, 95–97.

Raviv, Yael. "The Hebrew Banana: Local Food and the Performance of National Identity." Paper presented at the Association for the Study of Food and Society/Agriculture, Food and Human Values Joint Conference. New York University, New York, 2000.

Ray, Krishnedu. "'The East is East and the Yeast is West': Food and the Migrant Imagery of Place." Paper presented at the Association for the Study of Food and Society/Agriculture, Food and Human Values Joint Conference. New York University, New York, 2000.

———. "Migrant Food Practices." <asfs@listproc.umbc.edu> via <owner-asfs@listproc.umbc.edu> February 10, 2000.

————. "Migrant Food Practices (Again)." <asfs@listproc.umbc.edu> via <owner-asfs @listproc.umbc.edu> February 11, 2000.

Revel, Jean François. *Culture and Cuisine: A Journey Through the History of Food.* Trans. Helen R. Lane. Excerpted in *Cooking, Eating, Thinking: Transformative Philosophies of Food,* ed. Deane Curtin and Lisa Heldke. Bloomington: Indiana University Press, 1992. Originally published New York: Doubleday, 1982.

Richards, Janet and Charles Richards. *Classic Chinese and Japanese Cooking.* San Francisco: City Lights, 1958.

Riello, Mary Carmen. *Italian Cook Book Written in English.* New Haven, Conn.: n.p., 1936.

Roden, Claudia. *A Book of Middle Eastern Food.* New York: Vintage, 1974.

Romer, Elizabeth. *The Tuscan Year.* Berkeley: North Point Press, 1994.

Rosaldo, Renato. *Culture and Truth.* Boston: Beacon Press, 1989.

Rosicka, Marie. *Narodni Domaci Kucharka: Cesko-Amerika.* Omaha, Neb.: Narodni Tiskorna, 1904.

Rowland, Joan. *Good Food from the Near East: Five Hundred Favorite Recipes from Twelve Countries.* New York: M. Barrows, 1950.

Ruch, E. A. and K. C. Anyanwu. *African Philosophy: An Introduction to the Main Philosophical Trends in Contemporary Africa.* Rome: Catholic Book Agency, 1981.

Said, Edward. *Culture and Imperialism.* New York: Alfred A. Knopf, 1993.

————. *Orientalism.* New York: Vintage, 1979.

Scheman, Naomi. "Queering the Center by Centering the Queer: Reflections on Transsexuals and Secular Jews." in *Feminists Rethink the Self,* ed. Diana Tietjens Meyers. Boulder, Colo.: Westview Press, 1997.

Schindler, Roana and Gene Schindler. *Hawaii Kai Cookbook.* New York: Hearthside, 1970.

Sehlinger, Bob. "Etiquette Soup." In *Travelers' Tales: Food—A Taste of the Road.* Ed. Richard Sterling. San Francisco: Travelers' Tales, 1996.

Serra, Victoria. *Tia Victoria's Spanish Kitchen.* Trans. and with an introduction by Elizabeth Gili. Ed. and adapt. Nina Froud. South Brunswick, N.Y.: A. S. Barnes, 1963.

Shapiro, Laura. *Perfection Salad: Women and Cooking at the Turn of the Century.* New York: Henry Holt, 1986.

Shor, Ira and Paolo Freire. *A Pedagogy for Liberation: Dialogues on Transforming Education.* New York: Bergin and Garvey, 1987.

Shulman, Alix Kates. *Drinking the Rain.* New York: Penguin, 1996.

Smart-Grosvenor, Vertamae. *Vibration Cooking: Or Travel Notes of a Geechee Girl.* New York: Ballantine, 1986.

Smith, Andrew. "Re: Tacos." <asfs@listproc.umbc.edu> via <owner-asfs@listproc.umbc.edu> July 25, 2001.

Smith, Jeff. *The Frugal Gourmet Cooks Three Ancient Cuisines.* New York: Avon, 1989.

Smith, Valerie. "Split Affinities: The Case of Interracial Rape." In *Conflicts in Feminism,* ed. Marianne Hirsch and Evelyn Fox Keller. New York: Routledge, 1990.

Sokolov, Raymond. *Why We Eat What We Eat: How the Encounter Between the New World and the Old Changed the Way Everyone on the Planet Eats.* New York: Summit, 1991.

"Spam." www.brown.edu/Students/Brown_Hawaii_Club/About_Hawaii/spam.htm. June 8, 2001.

Spoerri, Daniel. *Mythology and Meatballs: A Greek Island Diary/Cookbook*. Trans. Emmett Williams. Berkeley: Aris Book, 1982.

Steingarten, Jeffrey. *The Man Who Ate Everything*. New York: Random, 1997.

Stern, Jane and Michael Stern. *American Gourmet*. New York: Harper Collins, 1991.

————. *Road Food and Good Food*. 1978 and 1983. Reprint, New York: Alfred A. Knopf, 1986.

Stoltenberg, John. *Refusing to Be a Man*. New York: Meridian, 1990.

Telfer, Elizabeth. *Food for Thought: Philosophy and Food*. New York: Routledge, 1996.

Thomas, Nicholas. *Colonialism's Culture: Anthropology, Travel and Government*. Princeton, N.J.: Princeton University Press, 1994.

Thompson, Paul B. *Food Biotechnology in Ethical Perspective*. London: Chapman & Hall, 1997.

————. *The Spirit of the Soil: Agriculture and Environmental Ethics*. New York: Routledge, 1995.

Thompson, Paul B. and Thomas Hilde, eds. *The Agrarian Roots of Pragmatism*. Nashville: Vanderbilt University Press, 2000.

Thorne, John with Matt Lewis Thorne. *Outlaw Cook*. New York: North Point Press, 1992.

Tomlinson, John. *Cultural Imperialism: A Critical Introduction*. Baltimore: Johns Hopkins University Press, 1991.

Trinh T. Minh-ha. *Woman Native Other: Writing Postcoloniality and Feminism*. Bloomington: Indiana University Press, 1989.

Trillin, Calvin. *The Tummy Trilogy*. Reprint (containing *Third Helpings*, 1983, *Alice Let's Eat*, 1978, and *American Fried*, 1974), New York: Noonday, 1994.

Urry, John. *The Tourist Gaze*. London: Sage, 1992.

Valldejuli, Carmen Aboy. *Puerto Rican Cookery*. Gretna, La.: Pelican, 1983.

Vizenor, Gerald. *The People Named the Chippewa*. Minneapolis: University of Minnesota Press, 1984.

Waldo, Myra. *The Art of South American Cookery*. Garden City, N.Y.: Doubleday, 1961.

Waters, Alice. *Chez Panisse Cafe Cookbook*. New York: Harper Collins, 1999.

————. *Chez Panisse Menu Cookbook*. New York: Random House, 1982.

————. *Chez Panisse Vegetables From Artichoke to Zucchini*. New York: Harper Collins, 1996.

Weatherford, Jack. *Indian Givers: How the Indians of the Americas Transformed the World*. New York: Fawcett Columbine, 1988.

Weinberger, Eliot. "The Camera People." *Transition* 55 (1992): 24–54.

Weiss, Caroline D. *A Collection of Creole Recipes*. New Orleans: Peerless, 1941.

Weismantel, Mary. *Food, Gender, and Poverty in the Ecuadorian Andes*. Philadelphia: University of Pennsylvania, 1998.

Wibisoni, Djoko and David Wong. *The Food of Singapore: Authentic Recipes from the Manhattan of the East*. Singapore: Periplus, 1995.

Wilk, Richard. "Food and Nationalism: The Origins of 'Belizean Food.'" Paper Presented at the Conference on Food and Drink in Consumer Societies, Wilmington, Del., 1999.

Yúdice, George. "We Are *Not* the World." *Social Text* 31/32 (1991): 203–16.

Zagat, Tim. 1995. Foreword to *The Restaurant Lover's Companion* by Steve Ettlinger with Melanie Falick. Reading, Mass.: Addison-Wesley, 1995.

Zibart, Eve, Muriel Stevens, and Terrell Vermont. *The Unofficial Guide to Ethnic Cuisine and Dining in America*. New York: Macmillan 1995.

# Index